Modern Residential Financing Methods

TOOLS OF THE TRADE 2nd Edition

Stephen R. Mettling
Gerald R. Cortesi

Real Estate
Education Company
a division of Dearborn Financial Publishing, Inc.

While a great deal of care has been taken to provide accurate and current information, the ideas, suggestions, general principles and conclusions presented in this text are subject to local, state and federal laws and regulations, court cases and any revisions of same. The reader is thus urged to consult legal counsel regarding any points of law—this publication should not be used as a substitute for competent legal advice.

Library of Congress Cataloging in Publication Data

Mettling, Stephen R.
    Modern residential financing methods : tools of the trade /
Stephen R. Mettling, Gerald R. Cortesi. — 2nd ed.
        p. cm.
    ISBN 0-88462-885-X
        1. Mortgage loans—United States.   2. Housing—United States-
-Finance.   3. Real property—United States—Finance.   I. Cortesi,
Gerald R. II. Title.
HG2040.5.U5M47 1990   89-10777
332.7'22'0973—dc20   CIP

Executive Editor: Richard A. Hagle
Development Editor: Margaret M. Maloney
Project Editor: Jack L. Kiburz
Copy Editor: Ronald J. Liszkowski
Cover Design: Sara Shelton

Cover illustration courtesy of First Union Mortgage Corporation of Charlotte, North Carolina

Table of Contents

Introduction

Residential real estate financing has been radically transformed in the past ten years, so much so that it would be barely recognizable by a person who had been out of the country during that time. For that matter, financing in general has changed—not just for housing but in every sector of our economy. Financing books and texts of every description have had to be rewritten as a result, with many of their etched-in-stone principles and axioms reshaped or thrown out altogether. Equally intriguing, new financial rules and laws have yet to fully emerge. Finance educators and authors face the prospect that the ever-changing financial picture will make their content obsolete almost immediately.

It would be pleasant and convenient to know for certain what the near future holds for the world of financing. Unfortunately, all we can state with any certainty is that the dynamics of change will continue and that only hindsight will accurately describe how credit works in our society. Be mindful, then, that what you learn in this text about mortgage financing is subject to change without notice.

ORGANIZATION OF THE BOOK

This text/workbook presents a technique analysis of the mortgage financing methods that have emerged in the 1980s. The techniques selected for study are those that have proven to be most widely accepted or that show the potential for wide appeal in the future. The list of financing methods includes both the major institutional loans that have been adopted and the most important seller-financed mortgages that in the early 1980s dominated residential financing.

In addition to technique analysis, this book presents an examination of the essential facet in contemporary financing: qualification. As financing has grown increasingly complex, the process of qualification has become increasingly important to effective mortgage lending. The chapter on qualification addresses not only financial qualification of the buyer but qualification of each principal component of the financing transaction: the buyer, the seller, the lender and the property itself.

For your reference, the workbook concludes with a comprehensive glossary of financing terms along with appendices containing essential mortgage loan tables.

LEARNING FORMAT

This workbook is designed to give students and readers:

1. a *conceptual understanding* of each financing technique presented, and
2. a rudimentary *level of skill* with the financial mechanics of each financing method examined.

These basic learning objectives will be achieved by systematically progressing through each financing method from:

1. identifying specific objectives; to
2. defining the techniques, including diagrams; to
3. identifying the techniques' key characteristics; to
4. explaining how the financial mechanics work; accompanied by
5. examples of the techniques; and ending with
6. questions and exercises at the end of each chapter.

HOW TO USE THIS BOOK

This workbook encourages your active involvement in order to maximize your learning experience. To complete the exercises in this workbook all you need is paper, pencil and a simple calculator. Mortgage loan tables have been printed in the appendices for your reference. In completing the various exercises, you are urged *not* to refer to the solutions provided at the end of the chapter until you have done your best to produce your answer. That way you'll get the most benefit from the material.

ACKNOWLEDGMENTS

We would like to thank the following reviewers for their valuable assistance on the new edition of this book: Laurence Beneke, First United Mortgage Corporation, San Antonio, Texas; Peter Glover, Austin Community College, Austin, Texas; William O'Malley, Equisure Mortgage Consultants, Sicklerville, New Jersey; Roger Zimmerman, Cleveland State University, Cleveland, Ohio.

Initiating the Loan

In recent years real estate finance has experienced dramatic changes that have brought about new challenges for lenders, real estate brokers, buyers and even sellers.

Prior to the 1970s mortgage lending was very different from what we have become accustomed to today. At that time the primary source of funds for home loans in the country came from savers' deposits in thrift institutions such as savings and loan associations (S&Ls) and mutual savings banks. Rates were adjusted infrequently, there was little variation in the type of loans offered, and few changes had been made in real estate lending since the 1930s. Lenders were able to pay low interest rates on their savings deposits, and the maximum rate paid to savers was regulated by state and federal governments. Many states also regulated the maximum interest rates that could be charged on mortgage loans, and federal regulations required thrifts to concentrate on making real estate loans.

The 1980s, however, brought deregulation of financial institutions and volatile interest rates. With deregulation lenders had to compete for deposits by setting competitive interest rates and investors moved their savings around looking for the highest return for their money. Because lenders no longer had a stable supply of inexpensive money to lend, they turned to the capital markets to fund their loans. Consequently interest rates for real estate loans became tied to fluctuations in the general economy. During this period new loan products were developed and new sources of real estate financing such as credit unions became available.

Deregulation of the lending industry, changes in state banking laws, introduction of new real estate loan products, new income tax rules, changes in interest rates and inflation are just some of the factors influencing the real estate financial market. This chapter presents some of the basic concepts and terminology used in real estate lending today including the critical process of qualifying the buyer, seller, lender and property. Without qualification, no loan can be made.

LEARNING OBJECTIVES

This chapter will help you learn to:

1. understand basic real estate lending concepts such as points and PMI,
2. identify sources of real estate financing and the distinctions between primary and secondary lenders,
3. qualify a prospective home buyer's borrowing capability and the amount of cash the borrower will need in addition to financing for conventional, FHA and VA loans,
4. determine what a home buyer can afford relative to his or her income, debt and available down payment,
5. qualify a seller's willingness to assist in home financing and identify the home seller's financial objectives,
6. qualify existing financing on a property, and
7. qualify lending sources as to the availability and terms of their mortgage financing programs.

SOURCES OF REAL ESTATE MORTGAGES

A variety of institutions and individuals are active within the mortgage lending system and play different roles in the process of providing funds for real estate mortgages.

Savings and Loan Associations

Despite all of the changes in the real estate lending market in the past few years the savings and loan (S&L) industry is still the largest single source of residential real estate lending. These specialized financial institutions have always been active lenders in the residential real estate market although in recent years regulatory changes have encouraged S&Ls to invest more of their funds in other types of loans. Also, many S&Ls recently have found themselves in financial difficulties forcing some to close or to merge with other financial institutions. Despite these developments, S&Ls are expected to continue to play a major part in financing residential real estate.

Commercial Banks

Commercial banks usually attract demand deposits (checking accounts) and make short-term loans primarily to businesses. Mortgage lending is an important but secondary activity for commercial banks, but they do initiate billions of dollars of mortgage loans each year. They are especially active in providing construction loans for medium to large-scale income properties because these loans will have shorter maturities. While some banks will offer real estate loans for up to 30 years, they will usually sell them to other financial institutions rather than keep them in their own investment portfolio.

Mutual Savings Banks

Probably less known than S&Ls and commercial banks, mutual savings banks number less than 1,000 and are concentrated on the East Coast. They are a hybrid of a bank and an S&L and invest a very high percentage of their available funds in mortgages. They compete aggressively for savings deposits and offer accounts similar to those offered by S&Ls.

Mortgage Companies

Mortgage companies, also known as mortgage bankers, represent funding sources such as life insurance companies and pension investors. Mortgage bankers locate borrowers who meet the qualifications of the loan investors, close the loans and then service them. They generally receive 1 percent to 3 percent of the loan when it is originated and ¼ percent to ½ percent of the outstanding balance each year to service the loan. Mortgage bankers are involved with every type of real estate loan and finance every stage of a real estate development. However, a large part of their business involves FHA and VA loans on owner-occupied single-family homes. After originating the loans, mortgage bankers generally sell the mortgages for an origination fee to financial institutions and large investors all over the country. Because of these activities they play an important role in VA and FHA lending.

Mortgage Brokers

Mortgage brokers match borrowers with investors. The mortgage broker does not lend money and usually does not service the loan, a duty often performed by commercial real estate brokers.

Credit Unions and Pension Funds

Federal regulations prevented credit unions from making mortgages until 1978. Since then credit unions have slowly increased their participation in the mortgage market. Because of their broad membership base and substantial assets, credit unions will probably become a larger factor in the mortgage market.

Pension funds have traditionally invested their money in high-grade corporate and government bonds and stock. In recent years they have begun to put more of their funds into real estate loans. They are active buyers in the secondary market and should become an important source of primary financing in the future. In some areas of the country, pension fund members can use their own pension funds for mortgage loans at reasonable rates.

Life Insurance Companies

Life insurance companies invest the premiums paid by their policyholders. Because premiums and policy payouts can be calculated, insurance companies are in an excellent position to invest money in long-term investments such as real estate. Although they invest large amounts of money each year in real estate financing, their major interest is in commercial financing for projects such as large apartment complexes, shopping centers or office buildings.

Sellers

Sellers of real estate often finance a part or all of the purchase of their property. Seller financing is more common in periods of high interest rates. For example, in the early 1980s when interest rates were in the teens it is estimated that more than half of all residential real estate transactions during this time involved some form of seller financing. Seller financing is usually for short terms and carries a balloon payment. (In a balloon loan the entire principal is due at maturity.)

THE SECONDARY MARKET

Most people are familiar with the primary lenders in the mortgage market such as banks and S&Ls that initiate and then service mortgages. Less well known is the secondary mortgage market that performs so critical a role in the mortgage system.

Primary lenders such as banks can give loans only if they have funds available for lending. If a heavy loan demand exceeded a bank's supply of funds, many potential borrowers would not be able to get loans and the real estate market in that area would suffer. Fortunately loans can be sold to other investors, and the secondary market provides an effective medium for buying and selling mortgage loans. Lenders can sell their loans in the secondary market, replenish their supply of funds and make additional loans.

With the development of the secondary mortgage market, real estate financing has become a national finance system. In order for the secondary mortgage market to function efficiently, however, investors must be able to buy and sell standardized loan products. The secondary lenders have accomplished this by developing guidelines that determine which loans they will accept from the local lenders. Because local lenders want to be able to resell most of their loans, they in turn tailor their loan requirements to match the secondary lenders' guidelines.

Lenders in the secondary market include: The Federal National Mortgage Association (Fannie Mae), the Government National Mortgage Association (Ginnie Mae) and the Federal Home Loan Mortgage Corporation (Freddie Mac).

The Federal National Mortgage Association (Fannie Mae)

Fannie Mae was created as a government agency in 1938 to provide a secondary market for FHA loans, also newly created at that time. Fannie Mae evolved with the housing market in the succeeding years and in 1952 began to purchase loans guaranteed by the Veterans Administration (VA). In 1968 Fannie Mae was rechartered and became a publicly held organization. In 1972 it began purchasing conventional loans (those not guaranteed or insured by the federal government) Fannie Mae is the largest institution in the secondary mortgage market and the largest investor in home mortgages in the country.

The Government National Mortgage Association (Ginnie Mae)

Ginnie Mae was created in 1968 and is a government agency that is part of the U.S. Department of Housing and Urban Development (HUD). Ginnie Mae was created when Fannie Mae became private and took on some of the functions that Fannie Mae had to surrender when it went private (e.g., federal guarantee of securities). Ginnie Mae pools FHA and VA mortgages and issues pass-through certificates, which are backed by the loans to investors. The investors who purchase the certificates receive monthly payments of both interest and principal. The pass-through certificates are guaranteed by the federal government, making them more attractive to investors.

The Federal Home Loan Mortgage Corporation (Freddie Mac)

Freddie Mac was created by the Emergency Home Finance Act of 1970. Freddie Mac is part of the Federal Home Loan Bank Board, which regulates federally chartered savings and loan associations. FHLMC is authorized to purchase conventional, FHA and VA loans, although its primary purpose is to develop a national secondary market for conventional home mortgage loans. To finance its operations it pools loans bought from lenders and sells "pass-through" securities, backed by the loans, to investors.

TAX CONSIDERATIONS

This section discusses income tax considerations pertaining to real estate financing. This is a complex topic, however, and the reader should always consult a tax attorney or CPA for further information or advice on the latest tax rules.

Interest Deductibility

Prior to 1987 mortgage interest on a qualified principal residence and a qualified second residence was generally fully deductible as an itemized deduction. Since 1987, however, the tax rules regarding deductibility have been changed more than once.

In 1988 Congress divided deductible mortgage interest into two categories: acquisition indebtedness and home equity indebtedness. Acquisition indebtedness includes money borrowed to buy, build or substantially improve a taxpayer's principal residence or second home. Home equity indebtedness includes money borrowed on the equity in the taxpayer's home for any use.

All interest on acquisition indebtedness secured by a qualified principal residence or second residence is generally deductible in either of these two situations:

1. The debt was incurred prior to October 13, 1987 and was not increased after that date. All interest is deductible regardless of the amount of the debt.
2. The debt is not more than $1,000,000 ($500,000 if married filing a separate return), provided the funds are used to buy, build or improve the home.

All interest on home equity loans is deductible if the debt is equal to or less than $100,000 ($50,000 if married filing a separate return). It does not matter how the taxpayer uses the loan proceeds.

Note that this only applies to loans that are secured by the residence. If a personal loan is taken and the proceeds used to improve the residence, the interest will not be deductible.

For example, a couple bought their home in 1988 for $100,000 and obtained a mortgage for $95,000. They now obtain a home equity loan for $45,000 and use the proceeds to make improvements in their house. Because all of the debt secured by the residence is used to purchase or improve the home and is less than $1,000,000 they can deduct all of the interest related to their mortgage and home-equity loans.

The new rules allowing interest on loans secured by the home while disallowing interest deductions on consumer loans may encourage homebuyers to reduce the amount of their down payment. This is illustrated by the choice a homebuyer might have of (1) adding

$15,000 to the down payment and then borrowing that amount to buy furniture or (2) increasing the mortgage by $15,000 and then using the cash to buy furniture. The second choice would be better for tax purposes because interest on the $15,000 would be deductible as acquisition indebtedness.

Refinancing and Taxation

If a taxpayer refinances his or her residence, the amount that will qualify as acquisition indebtedness is limited to the debt outstanding on the old loan plus any of the new loan money used for home improvements.

For example, a couple bought their home five years ago for $80,000 and their mortgage balance is $70,000. They now refinance their mortgage for $110,000 and end up with $40,000 cash ($70,000 was used to pay off the original mortgage). Interest on the first $70,000 of the new loan will be deductible since that equals the balance on the old loan. The deductibility of the remaining $40,000 depends on what the couple does with the money. Any part of this money spent for home improvements is treated as acquisition indebtedness and should be deductible. Any of the money not used to pay off the old mortgage or improvements will not qualify for acquisition indebtedness but can be treated as home equity indebtedness since it is secured by the home. This portion of the loan can also be deductible as long as the $100,000 limit on all equity loans on the property is not exceeded. If they use $25,000 to remodel the house and $15,000 to buy a new car, all of the interest related to the refinanced mortgage is deductible as illustrated below.

Balance on the previous loan	$ 70,000
Home improvement	+25,000
Loan amount interest deductible as acquisition indebtedness	$ 95,000
Loan amount interest deductible as home equity indebtedness	+15,000
Total refinanced mortgage	$110,000

Interest Deduction and Loan Qualification

While the allowance for interest deductions helps reduce the amount of income taxes a borrower pays, there is also another advantage. The reduction in tax liability resulting from the deductibility of interest can also assist a buyer in qualifying for a mortgage.

If a buyer is seeking a 30-year $100,000 mortgage at 10.5 percent, the monthly payments will be $915. If the lender's income-to-mortgage payment ratio is 30 percent, the borrower must have a monthly income of $3,050 to qualify for the loan. However, the amount of interest the borrower will pay in the first year will be approximately $10,500, which averages to $875 per month. If the borrower is in the 28 percent tax bracket, the borrower's tax savings in the first year will be $2,940 (28 percent of $10,500) or $245 per month. The borrower could reduce monthly withholding by the amount of the tax reduction and may now qualify for the loan.

POINTS

Points (sometimes referred to as discounts or loan fees) are a one-time charge that is used to raise the lender's yield on a loan. In addition to increasing the yield, points allow the lender to stabilize the effects of an ever-changing interest rate market. Lenders must take the current money market rates into consideration when determining the rates for their loans, but the market rates change several times each day. It would be too confusing to change loan rates each day. Instead, the lender adjusts the yield on the loan by changing the number of points that will be charged. This brings the yield on the loan in line with the current market rates.

Value of a Point

A point is equal to 1 percent of the loan amount and is paid to the lender at settlement or closing. For example, if the lender charges 3 points on a $75,000 loan, the one-time point charge due at closing would be $2,250 ($75,000 × .03 = $2,250).

The number of points charged on a loan will vary according to market conditions at the time the loan is made. If credit is tight the number of points (and yield to the lender) will increase. Other factors will also change the number of points charged. For instance, if the borrower takes out a higher rate on the loan the points will be lower. This is often done by mortgage lenders who will quote rates such as the following:

    10% interest rate with 4 points
    10¼% interest rate with 2 points
    10½% interest rate with 0 points

The yields on these three quotes are basically the same for the lender (although the lower rate may allow a borrower to qualify more easily for the loan). One point is not equal to the yield that 1 percent of interest would bring over the life of a 30-year mortgage. In terms of interest rates a point is usually valued as one-eighth of 1 percent over a 30-year fixed-rate loan. Thus if a loan is taken out with a rate of 10 percent and the borrower pays 4 points, the actual yield on the loan is 10.5 percent. Most buyers however do not keep their loans to the end of the 30-year term. In fact the average mortgage loan stays on the lender's books from about seven to 12 years. If the loan is not held for the full term, the yield on the loan will be higher since the points were prepaid at the start of the loan.

In our example of a 30-year fixed rate loan at 10 percent, a loan paid after seven years would yield 10.83 percent. If it were paid off after ten years, the yield would be 10.67 percent. The sooner the loan is paid the higher the yield is to the lender. Realizing that most loans will not be held to the end of their term, some lenders price the loan with fewer points. The number of points will depend on how long they expect the loan to stay on their books.

Interest Rate versus Points

Is it better to take a mortgage with a lower interest rate and more points or a higher interest rate with fewer points? This question must be answered whenever comparing a lender's loan products. For some borrowers there may be little choice because they may be able to qualify for the loan only if the lower interest rate is used. (Qualifying the borrower will be covered later in this chapter.) In most situations, however, the answer depends on how long the borrower intends to own the property and keep the loan.

For example, a lender offers a 30-year $80,000 loan at 10 percent interest with 2 points or a loan at 10¼ percent interest with 1 point. Which is the better loan for the borrower? The comparison of the two loans is listed in the table below. The difference in the monthly payment for a 10 percent loan and a 10¼ percent loan is $15.00 ($717 monthly versus $702). It would take almost 54 months to make up the difference in the points at the rate of $15 per month. Another consideration is that by paying out the additional point money at closing the borrower will lose the investment opportunity value (what could reasonably be expected to be earned on the money if it were invested) of the additional funds.

From this example if the borrower expects to keep the property longer than 54 months, the loan with the higher points would be more advantageous. If the borrower intends to keep the property less than 54 months, then the loan with the lower points would be better. In general, the longer the period the loan is held, the cheaper the cost of the additional points.

TABLE 1.1 Points vs. Interest

	Loan 1	Loan 2
Loan amount	$80,000	$80,000
Interest rate	10%	10¼%
Monthly payment	$702	$717
Extra monthly payment cost	—	$15
Number of points	2	1
Cash value of points	$1,600	$800
Extra cost for points	$800	—

Points can be paid by either the buyer or the seller unless restricted by state laws or if the loan involves the Veterans Administration (VA). The VA requires the seller to pay the points.

PRIVATE MORTGAGE INSURANCE (PMI)

Thousands of loans are taken each year by the buyer who has a very small down payment and who does not use either VA or FHA financing. These transactions would not be possible without a unique financial product called private mortgage insurance (PMI). Without PMI lenders would not ordinarily make these loans because of the excessive risk of making loans with such low down payments.

PMI is a plan that protects the lender against loss on the mortgage by insuring a portion of the loan. Private mortgage insurance companies offer PMI and guarantee loans that are conventional, that is, not government insured or guaranteed. If a loan is in default a claim is paid to the lender based on the percentage of the loan that is covered by the PMI.

As an example, a mortgage for $100,000 with a 20 percent PMI on it would be insured for $20,000. In the event that the borrower defaults and there is a loss on the property the first $20,000 of the lender's loss would be insured. If in this example the property sold in foreclosure for $90,000, the lender would not lose any money, because the lender would receive the $90,000 from the sale and $10,000 from the PMI company. If the property sold for only $75,000, however, the lender would receive $75,000 from the sale and $20,000 from the PMI company resulting in a $5,000 loss. In determining the amount of the loss the PMI company considers the "total claim." The total claim includes not only the mortgage balance but other items such as attorneys' fees and foreclosure costs. It might seem that because there is only 20 percent coverage the lender is still taking a considerable financial risk, but this is not the case. Besides the borrower's down payment (i.e., 5 percent to 20 percent of the property value) the loan balance is being reduced with each monthly payment (unless there is negative amortization). Another factor working to the advantage of the lender is that most properties appreciate in value. As the difference between loan value to property value increases, the risk to the lender decreases. *Appreciation*

The appreciation of property value raises the issue of whether the mortgage insurance coverage eventually could be removed because the loan-to-value ratio would be decreasing. In a period of rapid property appreciation, for instance, the loan-to-value ratio may quickly change from 95 percent when the loan was originally issued to less than 80 percent. Under these circumstances it would appear that the PMI could be removed automatically because the amount of equity in the property now exceeds the minimum guidelines set by the lender. However, PMI is not removed automatically. Usually the PMI must continue because it is based on the original appraised value of the property and not its current value. Some PMI policies state that the policy will exist for a specific time period regardless of the loan balance or property value. But when a borrower has reduced the loan balance to less than 80 percent of the original appraised value, the borrower can request and usually get the lender to remove the PMI.

[handwritten margin note: PMI can Remove only when the original loan is lowered to 80% LTV. Check Regulations with Lenders.]

The lender determines whether PMI will be required on a loan, and the requirements vary between lenders. As a general rule, however, lenders will require PMI if the down payment is less than 20 percent of the selling price. This however is only a general rule. If the lender feels that a particular type of loan is riskier than usual, the lender may require PMI even with a down payment of 20 percent or more. Some PMI companies may also have a requirement on "gift" money used for the down payment. For example, if the borrower is receiving the down payment as a gift from someone, the borrower may be required by the PMI company to also put down 5 percent to demonstrate financial stability and the ability to pay.

Private mortgage insurance companies charge a premium to cover expenses and claims. The amount of the premium is based on: the amount of the loan, the type of loan (i.e., fixed rate, ARM, GPM, etc.), the amount of the down payment and the length of coverage. Premiums can be paid either on an annual basis or as a lump sum at settlement although most borrowers choose to pay on an annual basis. Lenders determine how long the policies will remain in force, which as a general rule is usually seven years. Lenders may require longer policy terms in years when real estate takes a long time to sell or shorter terms in years when property is selling fast. In the last few years private mortgage insurers began adjusting their premium rates based on whether the loan payments were fixed or variable. Loans that do not have fixed payments—such as variable-rate and graduated-rate loans—are considered more risky and have a higher premium. For instance, a fixed-rate loan with 5 percent down might have a premium of 2.5 percent of the loan value while a variable-rate loan with the same down payment might have a 3 percent premium.

Private mortgage insurance can be purchased on either an annual or a multi-year basis. The premium on a multi-year policy is paid as one lump sum at closing while annual policy premiums are paid monthly. Of the two, buyers much prefer the annual over the multi-year policy.

Both buyers and lenders benefit from PMI. Besides reducing the risk to the lender, PMI helps the lender resell the loan in the secondary market. For profit and liquidity reasons this is an important consideration for most lenders in deciding whether to make a loan. PMI-backed loans are considered a secure mortgage investment because of the substantial reserves private mortgage insurers are required to maintain. Billions of conventional loans backed by PMI have been sold to secondary lenders such as Fannie Mae and Freddie Mac. PMI also helps borrowers. Without PMI the lender would require a larger down payment to reduce the risk of the loan thus prohibiting the potential buyer from making the purchase. The rates for a loan with PMI and other conventional loans are the same, and PMI charges no discount points at closing as is done in FHA and VA insured loans. Interest rates for conventional loans with or without PMI are identical. If conventional financing is available at 12 percent interest with a 20 percent down payment and 3 points, conventional financing with PMI would also be available at 12 percent interest with 3 points and only 5 to 15 percent down, plus the PMI premium. Since the rates for conventional loans with and without PMI are identical, no additional discount points are charged by the lender to equalize the rates, as is the case with VA and FHA loans. Also, unlike VA loans, there is no requirement that the seller pay all of the points in the transaction. Payment of the points can be negotiated by the parties in the transaction.

Private Mortgage Insurance companies became widespread in the 1920s but collapsed during the Great Depression. The mortgage insurance field was revitalized in the mid-1950s when the Mortgage Guarantee Insurance Corporation (MGIC) came into existence. Today there are several PMI companies insuring billions of dollars in mortgage loans.

Finally, private mortgage insurance should not be confused with mortgage life insurance. These are two different products. Mortgage insurance protects purchasers by paying the mortgage if they are unable to because of disability or death. Mortgage insurance can be obtained either through most lenders or insurance brokers.

FINANCIAL QUALIFICATION: WHAT IS IT?

It is axiomatic in residential brokerage that before any financing alternatives can be selected for a buyer, the circumstances surrounding the potential transaction must be analyzed. This process of analysis is called qualification. Although qualification is commonly understood as an assessment of the prospective *homebuyer's* financial condition, in actual practice qualification extends to analyzing *all* the important factors of the home sale, including the seller, the property and the available sources of financing. In each case, qualification means something a little different. When you qualify a buyer, you assess financial capability, housing objectives and logistical planning for the purchase. When you qualify the seller, you assess the seller's cash needs, overall objectives and willingness to finance. Qualifying a property entails analysis of the various data in the listing agreement plus the property's underlying financing. And finally, when you qualify a lender, you are examining the many financing programs available to your prospective buyer, interest rates, underwriting criteria and specific loan terms.

Only when these factors have been analyzed—qualified—can a practitioner claim to have qualified a potential transaction. In turn, it is only after the circumstances as such have been qualified that any of the financing alternatives available can be effectively put into use.

Financial qualification is thus defined as knowledge of (1) the buyer's financial situation; (2) the seller's financial situation; (3) what financing exists on the property for sale; and

✳ (4) what loan programs various lenders in the market are offering. The following sections detail what you need to know about these four qualification components in order to understand the qualification process as a whole.

QUALIFYING THE BUYER

Buyer qualification defines a buyer's purchasing capability in terms of *cash equity* and *income*. This capability is identified through the application of underwriting standards to the buyer's financial condition. Two such standards are most important:

- the debt-to-income ratio, and
- the loan-to-value ratio or LTV.

The debt-to-income ratio pertains to the ability to comfortably pay debt, and the LTV ratio defines how much cash is needed to keep the mortgage loan in a safe relationship to the value of the property securing it. Applying these two ratios to the buyer's condition constitutes the major portion of conventional financial qualification of the buyer.

Income Qualification

Two principal factors govern income qualification: the buyer's income level and long-term debt. In practice, both factors work hand in hand. A buyer with moderate income but little debt may be able to afford a larger home than a buyer with higher income but substantially higher debt. In principle, what you are looking for in income qualification is a family's level of available monthly funds for housing expressed typically as income minus long-term debt unrelated to housing.

There are two rule-of-thumb ratios in determining how much mortgage debt a borrower can reasonably afford. One is total long-term debt-to-income ratio, and the other is merely the mortgage debt-to-income ratio. The mortgage debt ratio includes the loan principal, interest, taxes and insurance premiums (called PITI for short) that the borrower pays to the lender every month. For our purposes, we call the first the long-term debt-to-income ratio, or *LT debt ratio*, and the second we term the *PITI debt ratio*.

The LT Debt Ratio.   Some homebuyers have substantial long-term debt and others don't. In either case, one of the first steps in qualifying for affordable debt—besides ascertaining income—is to determine each prospect's existing long-term debt and apply the LT debt ratio to determine how large a mortgage the buyer can afford. First, let's look at what the LT debt ratio is.

By conventional standards, the LT debt ratio is the ratio between long-term debt, including housing expenses, and the buyer's net effective income. Long-term debt is defined here as any debt that will continue to exist for another six months and beyond. Housing expenses here include mortgage principal and interest, taxes, insurance, utilities and maintenance, or PITIUM. Net effective income is defined as gross income minus withholding taxes.

The LT debt ratio is commonly used by VA and FHA underwriters as well as conventional, nongovernment underwriters. The LT debt ratio was recently set at a maximum of 50 percent, and long-term debt was defined as any debt beyond a six-month duration. Thus the LT debt ratio standard is currently:

$$
\begin{array}{ll}
\text{Loan Principal:} & \text{P} \\
+\ \text{Loan Interest:} & \text{I} \\
+\ \text{Property Taxes:} & \text{T} \\
+\ \text{Insurance:} & \text{I} \\
+\ \text{Utilities:} & \text{U} \\
+\ \text{Maintenance:} & \text{M}
\end{array}
\quad + \quad
\begin{array}{l}
\text{long-term debt} \\
\text{(nonhousing debt} \\
\text{over six months)}
\end{array}
\quad
\begin{array}{l}
\text{must be} \le .50 \times \text{(gross income} \\
\quad\quad\quad\quad\quad\quad\quad -\text{withholding} \\
\quad\quad\quad\quad\quad\quad\quad \text{tax)}
\end{array}
$$

Note that while the underwriting standard is 50 percent, this can fluctuate upwards or downwards depending on economic circumstances. For instance, recent statistics have revealed that Americans are spending an increasing percentage of their net income on housing expenses, so for our purposes we will use 55 percent.

Applying the LT Debt Ratio. To use the LT debt ratio, several assumptions must be made about the housing expenses to be incurred. Here, the long-term nonhousing debt is a total of actual dollar figures, as is withholding tax. But to plug in the housing expenses, one must assume:

- an interest rate,
- a loan term and loan type (interest-only or amortized),
- an estimate of taxes and insurance,
- utility costs, and
- anticipated maintenance costs.

This may sound like a lot of guesswork, but once a specific home has been selected, an estimate of loan rates and terms can be based on current market trends, and an estimate of nonmortgage housing expenses can be taken from comparable costs of an average home in the desired area. For example, if the buyers want a three-bedroom house in a given area, you can make a good estimate of prevailing taxes, insurance and utility costs.

Let's apply this ratio to determine how much debt load a fictitious buyer can carry. To review, our operable equation is (on a *monthly* basis):

$$
\begin{array}{c}
\text{P} + \text{I} + \text{T} + \text{I} + \text{U} + \text{M} + \text{nonhousing LT debt over 6 months} \\
\le .55 \times \text{(income} - \text{withholding)}
\end{array}
$$

Remember, what we're after here is the PI component, or the monthly principal and interest payment the buyer can afford. To determine this, we must move the equation around to solve for PI:

$$
\text{PI (affordable)} = .55 \times \text{(income} - \text{tax)} - \text{(T} + \text{I} + \text{U} + \text{M} + \text{LT debt)}
$$

Once we solve for PI, we can use mortgage tables to determine the maximum available mortgage loan. That amount plus the down payment equals the price of the home the buyer can afford.

For example, prospective buyers would like a three-bedroom home in one of your market areas. The buyers indicated to you that they do have some long-term debt. So you use the LT debt ratio qualification. Your assumptions and facts are:

- going interest rate: 15 percent,
- loan term and type: 30 years, amortized,
- taxes and insurance: $100/month (for a three-bedroom in that market),
- utilities: $75/month,
- maintenance: $40/month,
- buyer's gross income: $30,000 divided by 12 = $2,500/month,
- buyer's withholding tax: 24 percent of monthly income, and
- buyer's monthly nonhousing debt over six months = $300.

Then using our formula:

PI affordable = (ratio) (income − tax) − (T + I + U + M) − (LT debt)

PI affordable (@ 15%, 30 years) = 55% [$2,500 − (24% − $2,500)]
$$− ($100 + $75 + $40) − $300$$

PI affordable (@ 15%, 30 years) = $1,045 − $215 − $300 = $530

This buyer can afford a PI payment of $530. Now, using loan tables (in Appendices) the mortgage amount affordable at $530 per month for a 15 percent, 30-year loan is about $43,000. Thus, using the LT debt ratio, this prospect qualifies for a $43,000 loan.

The PITI Debt Ratio.   The PITI debt ratio is the ratio between a borrower's principal, interest, taxes and insurance (PITI) costs and his or her gross income. This ratio is commonly used as a quick indicator of borrowing capability but is more specifically used where a borrower has little or no long-term debt. Like the LT debt ratio, the PITI debt ratio is used to identify how much monthly housing debt the buyer can comfortably afford. Traditionally this ratio has stood at 25 percent with conventional lenders; that is, a home's PITI could not exceed 25 percent of gross income. Currently, however, it is acceptable to use a 28 to 30 percent ratio. For our purposes, we will use a 30 percent PITI ratio. Thus, we have:

P + I + T + I must be ≤ 30% gross income

As we did with the LT debt ratio, we must alter the PITI debt ratio in order to find how much debt a borrower can afford. To do this we move the taxes and insurance expenses to the other side of the equation:

P + I must be ≤ 30% gross income − T − I

Applying the PITI Ratio.   To use the PITI ratio, several assumptions must again be made about rates and terms. Here we must specifically assume (1) the interest rate, (2) the loan term and type and (3) taxes and insurance, then use them in the preceding equation.

Using our previous example, we can derive how much debt the borrower can afford under the following conditions:

- going interest rate: 15 percent,
- term and type: 30 years, amortized,
- taxes and insurance: $100/month, and
- buyer's gross income: $30,000 divided by 12 = $2,500/month.

Then, using our formula:

$$P + I \text{ affordable} = 30\% \, (\$2,500) - \$100 = \$650$$

The buyer's $650 per month PI capability will, from mortgage tables, allow him to qualify for a $50,000, 30 year, 15 percent mortgage. Note: Under guidelines set by the Federal National Mortgage Association (Fannie Mae), the PITI for a prospective home buyer should be no more than 28 percent of gross monthly income. Also the PITI plus other long-term debts with ten or more monthly payments outstanding should be no more than 36 percent of the monthly gross income.

The LT Debt Ratio and the PITI Debt Ratio: Which to Use? The PITI debt ratio can be quickly applied to derive a buyer's approximate mortgage borrowing capability. However, if a buyer has any substantial degree of long-term nonhousing debt, both ratios should be applied to the prospective borrower. Subsequently, the ratio yielding the lesser PI capability is the final debt qualification figure to use. From our example, for instance, we determined that, using the LT debt ratio, the prospect could qualify for a $43,000 mortgage and, using the PITI ratio, a $50,000 mortgage. In comparing the two, the lesser amount, or the $43,000 figure, is the correct amount of mortgage loan for which the buyer is qualified—not $50,000.

To be thorough in the qualification process, both ratios should be used and the lesser figure chosen—unless it is clear that the borrower's long-term debt is minimal.

Cash-on-Hand Qualification

In addition to income (or debt) qualification, buyers must be qualified for cash; that is, they must have enough cash to meet the minimum equity requirements for the particular loan to be obtained, plus cash needed for closing costs. The minimum cash needed is determined by what is called the loan-to-value ratio, or LTV ratio.

The LTV Ratio. The loan-to-value ratio for any mortgage is determined by the following equation:

$$\frac{\text{Mortgage amount (L)}}{\text{Home's market value (V)}} = \text{LTV}$$

or, simply

$$\frac{L}{V} = LTV$$

For example, the LTV ratio on a property with a $75,000 mortgage on it and a market value of $100,000 would have a 75 percent LTV:

$$\frac{\$\ 75,000}{\$100,000} = 75\%\ LTV$$

Usually lenders require a 75 to 80 percent LTV for their mortgages, but some will agree to a higher figure on the condition that private mortgage insurance (PMI) is obtained.

The cash required in a home purchase—excluding closing costs—is the price of the home minus the mortgage. Viewed in terms of the LTV ratio the cash required is:

$$\boxed{(100\% - LTV) \times Value = Cash}$$

In other instances it may be desirable to calculate how much a buyer can pay with a given amount of cash available and a particular LTV ratio. This can be determined by the following equation.

$$\boxed{Price \times (Value) = \frac{Cash\ down}{(100 - LTV\ ratio)}}$$

Let's look at an example for both equations. First calculate how much cash is required to purchase a $110,000 home using an LTV limit of 75 percent. Using the first equation, we see that $27,500 is required as a down payment:

$$\$110,000 - (\$110,000 \times 75\%) = \$27,500$$

Using the same example, we can calculate how much a buyer can afford in terms of the available down payment. Assuming the buyer has $27,500 to put down and lenders are using a 75 percent LTV ratio, we see that the buyer can purchase a $110,000 home:

$$\frac{\$27,500}{(100 - 75)} = \$110,000$$

The latter equation identifies maximum housing cost based on equity. However, because the LTV can vary substantially even in conventional circumstances, the equity qualification can render such a wide price range meaningless. Thus, it is preferable to perform the income qualification first and then determine how much cash would be required at a given LTV for that particular income level. Finally, to determine how much cash will be required to close a transaction, you must add an estimate of cash needed for closing costs to the cash needed for the down payment.

Selecting Income and Cash Ratio Amounts.   Perhaps most important when you qualify buyers is to be conservative when selecting the PITI debt ratio and LTV ratio you use. Obviously a buyer can purchase a much more expensive house if a 95 percent LTV is used along with a 45 percent PITI ratio. But then the buyer is more apt to default because other debt obligations may arise that may wipe out the borrower's ability to pay. Thus it is paramount that the underwriting ratios be conservative or be based on what institutional lenders themselves use.

Buyer Qualification and Fluctuating Interest Rates

Thus far we have reviewed the basics of conventional financial buyer qualification: identifying cash and income capabilities for mortgage debt derived under certain assumptions about loan terms, taxes, insurance and interest rates.

The advent of new financing alternatives, however, creates a new twist to the qualification process: widely varying rates of interest. Before, income qualification was usually a standard, routine procedure because institutional interest rates were fixed, give or take a point. Now, with seller financing, interest rates can vary within a remarkably wide range—as much as 10 to 17 percent. The related effect of such a rate range is a correspondingly wide range of purchasing power, depending on the ultimate rate procured. This in turn sets up a new dimension in qualification. Income qualification, by necessity, must determine a buying range based on several possible interest rates—not just "the going rate" as was assumed by our example. We saw earlier how the 15 percent interest rate affected the final price of the home the buyer could afford. Now, only a buying range, or rough purchasing capability, can be identified since varying rates create wide ranges of purchasing power—the lower the rate the bigger the buying power, and the higher the rate the smaller the buying power.

Buyer's Projected Income and Loan Term

Before going ahead with buyer qualification, consider one more new factor that eventually must go into the qualification process: the buyer's *projected* income. With seller financing and other new techniques, typical financing terms have shortened, in many cases down to three years. Because such financing tends to be cheaper than market rates, the buyer may have to refinance at much more expensive rates at the end of the short term. If the buyer's income hasn't increased, the buyer can be in trouble indeed. Thus a rough estimate of the buyer's projected income must be made to assess whether projected future interest rates will make financing unaffordable in the future.

As a rule, the shorter the term of a financing arrangement and the more its rates are below market, the greater the buyer's future income must be to avoid refinancing nightmares. For example, if the buyer's financing costs are projected to increase by 40 percent over the next three years and the buyer's income is projected to increase only 7 percent per year, the buyer is courting trouble. Thus, income projections are critical relative to the loan term involved in a possible financing package.

Quantitative Financial Qualification of the Buyer

Figure 1.1 is a form for qualifying a buyer. It shows how to derive the buyer's price range as a function of interest rates and the LTV. Once the range is established, a buyer can be matched up with real estate listings having various cash requirements and interest rates.

To use the buyer qualification form, start by positing the necessary assumptions and facts as shown. Each of these assumptions and facts affects the subsequent calculations. When completed, the process provides an income qualification, which is subsequently adjusted by the amount of cash either available or required, as described previously.

The price ranges derived in Section III can be subsequently used in matching the buyer with listings having various down payment and financing terms. In Figure 1.2 we will analyze a case example using this form. Remember, at this point, only rough qualification of the buyer has been undertaken. Only after a specific property has been identified can more specific qualification and loan structuring take place. Traditionally buyers would first find a home and then try to qualify for a loan. A growing trend today, however, is for the buyer to look for a loan and at the same time look for a home. Prequalification of the buyer for a loan by the lender is also a helpful selling point in negotiations with the seller.

Low-Docs and No-Docs

Another recent innovation is the low-documentation or no-documentation loan, also called "low-docs" and "no-docs." Depending on the lender's requirements, a borrower making a down payment of 20 to 30 percent may have the loan approved without all or some of the usual credit checks, job and income verifications and tax statements. This type of loan processing is especially attractive to self-employed borrowers who would normally face a time-consuming loan process.

Case Study Exercise: Financial Qualification of the Lincolns for a Conventional Loan

Mr. and Mrs. Lincoln, a couple in their fifties, walk into your real estate office and say they want to buy a house. After the usual discussion and nonfinancial qualification, it is time to figure out just what the Lincolns can afford. During your financial discussion, you learn that Mr. Lincoln, a mechanical engineer, makes $34,000 a year. Mrs. Lincoln works part-time at a flower boutique, and she earns about $6,000 a year. Mr. Lincoln relates that his income is fairly stable and goes up about 8 percent per year, depending on inflation. When the Lincolns sell their present home, they expect to have $30,000 to invest in the new home. They would like to move to Jewel Park, an old, established neighborhood where most of their friends live.

Further on, you learn that Mr. and Mrs. Lincoln pay about $900 per month in income taxes, and they have debts totalling $400 a month that will exceed 12 months' duration. Because Jewel Park is in your market, you know that taxes and insurance for homes run about $150 per month and that utilities and maintenance average about $100 per month.

To begin your calculation, you have to make a few assumptions. First, you assume that a 28 percent PITI debt ratio is usable because lenders in your area employ that figure in their calculations. Second, you assume that the long-term debt ratio to use with the Lincolns should be 55 percent, since a good part of their long-term debt will be paid up in

---

FIGURE 1.1: Quantitative Buyer Qualification Form

Buyer: _____

Essential data

A. Monthly income: $_____

B. Monthly taxes withheld: $_____

C. Projected change in annual income: _____%

D. Cash available for down payment: $_____

E. Long-term debt:_____/month

Assumptions

A. PITI ratio: _____%

B. LT debt ratio: _____%

C. Interest rate(s) used in analysis: _____

D. Loan term and type: _____ years; amortized/interest only (circle one)

E. Taxes and insurance estimate: _____

F. Utilities estimate: _____; maintenance estimate: _____ /month

  I. *Income (debt) qualification*

    A. PITI debt ratio qualification
      1. Income _____ /month $\times$ PITI debt ratio _____% =
         _____ PITI affordability
      2. PITI affordability _____ − Taxes and insurance = PI affordable _____

    B. LT debt ratio qualification
      1. Monthly income _____ − Monthly taxes withheld_____ =
         $_____ (1) Net effective income
      2. Net effective income _____ $\times$ LT ratio _____ =
         $_____
      3. Taxes + Insurance _____ + Utilities _____ +
         Maintenance _____ + Long-term debt _____ = $_____
      4. $_____(2) − $ _____(3) = $ _____PI affordable

    C. PI affordable: _____
       (enter amount from box in part A or part B, whichever is less)

II. *Mortgage loan range*

    A. Amortized vs. interest-only (circle one)

        • If amortized, use loan tables

        • If interest only, use the following equation for mortgage amount:

$$\text{(PI affordable} \times 12) \div \text{Rate} = \text{Mortgage amount}$$

    B. Mortgage loan range (compute at desired rates):

           11%   12%   13%   14%   15%

III. *Price range derivation*

    A. Select LTV ratios to be applied to mortgage range:

           75%   80%   85%   90%   95%

    B. Complete the buying range table below. To complete, divide each mortgage loan amount by each LTV ratio used.

    Price Range   Assumptions: term _____ type _____

Interest Rate

LTV	11%	12%	13%	14%	15%	other %
75% (25% down)						
80% (20% down)						
85% (15% down)						
90% (10% down)						
95% (5% down)						

IV. *Cash analysis and adjustment*

    A. Cash available: _____

    B. Cash required at _____ interest, _____% LTV (Price − Mortgage)

        1. If cash available exceeds required amount:

        Cash available _____ + Mortgage amount _____ =

        Price qualified for _____

        2. If cash available is less than cash required:

            a. Cash available $ _____ + Mortgage amount $ _____ =

            Tentative price qualified to buy $_____

            b. Compute new LTV: _____

            c. If acceptable, *a* is qualified amount

            d. If *b* is not acceptable, lower the mortgage amount until it is.

FIGURE 1.2: Quantitative Buyer Qualification Worksheet for Case Study Exercise

Buyer: _Lincolns_

Essential data

A. Monthly income: $ _3333.00_

B. Monthly taxes withheld: $ _900.00_

C. Projected change in annual income: _8_ %

D. Cash available for down payment: $ _30,000.00_

E. Long-term debt: _$400_ /month

Assumptions

A. PITI ratio: _28_ %

B. LT debt ratio: _55_ %

C. Interest rate(s) used in analysis: _11%, 13%, 15%_

D. Loan term and type: _30_ years; (amortized)/interest only (circle one)

E. Taxes and insurance estimate: _$150_

F. Utilities estimate: _$70_ ; maintenance estimate: _$30_ /month

I. *Income (debt) qualification*

   A. PITI debt ratio qualification
      1. Income _$3333_ /month × PITI debt ratio _28_ % = $ _933_ PITI affordability
      2. PITI affordability _$933_ − Taxes and insurance = PI affordable _$783_

   B. LT debt ratio qualification
      1. Monthly income _$3333_ − Monthly taxes withheld _$900_ = $ _2433_ (1) Net effective income
      2. Net effective income _2433_ × LT ratio _55_ = $ _1338_
      3. Taxes + Insurance _$150_ + Utilities _$70_ + Maintenance _30_ + Long-term debt _400_ = $ _650_
      4. $ _1338_ (2) − $ _650_ (3) = $ _688_ PI affordable

   C. PI affordable: _$688_

   (enter amount from box in part A or part B, whichever is less)

II. *Mortgage loan range*

A. Amortized vs. interest-only (circle one)

    • (If) amortized, use loan tables

    • If interest only, use the following equation for mortgage amount:

$$(\text{PI affordable} \times 12) \div \text{Rate} = \text{Mortgage amount}$$

B. Mortgage loan range (compute at desired rates):

    (11%)   12%   (13%)   14%   (15%)

    ? $72,500 $62,000 $54,000 ?

III. *Price range derivation*

A. Select LTV ratios to be applied to mortgage range:

    (75%)   80%   (85%)   90%   95%

B. Complete the buying range table below. To complete, divide each mortgage loan amount by each LTV ratio used.

Price Range   Assumptions: term ___30 yrs___ type ___Amort.___

Interest Rate

LTV	(11%)	12%	(13%)	14%	(15%)	other %
75% (25% down)	$96,700		$82,700		72,000	
80% (20% down)						
85% (15% down)	$85,300		$72,900		$63,500	
90% (10% down)						
95% (5% down)						

IV. *Cash analysis and adjustment*

A. Cash available: ___$30,000___

B. Cash required at ___13%___ interest, ___85___ % LTV (Price − Mortgage)

    1. If cash available exceeds required amount:

       Cash available ___$30,000___ + Mortgage amount ___$62,000___ =

       Price qualified for ___$92,000___

    2. If cash available is less than cash required:

       a. Cash available $ _____ + Mortgage amount $ _____ =

          Tentative price qualified to buy $_____

       b. Compute new LTV: _____

       c. If acceptable, *a* is qualified amount

       d. If *b* is not acceptable, lower the mortgage amount until it is.

three years. Finally, because you see the Lincolns have a sizable amount of cash, you decide to at least initially determine their purchasing power based on two loan-to-value ratios: 75 percent and 85 percent.

After getting the foregoing data and making the various assumptions, you determine what the Lincolns can afford based on the various interest rates in your quantitative buyer qualification table.

Determine the Lincolns' buying range by completing the following quantitative buyer qualification worksheet (Figure 1.2). In deriving the mortgage range, use 30-year amortized loans and interest rates of 11 percent, 13 percent, and 15 percent. Also, complete the cash analysis and adjustment section (Section IV) using the middle interest rate, 13 percent, and an 85 percent loan-to-value ratio. Remember, don't study the solution till you have worked through the qualification exercise yourself.

Discussion of the Financial Qualifications of the Lincolns.   From the qualification form (Figure 1.3), you learn that the Lincolns have an affordability range of $63,500 at 15 percent interest and 85 percent LTV to $96,700 at 11 percent interest and 75 percent LTV. However, since the Lincolns have more cash than those loans require, their cash-adjusted price range is the $72,500 mortgage plus $30,000 or $102,500 at 11 percent interest down to $54,000 plus $30,000, or $84,000 at 15 percent interest. The cash-adjusted mid-range, at 13 percent, is $62,000 + $30,000, or $92,000.

In terms of rough qualification, the Lincolns can afford a home priced between $84,000 and $102,500, depending on what financing they can get.

Qualitative Buyer Qualification

To conduct a thorough financial qualification of the buyer, several qualitative factors should be covered in addition to the quantitative analysis. This is necessary because contemporary financing has generated a need for certain types of additional information. These are discussed in the following paragraphs.

The Buyer's Income Potential.   A detailed discussion should take place with the buyers about future income potential, particularly if seller financing is to be arranged. As pointed out earlier, cheaper, short-term financing, or techniques that initially lower financing costs, can create onerous affordability problems at the short-term loan's maturity. The higher costs of refinancing or obtaining permanent financing can be difficult if the buyer's income has not increased. For that reason it is advisable to arrive at a solid income projection for each contributing wage earner in the household.

The Buyer's Planning Horizon.   Given the possibility of short-term financing, the length of time the buyers plan to live in the residence takes on added importance. If they plan on a short residency, say three to five years, short-term financing may be attractive since refinancing may not be necessary; they can just sell the home. If they plan to stay five or six years, four-year balloon financing could be an aggravation, if not a serious problem, because something would have to be arranged for a mere one to two years after the initial four-year period. If they plan on a long-term occupancy, either short-term or long-term financing might be acceptable.

FIGURE 1.3:   Quantitative Buyer Qualification (Solution to Case Study Exercise)

Buyer: _____Lincolns_____

Essential data

A. Monthly income: $ _____3,333_____

B. Monthly taxes withheld: $ _____900_____

C. Projected change in annual income: ____8_____%

D. Cash available for down payment: $ ____30,000_____

E. Long-term debt: ___$400_____/month

Assumptions

A. PITI ratio: _____28_____%

B. LT debt ratio: _____55_____%

C. Interest rate(s) used in analysis: ___11%, 13%, 15%_____

D. Loan term and type: ____30_____years; (amortized)/interest only (circle one)

E. Taxes and insurance estimate: _____$150_____

F. Utilities estimate: ____$70_____; maintenance estimate: ____$30_____/month

I. *Income (debt) qualification*

    A. PITI debt ratio qualification

        A. Income ____$3,333_____/month × PITI debt ratio ____28_____% =
           ____$932_____ PITI affordability

        2. PITI affordability ____$932____ − Taxes and insurance = PI affordable ____$782____

    B. LT debt ratio qualification

        1. Monthly income ___$3,333_____ − Monthly taxes withheld ___$900_____ =
           $___2,433_____ (1) Net effective income

        2. Net effective income ___$2,433_____ × LT ratio ___55%_____ =
           $___1,338_____

        3. Taxes + Insurance ___$150_____ + Utilities ___$70_____ +
           Maintenance ___$30_____ + Long-term debt ___$400_____ = $ ___650_____

        4. $ ___1,338_____ (2) − $ ___650_____ (3) = $ ___688_____ PI affordable

    C. PI affordable: _____$688_____

    (enter amount from box in part A or part B, whichever is less)

II. *Mortgage loan range*

A. Amortized vs. interest-only (circle one)
  - If ~~amortized~~, use loan tables
  - If interest only, use the following equation for mortgage amount:

    (PI affordable × 12) ÷ Rate = Mortgage amount

B. Mortgage loan range (compute at desired rates):

    (11%)   12%   (13%)   14%   (15%)
    $72,500 $62,000 $54,000

III. *Price range derivation*

A. Select LTV ratios to be applied to mortgage range:

    (75%)   80%   (85%)   90%   95%

B. Complete the buying range table below. To complete, divide each mortgage loan amount by each LTV ratio used.

    Price Range   Assumptions: term __30 yrs.__ type __amort.__

Interest Rate

	11%	12%	13%	14%	15%	other %
LTV						
75% (25% down)	96,700		82,700		72,000	
80% (20% down)						
85% (15% down)	85,300		72,900		63,500	
90% (10% down)						
95% (5% down)						

IV. *Cash analysis and adjustment*

A. Cash available: ___$30,000___

B. Cash required at ___13%___ interest, ___85___ % LTV (Price − Mortgage)

  1. If cash available exceeds required amount:
     Cash available ___$30,000___ + Mortgage amount ___$62,000___ =
     Price qualified for ___$92,000___

  2. If cash available is less than cash required:
     a. Cash available $ _____ + Mortgage amount $ _____ =
        Tentative price qualified to buy $_____
     b. Compute new LTV: _____
     c. If acceptable, *a* is qualified amount
     d. If *b* is not acceptable, lower the mortgage amount until it is.

Risk Acceptance.   Certain unavoidable risks attend the noninstitutional financing arrangement, and these risks (default, remedying default, refinancing at higher costs, possible financial losses, etc.) must be disclosed to, understood and accepted by the buyer. The degree of risk the buyer agrees to accept directly influences the type of financing and the source of financing to be used.

Tax Impacts.   In some instances, the buyer may have taxation objectives relating to capital gains, gains tax deferment or ordinary income tax shelter. For example, a seller might be willing to trade off a higher price for a lower interest rate in a wraparound; the buyer may be income-short for the time being and may be willing to take a higher adjusted basis in exchange for lower monthly payments. Or the buyer may want maximum interest writeoffs and a minimum capital gain, in which case he or she might negotiate for a lower price offset by a higher interest rate. These objectives should be ultimately engineered by the buyer's legal or tax counsel.

Equity Objectives.   Closely related to the buyer's planning horizon are the buyer's objectives for the amount and speed of equity generation from their real estate investments over a period of time. A recent trend has developed among buyers to generate more home equity at a more rapid pace rather than opt for cheaper, interest-only loans or long-term amortized loans. The monthly costs may be higher, but in the final summary fewer total interest dollars are paid and the homeowner owns the home sooner. This new alternative can be explored when discussing the buyer's equity objectives.

Buyer Qualification—FHA Loans

The Federal Housing Administration (FHA) was established in 1934 under the National Housing Act and helps home buyers secure financing by insuring loans. Because the government insures the loans they can be obtained in most cases with smaller down payments and lower interest rates than conventional loans. Consequently buyers unqualified for a conventional loan may be able to qualify for an FHA-backed loan. For most FHA loans the minimum down payment is three percent on the first $25,000 of the loan and five percent on the rest of the loan. The FHA sets maximum loan amounts that vary in different parts of the country. Currently FHA-backed loans can not exceed $67,500 although higher limits are set for certain "high cost" areas of the country. The qualifying process for FHA loans is illustrated in the following case study and is explained below.

The primary difference in qualifying the buyer for an FHA loan as opposed to a conventional loan is the income figure used in the underwriting ratio. The FHA uses net monthly income instead of the gross monthly income used in conventional qualification. To calculate the monthly net income, deduct the amount of income tax paid each month from the gross income.

Next calculate the proposed housing expense by determining the proposed monthly mortgage payment. This includes: principal, interest, property taxes, hazard insurance, and any homeowner's dues, if applicable. A monthly "Maintenance and Repair" and "Utility" expense must also be included. These are based on the square footage of the house and can be determined by using FHA tables. The amounts in the FHA tables vary across the country.

Next you must calculate the other monthly expenses. These include:

- social security and retirement deductions,
- child support,
- child care,
- insurance premiums,
- union dues, and
- debts that will not be paid off before closing or in six months (monthly payments of $100 or more should be included even if the debt will be paid off in less than six months).

Next apply the qualifying ratios. For FHA loans the front-end qualifying ratio is 38 percent and the back-end qualifying ratio is 53 percent. To find the front-end ratio divide the total monthly housing expense by the net income. To find the back-end ratio divide the total of housing and other expenses by the net income. The calculated results for both must be less than the FHA qualifying ratios to qualify for the loan.

Residual Income Formula—FHA Loans

If the borrowers do not qualify for the loan using the 38/53 percent ratios, an alternate method called the "residual income formula" can be used to qualify the borrowers. With this method the monthly housing expenses and other expenses are subtracted from the net income to find the borrowers' "residual income." This amount is checked against the FHA residual income chart. If the borrowers' residual income exceeds the amount allowed on the FHA chart, they will qualify for the loan. The income chart takes into account the number of family members and may vary in different areas of the country.

Case Study Exercise: Financial Qualification of the Lincolns for an FHA Loan

From the preceding qualification exercise we know most of the information that is needed to qualify the Lincolns for an FHA loan. We already know that Mr. Lincoln earns $34,000 a year and Mrs. Lincoln earns $6,000. They pay about $900 a month in income taxes. They pay $400 a month on debts that are longer than six months. Taxes and insurance for homes in the area they are looking at are $150 per month, and utilities and maintenance costs average $100 per month.

They are purchasing a house for $79,000 and have a down payment of $4,000 (approximately 5 percent down) leaving a balance of $75,000 to finance. They are seeking a 30-year loan for 10 percent.

Using this information, an FHA qualification analysis for the Lincolns is illustrated in Figure 1.4.

Buyer Qualification—VA Loans

The Veterans Administration (VA) loan guarantee program was established in 1944 as part of the GI Bill of Rights. Originally the program was established for World War II veterans, but it has been expanded to include veterans of the Korean and Vietnam wars. Because they are guaranteed by the government, the loans can be offered with little or no

---

FIGURE 1.4:   FHA Quantitative Buyer Qualification (Solution to Case Study Exercise)

Buyer: The Lincolns

Step 1.   Borrowers' net monthly income

> $2,833   Borrower's income (34,000 ÷ 12)
> <u> $500</u>   Co-borrower's income (6,000 ÷ 12)
> $3,333   Total gross income
>
> <u> $900</u>   Minus federal taxes withheld
> $2,433   Net income

Step 2.   Proposed monthly payment

> $658   Principal and interest (based on a 30-year loan of $75,000 @ 10%)
> $120   Taxes
> <u> $30</u>   Hazard insurance
> $808   Total mortgage payment
>
> <u>$100</u>   Maintenance & utilities
> $908   Total proposed housing expense

Step 3.   Other monthly expenses

> $250   Social security and retirement payments (may vary based on borrower's employment situation. In this case the social security rate is used: 0751 × $3,333).
> <u>$400</u>   Monthly debt obligations
> $1,558   Total obligations

Step 4.   Apply ratios

Allowable housing expense ratio (front-end ratio)

> $925   Allowable housing expense (net income $2,433 × .38) — *front-end ratio*
> Since the allowable housing expense ($925) is more than the proposed housing expense ($908) the Lincolns would qualify for the loan.

Allowable expense ratio (back-end ratio)

> $1,289   Amount of allowable obligations (net income $2,433 × .53) — *back-end ratio*
> Since the allowable expense ($1,289) is less than the total obligation expense ($1,558) the Lincolns would <u>not</u> qualify under this ratio.

Residual income formula

> $3,333   Gross income
> $900   Subtract federal taxes
> $908   Subtract housing expense
> $250   Subtract social security expense
> <u>$400</u>   Subtract debt expense
> $875   Residual income

Using the sample Residual Income Chart below we see that the minimum residual amount for a two-person family is $643. Since the Lincolns' residual income is more than that ($875) they will qualify for the loan under this formula.

Residual Income Chart

> $409   One person
> $643   Two persons
> $781   Family of 3
> $868   Family of 4
> $946   Family of 5
> $1,026   Family of 6
> $1,096   Family of 7

down payment and a lower interest rate than conventional loans. Although the VA does not limit the amount of loan an eligible veteran may obtain, lenders generally establish the maximum loan amount based on the entitlement amount. Veterans who qualify for a certificate of eligibility are currently entitled to a loan guarantee of $27,500. Most lenders who make VA guaranteed loans will loan up to four times the amount of entitlement (i.e., $110,000). By making a larger down payment a veteran may be able to obtain a larger loan from the lender.

The qualifying process for VA loans is illustrated in the following case study and is explained below. The primary difference between qualifying the buyer for a VA loan and an FHA loan is the income figure used in the qualifying ratio. The VA uses gross monthly income; the FHA uses net monthly income.

First calculate the borrower's monthly gross income. Next figure out all of the monthly expenses of the borrower. These include:

- federal income taxes withheld,
- social security and retirement deductions,
- debts that will not be paid off before closing or in six months (Monthly payments of $100 or more should be included even if the debt will be paid off in less than six months.),
- child support and alimony payments,
- child care payments (children under ten),
- job-related expenses (minimum of $50 per working person), and
- proposed house payments.

The proposed house payment includes: principal, interest, property taxes, hazard insurance, and any homeowner's dues, if applicable. A monthly "Maintenance and Utility" expense must also be included, is based on the square footage of the house and can be determined by using VA tables.

Next apply the qualifying criteria. First the "Residual Income Formula" is used to qualify the borrowers. Under this method the monthly housing expenses and other expenses are subtracted from the gross income to find the borrowers' residual income. This amount is compared to the VA residual income chart. If the amount of residual income exceeds the amount allowed on the VA chart they will qualify for the loan. The income chart takes into account the number of family members and the chart may vary in different areas of the country.

Next work out the expense-to-gross-income ratio. To calculate the ratio, divide the total of housing and other expenses (do not include federal tax and social security expenses) by the gross income. The calculated ratio must be less than the 41 percent factor set by the VA to qualify for the loan.

Case Study Exercise: Financial Qualification of the Lincolns for a VA Loan

From the preceding qualification exercises you have most of the information needed to qualify the Lincolns for a VA loan. In addition, the Lincolns have no children and the home they are buying is brick, has central air-conditioning and is 1,100 square feet. A VA qualification analysis for the Lincolns is illustrated in Figure 1.5.

FIGURE 1.5: VA Quantitative Buyer Qualification (Solution to Case Study Exercise)

Buyer: The Lincolns

Step 1. Borrowers' net monthly income

$2,833 Borrower's income (34,000 ÷ 12)
$500 Co-borrower's income (6,000 ÷ 12)
$3,333 Total gross income

Step 2. Subtract all monthly expenses

$900 Subtract federal taxes withheld
$250 Subtract social security/retirement payments (may vary based on borrower's employment situation. In this case the social security rate will be used: .0751 × $3,333).
$400 Subtract monthly debt obligations
$ 0 Subtract child support alimony payments
$ 0 Subtract child care payments
$100 Subtract job-related expenses
   $658 Principal and interest (based on a 30-year loan of $75,000 @ 10%)
   $120 Taxes
    $30 Hazard insurance
   $149 Maintenance & utilities
$957 Subtract total house payment
$726 Amount remaining for family support

Step 3. Apply qualification criteria

Residual income — $726. Because this is more than the residual income for a veteran and spouse in the chart ($570) the Lincolns would qualify under this criterion.

Expense to income ratio

$41% Allowable expense to gross income ratio
$44% Borrowers expense to gross income ratio
   expenses = $1,457 ($400 + $100 + $957)
   expenses $1,457/gross income $3,333

Since the allowable expense ratio (41) is less than the expense/gross income ratio (44) the Lincolns would not qualify under this ratio.

Maintenance and Utilities Chart

	Frame	Frame w/AC	Brick	Brick w/AC
1,100 sq. ft. or less	10.5	15.0	9.0	13.5
1,101–1,700 sq. ft.	11.2	15.0	10.2	14.0
1,700 sq. ft. or more	9.5	12.7	8.0	11.2

Residual Income Chart

$ 400 One person
$ 570 Veteran and spouse
$ 670 Family of 3
$ 760 Family of 4
$ 850 Family of 5
$ 940 Family of 6
$1,030 Family of 7
$1,120 Family of 8

QUALIFYING THE SELLER AND PROPERTY

Qualifying the Seller

Qualifying the seller does not involve the financial computations and capabilities assessments that characterize buyer qualification. Rather, the purpose of seller qualification is to uncover (1) how much cash the seller needs from the sale, (2) how much of the financing the seller will provide, if any, and (3) what the seller's other, more qualitative objectives are, such as tax strategies and purchasing plans.

In residential brokerage, there are essentially two types of sale: the new home sale and the resale. New home sales are most likely conducted through professionally designed and engineered programs constructed by the builder and associated marketing experts. The large resale market—if its transactions involve seller financing—entail certain commitments from a new, inexperienced party: the homeseller.

In view of the two types of homeseller, two different sets of information are needed to set the brokerage process in motion. From builders, practitioners need to know only the various elements of the offering: prices, financing terms and buyer qualification standards. Thereafter it's a matter of matching pre-existing seller data with the buyer's situation and following through with whatever brokerage participation may be involved.

On the other hand, the resale seller's selling data may not exist prior to the marketing process. The seller's asking price, selling terms and timing plans, for example, may at best be only tentatively surmised before the broker or agent comes on the scene. Thus the broker/agent is more actively involved in developing the seller's marketing terms. Here, the broker must steer a cautious yet positive course in generating the necessary information that will best meet the seller's objectives.

The Seller and Property Qualification Summary.   Figures 1.6 and 1.7 outline the data that must be obtained and maintained from both owner/sellers and builders. Information about the property itself is also included.

The Property Qualification Summary has been integrated into the Seller Qualification Summary as shown in Figure 1.6. The integration of these summaries is done to facilitate reference to both the seller's commitments and the property's financial data.

The most important information for qualifying the resident homeseller is the amount of cash needed from the sale proceeds and, of course, the price range.

Of secondary import is to know the seller's commitment to finance the sale and the specific terms, if any. Today, selling a home may depend on the seller's agreement to finance all or part of the purchase price. Part IB of Figure 1.6 details these terms, if any, including how much the seller will finance, for how long, and at what interest rate. When this data is obtained, the real estate practitioner is in a position to know just what forms of non-institutional financing are available in addition to bank and savings and loan association offerings.

FIGURE 1.6: Seller Financial Qualification Summary

Seller: _____

I. Homeseller data

    A. Quantitative needs

        1. Price: _____

        2. Cash at sale: _____

    B. Financing commitments:

        1. Is the seller able to finance according to his/her mortgage documents? Yes___No___

        2. Is he or she willing to do so?

        3. Amount will finance: $ _____

        4. Minimum cash down: _____

        5. Type of financing preferred: _____

        6. Maximum term: _____

        7. Interest rate: _____

        8. Interest-only with balloon or amortized with balloon?

        9. Will/will not roll over balloon for added term (circle)

II. Property Qualification Summary

    A. CMA valuation: _____

    B. Underlying financing: type _____priority _____remaining term _____

        1. Principal balance $ _____

        2. Interest rate _____%

        3. Assumable?   yes   no

FIGURE 1.7:   Builder Financial Program Summary

Builder:_____ Name of property(ies):_____

I. *Price range:* $_____ to $_____

Down payment range _____% to _____%

II. *Financing terms:*

Amount (% or $): _____

Rate: _____ APR _____%

Term/type _____years; amortized/interest only

Special arrangements/conditions:

Buydown subsidy/second mortgage program:

III. *Qualification parameters*

Minimum down payment $ _____ / _____%

Qualifying income method: _____

_____

Other:

In addition to this financial data, item IB(9) in Figure 1.6 asks a key question about an extension of the potential balloon loan. Balloon loans—being short-term loans with the entire balance due at maturity—can cause problems if the borrower can't refinance the principal balance. For that reason, it is a good safeguard to determine in advance whether the seller will extend the loan term—"roll it over"—should the borrower be unable to obtain permanent long-term financing.

Aside from quantitative financial data, a number of qualitative objectives should be sought. They include (1) urgency, (2) the seller's plans for purchasing (or renting) the next residence, and (3) their more general attitudes about financing.

The astute real estate practitioner will explore these qualitative areas for two reasons: first, in order to know the seller's plans and motivations; and second, in order to evaluate whether such plans are realistic and feasible in view of the desired selling price, cash needed from the sale and the financing commitments (or lack thereof) the seller has made.

In a hypothetical situation that could easily occur, an owner must sell his home quickly, within 30 to 45 days. The seller doesn't know the market yet wants top dollar. In addition, the seller needs all of the selling price in cash and will not participate in financing. Given these circumstances, most practitioners will recognize that this seller's objectives are not very realistic in a tight market. To get top dollar—and all in cash—in a tight market requires more than 30 to 45 days in all probability. Or if the property must be sold in 30 to 45 days, some compromise in pricing or financing will almost certainly be necessary.

Qualifying the Resale Property

Qualifying the existing financing on the seller's property enables the agent to evaluate the marketability of the property from a financial standpoint.

As shown in the Property Qualification Summary (Figure 1.6, Part II), three items of information are needed: the property's value, its estimated appreciation rate and its underlying financing.

Item IIA, the CMA valuation, or the value of the property derived from competitive market analysis, renders a realistic market value of the property being sold. The CMA in residential brokerage consists of a price comparison of recently sold homes of comparable size and condition in comparable locations. This price analysis effectively indicates what a buyer is likely to pay for the property—the property's market value.

It is important to note, however, that the CMA should in no way be construed as a formal property appraisal. Such appraisals are done by qualified specialists and represent truer estimates of property value than the CMA. The CMA is a valuable tool but only for obtaining a rough estimate of value.

The CMA, in addition to establishing a market price guide, is useful in getting the homeseller to understand how home values are determined. Obviously sellers want maximum money for their homes and they often feel their homes are worth more than market price. But in residential brokerage, the price is set not by the emotions of a seller but by what a buyer will pay. Thus the CMA valuation is a key tool in pricing the property realistically enough to sell.

The property's underlying financing is a key factor in the pricing and salability of a home. As indicated earlier, a home is worth what a buyer will pay, and this is determined by not only the property's price but also by the monthly payments. A buyer can more easily afford a $75,000 home than a $65,000 home if financing on the $75,000 home is at 10 percent and financing on the $65,000 home is at 15 percent. If a buyer put $10,000 down on either property and got a 30-year loan, payments on the $75,000 home would be $570.43 and payments on the $65,000 home would be $695.45.

There are three important things to ascertain regarding the underlying financing: whether the buyer can assume the loan, how much unpaid principal balance remains on the loan and the loan's interest rate. If the loan is assumable (such as FHA or VA loans), the buyer may benefit from an interest rate lower than current conventional rates. Moreover, if the remaining loan balance is high in relation to the price, the buyer further benefits because less financing will be needed at the higher current rates.

From the seller's perspective, an assumable high-balance, low-rate loan greatly improves the likelihood that a higher price can be obtained for the property. Conversely, if the seller's underlying mortgage is not assumable, or has a very low balance, the buyer has to procure a larger mortgage elsewhere at higher rates. This in turn creates higher monthly payments and hurts the buyer's chance to qualify as well as the seller's chance of receiving the highest possible price.

Qualifying the New Homebuilder

Figure 1.7, Builder Financial Program Summary, is a straightforward data sheet for summarizing a builder's financial program on a given development. Like the Seller Summary, this worksheet can be completed for all active builders and used in the process of matching buyers with properties from a financial standpoint. Obviously, these are valuable when working with buyers who strictly want to purchase brand new houses.

As indicated earlier, qualifying new developments requires less effort than does qualifying occupied resale residences. Builders formulate their own pricing and financing standards and generally have determined specific qualifying ratios to apply to potential buyers. As a result, qualifying builders amounts essentially to organizing records and files on the builders in a market area and to keeping track of their financing programs. Once you have this information on record—using, for example, the Builder Financial Program Summary —you can match prospective buyers with the builder's property data.

QUALIFYING THE MORTGAGE LENDER

Besides the seller and the builder, the remaining principal source of residential mortgage financing is the institutional lender, who, like seller, builder, buyer and property, must be qualified. Qualifying the institutional lender is in reality doing a market survey of available mortgage programs offered by lenders in your market area.

Survey of the Local Mortgage Market

There are three lenders to be primarily concerned with: (1) the seller's lender, (2) the buyer's lender, and (3) the lenders you are familiar with who have competitive market rates and programs. All of these organizations will be interested in obtaining the buyer's business if he or she is qualified under specified terms. It is the practitioner's role to know who these lenders are and what terms they are offering, so one can identify various institutional programs that are attractive or promise to help complete a transaction successfully.

Knowing the various programs offered in an area is not difficult if one is organized and can develop a method for maintaining updated information. The Lender Market Summary, Figure 1.8, is one such way to concisely compile and maintain mortgage programs in a market area.

The Lender Market Summary.   The Lender Market Summary presents a matrix that asks for the lender's various terms and conditions on a range of major mortgage financing alternatives. By and large, the five alternatives shown represent most of the instruments used by lenders.

For each of these mechanisms, six key questions are asked about the loan products themselves and the qualifications required to obtain them: how much the lender will lend, at what rate, points chargeable, the loan term, and the two qualifications we've worked with—the maximum LTV allowed and the debt ratio used. At the bottom of the Lender Market Summary is space for the lender or broker's other comments that may be pertinent to the various loans—the due-on-sale policy of the lender, any short-term call provisions of the various loans, and so on.

Computerized Mortgage Services

A recent innovation that is becoming very popular is computerized mortgage services. In the past when borrowers wanted to find a loan with the best rate and terms to fit their situation, they would have to laboriously make contact with and collect information from each lender. Also, when lenders wanted to enter a particular mortgage market, they would have to go through the costly and time-consuming process of hiring qualified personnel and setting up an office in the market area. These problems are alleviated with the development of computerized mortgage services. Borrowers can now collect and compare loan information on many lenders easily and quickly including lenders in other parts of the country, while lenders can access markets all over the country without the need to maintain costly offices and staff in each area. Another benefit of this approach is that it increases competition among lenders.

There are several computerized mortgage networks. One of them is Rennie Mae®, developed by the National Association of REALTORS®. It is marketed nationwide to real estate brokers and is open to participation by any lender in the country. Some of the other mortgage networks offer mortgages from a small group of lenders who jointly market their individual mortgage programs.

Mortgage networks not only can be used to compare loan programs but also to prequalify buyers and assist in the loan application process. Information provided by the buyer is entered into the computer system, which produces a range of prices that the buyer can afford. The buyer can then review mortgages that are sorted by loan type, interest rate, annual percentage rate, down payment requirements or other variables. After reviewing all of the loan options, the buyer can select a mortgage and fill out a loan application. Verification forms are electronically transmitted by the computer to the lender, and the original loan documents are sent by messenger service. This system allows the lender to begin processing the loan immediately.

FIGURE 1.8: Lender Market Summary

Lender _____   Date completed _____

Updating _____

_____

Mortgage Loan Programs Offered	Maximum Amount	Rate	Terms/Conditions		Maximum LTV	Debt Ratio
			Points	Term		
Fixed-rate (conventional)						
AML/ARM						
Blends						
Assumptions (with DOS clauses)						
VA						
Other (including GPMs)						

Notes/Other Comments:

Due-on-sale policy:

Call provisions:

Other:

2

Fixed-Rate Mortgages and Blended-Rate Mortgages

The traditional fixed-rate amortized mortgage is the grandfather loan of mortgage financing as it exists today. As its name implies, the fixed-rate mortgage has an interest rate that remains unchangeable for the mortgagor over the entire term of the loan. The loan's monthly payments are a fixed and constant amount whether the loan is amortized or is interest-only with a balloon. A more recent introduction, the blended-rate mortgage, responds to today's less-stable financial environment. Blended-rate mortgages vary their interest rates over the term of the loan to reflect current market interest rates. This chapter will examine and compare the two mortgage approaches and explain how to apply each to typical real estate situations.

LEARNING OBJECTIVES

This chapter will help you learn to

1. define the conventional fixed-rate mortgage and describe its key characteristics,
2. describe the mechanics of fixed-rate mortgages,
3. define blended-rate mortgages and describe their key characteristics, and
4. calculate the interest rate on blended-rate mortgages.

THE FIXED-RATE MORTGAGE

Because it lets borrowers know in advance what their monthly payments will be, the fixed-rate loan has remained by far the most popular mortgage loan available today. Borrowers also know how much equity is increasing in the property as the loan is paid. A potential disadvantage here is that in a period of declining interest rates the borrower is locked into a fixed-rate loan. In recent years the fixed-rate mortgage has lost some of its appeal among lenders because interest rate payments on deposits have become more volatile. In some cases, short-term deposit payments have risen above the lender's income from long-term, fixed-rate loans creating a financial loss for the institution. Thus the fixed-rate mortgage loan today carries a higher interest rate than newer types of loans such as the adjustable-rate loan.

What Is a Fixed-Rate Mortgage?

The fixed-rate mortgage is a loan having a predetermined rate of interest that cannot be changed throughout the term of the loan for the original mortgagor. The fixed-rate loan that is called "conventional" is typically an amortized loan issued by a nongovernment lender such as a bank, savings and loan association or mortgage banking company. Note that the interest rate on the conventional fixed-rate mortgage *can* be changed should a transfer of interest take place on the secured property—unless the loan document contains an acceleration clause prohibiting such a transfer. Practically all conventional mortgages issued over the past ten years carry such a clause. Mortgages insured or guaranteed by a government agency such as the FHA and VA do not carry an acceleration clause and are thus assumable.

Sources of Fixed-Rate Mortgages

There are numerous sources for the fixed-rate mortgage including banks, savings and loans, mortgage companies, credit unions, builders and homesellers themselves. In addition, the institutional fixed-rate loan (amortized) has long been insurable by the Federal Housing Authority (FHA) or guaranteed for veterans by the Veterans Administration (VA). Finally, secondary market organizations such as the Federal National Mortgage Association (Fannie Mae) and The Mortgage Corporation (formerly Freddie Mac) have had long-standing programs to purchase fixed-rate mortgages from primary lending institutions.

Components of the Fixed-Rate Loan

Interest Rate.   The interest rate is fixed for the life of the loan. The rate itself will tend to be higher than variable-rate loans.

Loan Term.   The traditional fixed-rate loan is issued for 25 to 30 years. Such long-term loans now have competition from five- to ten-year loans or 25 to 30-year loans with short-term call provisions of 5 to 10 years that give a lender the option to continue the loan, accelerate it or change the interest rate. The advantage of the "long-term" loan with a short-term call provision is that payments are amortized over 25 to 30 years even though the loan may be "called in" after five to ten years. The lengthier amortization reduces monthly payments thereby allowing borrowers to qualify. In some states the 15-year mortgage has recently become very popular. This mortgage is discussed in Chapter 8.

Loan Payments.   The typical fixed-rate loan as issued by institutions is an amortized loan, that is, payments contain both an interest and a principal amount that will eventually retire the outstanding balance over the loan period. However, it is not uncommon to obtain a fixed-rate loan with interest-only payments and a balloon payment of the whole principal at the end.

Lien Priority.   The fixed-rate loan can either be a senior *or* a junior lien against a property's title. Senior, or first, liens carry a lower rate of interest than junior liens because a junior lien does not have first claim on the proceeds in a foreclosure sale. Junior fixed-rate liens are commonly called conventional second mortgages or "seconds," "thirds," or "fourths."

Loan-to-Value Ratio.   The loan-to-value ratio (LTV) for conventional senior fixed-rate mortgages runs between 75 and 90 percent. In some cases, such as FHA mortgages, a 95 to 97 percent value is permitted. Among conventional lenders a 90 percent LTV mortgage may be granted provided that private mortgage insurance is obtained.

Mechanics of the Fixed-Rate Mortgage

The financial mechanics of the fixed-rate mortgage are the least complicated of all mortgages available today. Simply stated, the homebuyer invests a certain percent of the sales price as a down payment, gives the lender a promissory note secured by the mortgage, and the lender loans the buyer the money. Subsequently the mortgagor makes his or her fixed-level monthly payment to the lender, and that is that.

In understanding how the mechanics of fixed-rate mortgages work, it is necessary to learn:

- what the monthly payments will be on the loan,
- what the remaining principal balance is on the loan period, and
- how much principal and/or interest has been paid over a given period of time.

The following sections detail how these three factors are calculated, both for amortized and interest-only loans.

Calculating the Monthly Payment on the Fixed-Rate Loan

Amortized Payments.   On an amortized fixed-rate loan, a portion of the level payment goes to principal on an ever-increasing basis and a portion is allocated to interest on an ever-decreasing basis. Because the principal and interest portions of the payment change every month—even though the payment amount does not—it is virtually impossible to calculate amortized loan payments without a computer. For that reason, amortized loan tables were created so that practitioners need only refer to charts to find the monthly or annual payment on an amortized loan. Such charts are also useful for determining how much money a buyer could borrow assuming a given payment level, interest rate and loan term.

For example, if a borrower could afford $500 per month for PI payments and 30-year loans were going for 14 percent interest, one would refer to the 14 percent table under the 30-year column to see that the borrower could obtain roughly a $42,000 mortgage. Sample fixed-rate mortgage payment charts are printed in the Appendix. If you are not familiar with such charts, refer to the Appendix to see how they work.

Interest-Only Monthly Payments.   The other type of fixed-rate loan payment is the interest-only monthly payment. Usually, interest-only monthly payments are calculated by multiplying the interest rate times the principal balance and dividing by 12:

$$\frac{\text{Rate} \times \text{Principal Balance}}{12}$$

This equation yields a noncompounded monthly payment rate that is typical of interest-only mortgage loans. Using our foregoing example, for instance, if a borrower obtained a $42,000 interest-only mortgage at 14 percent, the monthly payments (regardless of the loan term) would be:

$$\frac{14\% \times \$42,000}{12} = \frac{\$5,880}{12} = \$490$$

See HP Guide Book pg 13-15

Using Loan Constants to Determine Amortized Payments.   It can be observed from the amortized loan charts in the Appendix that the monthly payments are indicated for loan amounts having a rounded figure, e.g., $40,000, $55,000, etc. What happens if you want to know the amortized monthly payment for an unrounded amount, for example $41,250? You can use what are called loan constants. Shown on the next page is a sample loan constant table, Table 2.1, entitled "Monthly Payment Needed to Amortize a $1,000 Loan."

The table shows the interest rates along the top and the number of years in the loan term down the left side. The number where an interest column and a year intersect is the loan constant. For example, for a ten-year loan at 13.50 percent, the loan constant is 15.2274.

The loan constant is a figure that when multiplied by any loan amount *in thousands* will produce the monthly payment that will amortize the loan over the indicated loan term. Use this equation:

Constant × Loan Amount in Thousands = Monthly Payment

Taking the example of a $41,250 loan for ten years at 13.5 percent interest, we get:

15.2274 × 41.250 = $628.13

Thus the monthly payment needed to amortize our $41,250 ten-year loan at 13.50 percent interest is $628.24. (Note the use of the decimal point to express the loan amount in $1,000s.) This equation can be used for any loan amount for any time period and rate of interest on an amortized loan. For your reference, additional loan constant charts can be found in the Appendix. Each payment of a fixed-rate mortgage loan is comprised of a portion that pays down the balance of the loan and a portion that is payment of interest. While the monthly payment amount is constant, the portion allocated to interest and principal changes with each payment. As payments are made, the amount of interest decreases and the amount of money used to pay down the loan increases. It is possible to

TABLE 2.1:   Monthly Payment Needed to Amortize a $1,000 Loan

Interest Rate	Term of Loan							
	9 Years	10 Years	11 Years	12 Years	13 Years	14 Years	15 Years	16 Years
12.000%	15.1842	14.3471	13.6779	13.1342	12.6867	12.3143	12.0017	11.7373
12.125%	15.2548	14.4194	13.7520	13.2100	12.7641	12.3933	12.0822	11.8193
12.250%	15.3256	14.4920	13.8263	13.2860	12.8417	12.4725	12.1630	11.9015
12.375%	15.3965	14.5647	13.9007	13.3622	12.9196	12.5520	12.2440	11.9840
12.500%	15.4676	14.6376	13.9754	13.4386	12.9977	12.6317	12.3252	12.0667
12.625%	15.5388	14.7107	14.0503	13.5152	13.0760	12.7116	12.4067	12.1496
12.750%	15.6102	14.7840	14.1254	13.5920	13.1545	12.7917	12.4884	12.2328
12.875%	15.6818	14.8574	14.2006	13.6690	13.2332	12.8721	12.5703	12.3162
13.000%	15.7536	14.9311	14.2761	13.7463	13.3121	12.9526	12.6524	12.3999
13.125%	15.8255	15.0049	14.3518	13.8237	13.3912	13.0334	12.7348	12.4837
13.250%	15.8976	15.0789	14.4276	13.9013	13.4706	13.1144	12.8174	12.5678
13.375%	15.9699	15.1531	14.5036	13.9791	13.5502	13.1956	12.9002	12.6521
13.500%	16.0423	15.2274	14.5799	14.0572	13.6299	13.2771	12.9832	12.7367
13.625%	16.1149	15.3020	14.6563	14.1354	13.7099	13.3587	13.0664	12.8214
13.750%	16.1877	15.3767	14.7329	14.2138	13.7901	13.4406	13.1499	12.9064
13.875%	16.2606	15.4516	14.8097	14.2925	13.8704	13.5226	13.2335	12.9916
14.000%	16.3337	15.5266	14.8867	14.3713	13.9510	13.6049	13.3174	13.0770

manually calculate the amount allocated to interest and principal for each mortgage payment. This calculation is shown for the first three loan payments of a $41,250 loan at a rate of 13.5 percent with a ten-year term.

Payment #1

$$\$41,250 \times .135 \div 12 = \$464.06 \text{ interest}$$
$$\$628.13 - \$464.06 = \$164.07 \text{ principal}$$

Payment #2

$$\$41,250.00 - \$164.07 = \$41,085.93 \text{ new balance}$$
$$\$41,085.93 \times .135 \div 12 = \$462.22 \text{ interest}$$
$$\$628.13 - \$462.22 = \$165.91 \text{ principal}$$

Payment #3

$$\$41,085.93 - \$165.91 = \$40,920.02 \text{ new balance}$$
$$\$40,920.02 \times .135 \div 12 = \$460.35 \text{ interest}$$
$$\$628.13 - \$460.35 = \$167.78 \text{ principal}$$

See HP Guide Pg. 13-15

All of the payments for the loan are shown in Table 2.2. Notice that the reduction of the loan balance accelerates later in the loan period because the amount of interest for a payment is calculated on the remaining balance. As the balance decreases with each payment the amount of interest also decreases leaving a greater amount of the next payment to be applied toward the principal.

Calculating the Remaining Balance on the Amortized Fixed-Rate Loan

The mechanics of amortized fixed-rate loans are such that the remaining principal balance on the loan decreases by a slightly greater amount every month until the balance is entirely paid off. In working with this type of loan, it is important to know how much of the loan has been paid off at any given time—or conversely how much of the loan at such a time remains unpaid. Since this calculation is also very complex, charts called "Loan Progress Charts," which make use of "loan progress constants" to derive a loan's remaining balance, are used. A sample chart is displayed in Table 2.3.

TABLE 2.2: Amortization of a Ten-Year $41,250 Loan at 13.5% Interest

Payment	Principal	Interest	Balance	Payment	Principal	Interest	Balance
1	$164.07	$464.06	$41,085.93	61	$321.02	$307.11	$26,977.50
2	165.91	462.22	40,920.02	62	324.63	303.50	26,652.87
3	167.78	460.35	40,752.24	63	328.29	299.84	26,324.58
4	169.67	458.46	40,582.57	64	331.98	296.15	25,992.60
5	171.58	456.55	40,410.99	65	335.71	292.42	25,656.89
6	173.51	454.62	40,237.48	66	339.49	288.64	25,317.40
7	175.46	452.67	40,062.02	67	343.31	284.82	24,974.09
8	177.43	450.70	39,884.59	68	347.17	280.96	24,626.92
9	179.43	448.70	39,705.16	69	351.08	277.05	24,275.84
10	181.45	446.68	39,523.71	70	355.03	273.10	23,920.81
11	183.49	444.64	39,340.22	71	359.02	269.11	23,561.79
12	185.55	442.58	39,154.67	72	363.06	265.07	23,198.73
13	187.64	440.49	38,967.03	73	367.14	260.99	22,831.59
14	189.75	438.38	38,777.28	74	371.27	256.86	22,460.32
15	191.89	436.24	38,585.39	75	375.45	252.68	22,084.87
16	194.04	434.09	38,391.35	76	379.68	248.45	21,705.19
17	196.23	431.90	38,195.12	77	383.95	244.18	21,321.24
18	198.43	429.70	37,996.69	78	388.27	239.86	20,932.97
19	200.67	427.46	37,796.02	79	392.63	235.50	20,540.34
20	202.92	425.21	37,593.10	80	397.05	231.08	20,143.29
21	205.21	422.92	37,387.88	81	401.52	226.61	19,741.77
22	207.52	420.61	37,180.36	82	406.04	222.09	19,335.73
23	209.85	418.28	36,970.51	83	410.60	217.53	18,925.13
24	212.21	415.92	36,758.30	84	415.22	212.91	18,509.91
25	214.60	413.53	36,543.70	85	419.89	208.24	18,090.02
26	217.01	411.12	36,326.69	86	424.62	203.51	17,665.40
27	219.45	408.68	36,107.24	87	429.39	198.74	17,236.01
28	221.92	406.21	35,885.32	88	434.22	193.91	16,801.79
29	224.42	403.71	35,660.90	89	439.11	189.02	16,362.68
30	226.94	401.19	35,433.95	90	444.05	184.08	15,918.63
31	229.50	398.63	35,204.45	91	449.05	179.08	15,469.58
32	232.08	396.05	34,972.38	92	454.10	174.03	15,015.48
33	234.69	393.44	34,737.68	93	459.21	168.92	14,556.27
34	237.33	390.80	34,500.36	94	464.37	163.76	14,091.90
35	240.00	388.13	34,260.36	95	469.60	158.53	13,622.30
36	242.70	385.43	34,017.66	96	474.88	153.25	13,147.42
37	245.43	382.70	33,772.23	97	480.22	147.91	12,667.20
38	248.19	379.94	33,524.04	98	485.62	142.51	12,181.58
39	250.98	377.15	33,273.06	99	491.09	137.04	11,690.49
40	253.81	374.32	33,019.25	100	496.61	131.52	11,193.88
41	256.66	371.47	32,762.59	101	502.20	125.93	10,691.68
42	259.55	368.58	32,503.04	102	507.85	120.28	10,183.83
43	262.47	365.66	32,240.57	103	513.56	114.57	9,670.27
44	265.42	362.71	31,975.15	104	519.34	108.79	9,150.93
45	268.41	359.72	31,706.74	105	525.18	102.95	8,625.75
46	271.43	356.70	31,435.31	106	531.09	97.04	8,094.66
47	274.48	353.65	31,160.83	107	537.07	91.06	7,557.59
48	277.57	350.56	30,883.26	108	543.11	85.02	7,014.48
49	280.69	347.44	30,602.57	109	549.22	78.91	6,465.26
50	283.85	344.28	30,318.72	110	555.40	72.73	5,909.86
51	287.04	341.09	30,031.68	111	561.64	66.49	5,348.22
52	290.27	337.86	29,741.41	112	567.96	60.17	4,780.26
53	293.54	334.59	29,447.87	113	574.35	53.78	4,205.91
54	296.84	331.29	29,151.03	114	580.81	47.32	3,625.10
55	300.18	327.95	28,850.85	115	587.35	40.78	3,037.75
56	303.56	324.57	28,547.29	116	593.96	34.17	2,443.79
57	306.97	321.16	28,240.32	117	600.64	27.49	1,843.15
58	310.43	317.70	27,929.89	118	607.39	20.74	1,235.76
59	313.92	314.21	27,615.97	119	614.23	13.90	621.53
60	317.45	310.68	27,298.52	120	621.14	6.99	0.39

TABLE 2.3:   Loan Progress Chart   11.75%   Showing Remaining Balance on $1,000 Loan

For Mortgages with an Interest Rate of 11.75% and an Original Term of:

Age of Loan in Years	5 Years	6 Years	7 Years	8 Years	9 Years	10 Years	11 Years	12 Years	15 Years	20 Years	25 Years	30 Years	35 Years	40 Years
1	0.844	0.878	0.902	0.920	0.933	0.944	0.953	0.960	0.974	0.987	0.993	0.996	0.998	0.999
2	0.668	0.741	0.792	0.830	0.859	0.881	0.899	0.914	0.945	0.972	0.985	0.992	0.996	0.998
3	0.471	0.587	0.668	0.729	0.775	0.811	0.840	0.863	0.912	0.955	0.976	0.987	0.993	0.996
4	0.249	0.414	0.529	0.615	0.680	0.731	0.772	0.806	0.875	0.936	0.966	0.982	0.990	0.994
5	0.000	0.219	0.373	0.487	0.574	0.642	0.697	0.741	0.834	0.915	0.955	0.975	0.987	0.993
6		0.000	0.197	0.343	0.455	0.542	0.612	0.669	0.787	0.891	0.942	0.969	0.983	0.990
7			0.000	0.182	0.320	0.429	0.516	0.587	0.735	0.865	0.928	0.961	0.978	0.988
8				0.000	0.170	0.302	0.409	0.495	0.676	0.835	0.912	0.952	0.974	0.985
9					0.000	0.160	0.288	0.392	0.610	0.801	0.894	0.942	0.968	0.982
10						0.000	0.152	0.276	0.535	0.763	0.874	0.931	0.962	0.979
11							0.000	0.146	0.452	0.720	0.851	0.919	0.956	0.975
12								0.000	0.358	0.672	0.826	0.905	0.948	0.971
15									0.000	0.490	0.729	0.852	0.919	0.955
20										0.000	0.468	0.711	0.841	0.912
25											0.000	0.456	0.701	0.835
30												0.000	0.450	0.696
35													0.000	0.447
40														0.000

Each Loan Progress Chart is set up for a particular interest rate. The one shown is for a rate of 11.75 percent. On the top row of the chart is the loan's original term in number of years. The vertical column on the left gives the current age of the loan. Following the proper row and column to their intersection gives a constant. This loan progress constant is in reality the *percentage of the original loan amount that remains unpaid* per $1,000. Therefore, to identify the remaining balance on any loan, multiply the constant times the original loan amount in thousands. Or:

Constant × Original Loan Amount (1,000s) = Remaining Balance

Take a $42,000 loan, for example. Let's assume the $42,000, originally issued at 11.75 percent interest for 25 years, is now ten years old. What is the remaining principal balance of the loan?

By using Table 2.3 we find the remaining balance constant for an 11.75 percent, 25-year loan which is ten years old is 874. Thus:

874 × $42.000 = $36,708 remaining unpaid balance

To determine how much principal has been paid on the loan, subtract the remaining loan balance from the beginning loan balance. For example, the principal already paid on the foregoing $42,000 loan is $42,000 − $36,708, or $5,292. Note that the chart provided requires that the age of the loans be in whole years.

Calculating Interest and Principal Paid During a Given Time Period

In residential brokerage, it is very often necessary to estimate how much interest and how much principal was paid on an amortized fixed-rate loan during a given time period. For example, an individual might want to estimate his or her interest deductions in a given tax year.

To determine how much principal on a loan has been paid, use the loan progress chart as follows:

$(\text{Constant}_1 - \text{Constant}_2) \times$ Original Loan Amount in 1,000s

where:

Constant_1 is found for the age of the loan at the beginning of the period, and Constant_2 is found for the age of the loan at the end of the period.

Let's use the same $42,000 loan at 11.75 percent to illustrate. Assume a homeowner wants to know how much principal was paid on the 25-year loan during the tenth year of the loan period. To calculate this, we first recognize that the beginning constant is for a nine-year-old loan, and the ending constant is for a ten-year-old loan. Thus:

$$(894 - 874) \times \$42.000 = \text{principal paid during tenth year.}$$
$$20 \times \$42 = \$840$$

During the tenth year, the borrower paid 2 percent, or $840 of the principal.

It is also possible to calculate how much interest was paid on an amortized loan over any period using the loan constants already discussed. To do this, take the *entire* principal and interest amount paid, and subtract the principal paid:

$$\text{Interest paid} = (\text{PI payments}) - ([\text{Constant}_1 - \text{Constant}_2] \times \text{Original Loan Amount in 1,000s}$$

To illustrate, let's assume our borrower wants to know how much interest was paid on the foregoing loan in the tenth year. The monthly payment on the $42,000 loan for 25 years at 11.75 percent interest is $434.70. Total payments during the year, then, are $434.70 × 12 or $5,216.40. Now we plug figures into our equation:

$$\text{Interest paid} = \$5,216.40 - ([.894 - .874] \times \$42,000)$$
$$= \$5,216.40 - 840 = \$4,376.40$$

NOTE: The foregoing calculations are for the purpose of making rough estimates only. It is not the role of the broker to act in a lender's capacity by representing that such figures are "true and accurate."

Summary of Fixed-Rate Loan Mechanics

As we have seen, the mechanics of fixed-rate amortized or interest-only loans are straightforward principal and/or interest payments to the lender as established by loan charts and/or loan constants. To understand how amortized fixed-rate loans work, you need to know:

Study

Equations

1. Monthly payments on the loan:

    Constant × Loan Amount (1,000s)

    From the Monthly Payment Needed to Amortize a $1,000 Loan Chart (Table 2.1)

2. The remaining principal balance:

    Constant × Original Loan (1,000s)

    From the Loan Progress Chart (Table 2.3)

3. How much principal was paid in a given time period:

    $Constant_1 - Constant_2$ × Original Loan Amount in 1,000s

    From the Loan Progress Chart (Table 2.3)

4. How much interest was paid in a given time period:

    (Yearly PI Payment) − $(Constant_1 - Constant_2)$ ×

    Original Loan Amount in 1,000s

    From the Loan Progress Chart (Table 2.3)

SELF-QUIZ: FIXED-RATE MORTGAGES

1. Can the interest rate on a fixed-rate mortgage be changed during the loan term?

2. An amortized 30-year fixed-rate mortgage with a 5-year call provision is amortized over the initial 5 years. True or false?

3. Why do "second" mortgages have a higher interest rate than "first" mortgages?

    Risk

4. Loan-to-value ratios on conventional mortgages rarely exceed 90 percent without private mortgage insurance. Why is this?   *Risk*

The following exercises concern a $73,500 fixed-rate loan amortized at 11.75 percent interest for 30 years. Refer to the loan charts in the Appendix to complete your answer.

5. What are the principal and interest payments on this loan?

    $742

6. If this loan were interest-only, what would the monthly payments be?

$720

7. What is the remaining balance on this loan after 8 years?

8. How much principal was paid on this loan during the 8th year?

9. How much interest did the borrower pay during the 8th year?

ANSWERS TO SELF-QUIZ: FIXED-RATE MORTGAGES

1. Yes. In the event the property is sold or the mortgage loan is assumed by another party, the lender can accelerate a loan or adjust the interest rate, provided the loan documents contain such acceleration/assumption provisions.

2. False. A 30-year amortized loan is amortized over its original term of 30 years.

3. Because "seconds" only have a junior lien priority which places their claim against the secured property *behind* senior liens. Since a secondary claim stands less chance of being satisfied in foreclosure, the loan is riskier, hence more expensive.

4. Should the loan ever exceed the property value, a foreclosure sale would never recover the entire balance of the defaulted loan.

_____

5. Constant of 10.0941 × $73.500 = $741.92

6. (11.75% × $73,500) ÷ 12 = $719.69

7. (Constant 952) × $73.500 = $69,972

8. (Constant$_1$ = .961) − (Constant$_2$ = .952) × $73.500 = $661.50

9. ($742.35) × (12 months) − $661.50 (calculated above in questions 6 and 9) equals interest paid. $8,908.02 − $661.50 = $8,246.70

BLENDED-RATE MORTGAGES

Mortgage lenders in the late 1970s and early 1980s found themselves in a very difficult position. Over the prior 25 years they had issued thousands of conventional fixed-rate mortgages at pre-inflation interest rates for loan periods of up to 30 years. The decade of 1970s, however, brought with it a high rate of inflation. When high inflation persisted, interest rates began increasing for both loans and deposits. Suddenly mortgage lenders found themselves having to pay 10 percent, 11 percent, and 12 percent interest rates in order to attract depositors to their institutions. These lenders were earning only 7 to 9 percent from their long-term, fixed-rate mortgages. So they began to lose money.

At the same time, mortgage loan rates were going higher and higher, primarily because there was tremendous competition in the credit markets for financing. What little cash was available was being loaned out at 16 to 20 percent interest. This credit squeeze of the early 1980s put mortgage lenders in a second predicament. With interest rates at 16 to 17 percent, prospective homebuyers could no longer afford the financing costs. Not only were lenders losing money on term loans that they couldn't get off their books, they had no marketplace for new loans at current interest rates.

This severe financial crisis in mortgage lending called for a swift, effective solution. On the one hand, lenders had to get the low-yield loans off their books; on the other, they had to offer an affordable loan product that homeowners could afford and would accept. One of the most effective solutions was the blended-rate or consolidated-rate mortgage. The purpose of the blended-rate mortgage—or simply "the blend"—was to offer the new mortgage borrower a loan that reflected the weighted average of the interest rate on a property's underlying mortgage and the current market rate of interest for new money borrowed. By offering a new "blended" rate loan, the lender would upgrade his or her low-yielding loan portfolio while offering a product that homeowners could afford.

The "blend" became popular very quickly and is now offered by mortgage lenders throughout the country. In the following pages we will examine the blended-rate mortgage and see how it works.

What is a Blended-Rate Mortgage?

The blended-rate mortgage is *a mortgage loan, usually of senior lien priority and issued by institutional lenders, that carries an interest rate reflecting the approximate weighted average between the interest rates on a property's existing senior mortgage and the current market interest rate on additional funds needed to finance the property at its current value.* The blend is typically issued by the same lender who holds the property's existing senior mortgage.

Other names for the blended-rate mortgage, or blend, are:

- consolidated-rate mortgages (CRMs),
- weighted average money mortgages (WAMMs),
- FNMA resale/refinance mortgages, and
- the lender's wraparound.

The Blend: An Illustrated Scenario

This is how the blend works in a hypothetical situation. A married couple bought a home six years ago for $60,000. They obtained a $50,000 mortgage at 8 percent interest. They now want to sell their home for $75,000. They have a remaining balance on their old loan of about $48,000. Eventually a buyer comes along who wants the home. The buyer has the standard 20 percent, or $15,000, down, so the buyer has to finance the balance, $60,000. Since current interest rates are 16 percent, the buyer cannot (hypothetically) qualify for a $60,000 loan. The lender, however, wants to retire the unprofitable 8 percent loan and so agrees to a blend.

To blend the new loan, the lender offers the borrower an interest rate of 9 percent on the "old" $48,000 plus an interest rate of 16 percent for the additional $12,000 the buyer must borrow. He then averages these two dollar amounts and rates to find the new interest rate for the "blended" loan:

$$\frac{(\$48,000 \times 9\%) + (\$12,000 \times 16\%)}{\$60,000} = \frac{\$6,240}{\$60,000} = 10.4\% \text{ interest rate}$$

Rounding the averaged interest rate, the lender offers the borrower a 10.5 percent blended-rate mortgage for $60,000. The borrower (hypothetically) qualifies under this new rate, and the lender is able to upgrade the loan by 2½ percent.

The foregoing narrative demonstrates the essential mechanics of the blend. Quite simple in structure, the blend can be visualized diagrammatically as in Figure 2.1, where X equals the balance left on the old mortgage, Y equals the old rate, A equals the new money needed and B equals the new rate.

As the diagram indicates, the blended mortgage is a new senior mortgage for the entire amount of needed financing. The interest rate on the blend reflects the weighted averages of the old and new dollar amounts and loan rates. In the process of originating the new blended mortgage, the lender retires the seller's old loan.

Sources for Blended-Rate Mortgages

Typical sources for blended-rate mortgages are banks, savings and loan associations and mortgage companies. In addition, Fannie Mae recently introduced a blended-rate mortgage program that is offered through participating lenders. This program is called the

FIGURE 2.1:   The Blend

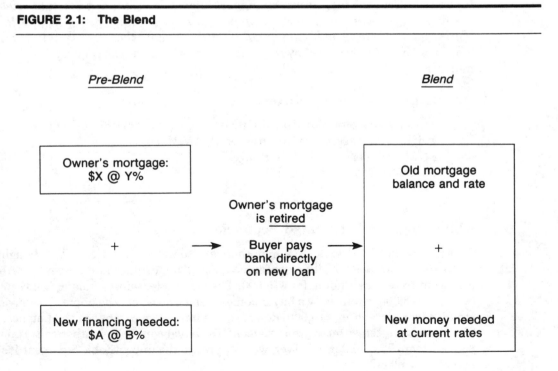

FNMA ReSale/Refinance program and offers blended-rate mortgages for both the homebuyer (Resale program) and for homeowners who merely wish to borrow on their home equity (Refinance program).

Components of the Blended-Rate Mortgage

Interest Rate.   The interest rate reflects an approximate weighted average based on the rate and balance of the old loan and the rate and balance of the new loan amount. It may, however, be adjusted to meet a lender's minimum blended-rate requirement. In other words, a lender may set the new rate at the straight average rate *plus* 1½ or 2 percent. Even in that case, however, the borrower will obtain a below-market interest rate.

The *type* of interest rate for a blend can either be fixed or variable. Once the initial averaged rate is determined, the blended-rate mortgage can be structured as a conventional fixed-rate loan or as an adjustable-rate loan where the rate is lowered or raised in synchronization with a financial economic index over the loan's term.

Loan Term.   Once the blended interest rate is established, the mortgage can become any type of loan for any duration. Commonly, the blend will have a 25- to 30-year amortization period with a three- to ten-year call provision.

Loan Payments.   Loans with blended interest rates can either be amortized with monthly payments of principal and interest or they can be interest-only loans with a balloon.

Lien Priority.   The blended-rate mortgage is predominantly a newly originated loan having senior lien priority.

Calculating the Blended Rate

To calculate the interest rate on the blended loan we use the following equation:

$$\frac{\text{I:} \quad (\text{Old \$} \times \text{Old Rate}) + (\text{New \$} \times \text{New Rate})}{\text{P:} \qquad\qquad (\text{Old \$} + \text{New \$})} = R \text{ (Blended)}$$

Note that to derive how much interest is paid on a loan you multiply the rate of the loan by the principal balance. In our formula for blends, this equals the annual interest on the old loan plus the new loan. Dividing this sum by the total principal balance produces the new blended rate.

Let's take another example. Assume that on a $100,000 home a homeseller had an old 9¼ percent mortgage for $47,000. A buyer with a $27,000 down payment needs to finance

$73,000. Current interest rates are 14 percent. If the buyer were to get a $73,000 mortgage which blended the old mortgage, the blend's interest rate would be:

$$\frac{(\$47,000 \times 9.25\%) + (\$26,000 \times 14\%)}{\$73,000} = \frac{\$4,347.50 + 3,640}{\$73,000}$$

$$= \frac{\$7,987.50}{\$73,000} = 10.94\%$$

SELF-QUIZ: BLENDED-RATE MORTGAGE

1. Why would a lender want to make a mortgage loan at rates of interest below current market levels?

2. A homeowner bought his home 7 years ago and obtained a 30-year senior mortgage of $62,000 for 9% with a 15% down payment. The home is now for sale for $100,000. The lender wants to retire the 9% loan and agrees to a blended mortgage. He will loan new funds at 16½% and will grant a blended interest rate that is a straight average plus 1½%. What will the new buyer's blended rate be?

ANSWERS TO SELF-QUIZ: BLENDED-RATE MORTGAGE

1. Lenders write blended mortgages to retire old, low-yielding loans that are losing money in view of high rates of interest those lenders must pay on deposits and to offer a loan that is within the homebuyer's affordability range.

2. a. The remaining balance on the old loan is $58,032.*

   b. Total funds needed to be financed is $85,000.

   c. *New* funds to be financed are $85,000 − $58,032, or $26,968.

   d. The straight average rate is:

   $$\frac{(\$58,032 \times 9\%) + (\$26,968 \times 16\frac{1}{2}\%)}{\$85,000} = \frac{\$5,223 + \$4,450}{\$85,000} = \frac{\$9,673}{\$85,000} = 11.38\%$$

   e. The new blended rate = 11.38% + 1.50% = 12.88%.

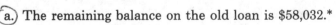

*The remaining loan balance is found by using the loan progress chart in Appendix III. The loan progress constant for a 30-year loan at 9% is 936.
.936 × $62,000 = $58,032.

3

Assumptions and Purchase-Money Mortgages

In Chapters 2 and 3 we examined the classic fixed-rate conventional mortgage and how it came to dominate residential mortgage financing over the last 40 years. We also learned how these loans—originated with terms of 30 years—dealt a severe blow to the mortgage lender when interest rates on them remained well below profitable levels.

With housing costs rising sharply, however, would-be buyers and sellers took a different point of view: for them bargain-rate financing was the only way they could buy the house or make the sale. Out of these opposing interests arose a war of buyers and sellers aligned against the institutional lenders. The focus of this war was the buyer/seller wish to keep the old fixed low-rate financing intact versus the lender's determination to get those cheap loans off the books.

It became standard for buyers to look for a way to assume the seller's mortgage. When this happened, the purchase became affordable; the buyer got the house, and the seller got the sale. In a very short time the assumption became the most sought-after financing technique of all. In a survey conducted by the National Association of REALTORS® Economics and Research Division, it was found that mortgage assumptions were involved in four out of every ten residential financing transactions in the first two years of the 1980s.

In addition to the assumption of old mortgages, home buyers and sellers developed a second battleline against prohibitively high institutional interest rates: the so-called practice of "seller financing." If the mortgage assumption still left the property unaffordable, the seller would step in and loan the buyer money at below-market rates. For instance, if a buyer needed $50,000 in financing and the assumption covered $35,000, the seller would loan the buyer the additional $15,000. More precisely, the seller would agree to defer receipt of the $15,000 in exchange for the buyer's payment of interest. This method of seller financing, called the purchase-money mortgage, became at least as popular in the late 1970s and early 1980s as mortgage assumptions. In the survey cited above, it was found that purchase-money mortgages were involved in almost 50 percent of all residential financing transactions in 1980—a remarkable phenomenon in view of the fact that in the early 1970s purchase-money mortgages were almost unheard of.

These new-style loans, in the form of purchase-money "seconds," were highly compatible with the assumption technique. Consequently the assumption accompanied by a purchase-money mortgage became the cheapest financing package a homebuyer could find: an old mortgage assumed at 8 percent, for example, when averaged with an 11 percent purchase-money mortgage, created a mortgage rate of about 9½ percent. Contrast this with the 15 to 16 percent financing offered by lenders in the early 1980s and the reason for the new technique becomes clear.

Needless to say, lenders had a problem. To counter "seller financing," they concocted two strategies. To fight assumptions, they introduced the due-on-sale clause (DOS clause), which effectively made assumption legitimate grounds for acceleration of the balance due. To fight both the assumption and purchase-money mortgage, the lender invented the blend as a "compromise mortgage" that averaged the rate and balance on the old loan amount with the rate and balance on the new loan amount.

In this chapter (and the next two) we will look at the assumption and the purchase-money mortgage. We will examine each technique separately, then see how the two techniques work in unison. Note that a slightly different kind of purchase-money mortgage, the wraparound, has also become very popular. This form will be treated in Chapter 4.

LEARNING OBJECTIVES

When you have completed this chapter, you should be able to:

1. define and describe the process of assuming a mortgage,
2. discuss the concept of "assumability" and how assumability is determined by the due-on-sale clause,
3. understand the mechanics and key characteristics of assumptions with and without the presence of due-on-sale clauses,
4. discuss the various types of purchase-money mortgages and their key characteristics,
5. understand the financial mechanics of purchase-money mortgages,
6. discuss the legal pitfalls and considerations of PMMs and the problems they can create, and
7. discuss why the assumption and purchase-money mortgage is attractive to buyers.

ASSUMPTIONS

Assumption is the financing technique wherein a homebuyer assumes the primary obligation for payment of the homeseller's existing mortgage loan.

Figure 3.1 depicts the assumption transaction, with or without additional financing. In the transaction, the buyer becomes the new mortgagor on the seller's original senior mortgage loan. He or she gives the lender the note and security instrument and begins monthly payments directly to the lender. The seller receives the purchase price less the mortgage balance (less any financing he or she has transacted with the buyer) in cash, then deeds title to the buyer. The buyer then takes possession of the property.

Assumption of a mortgage and taking title "subject to" a mortgage are similar but not exactly alike. With an assumption of a mortgage a buyer acquires title to property that has

FIGURE 3.1:   Assumption Transaction

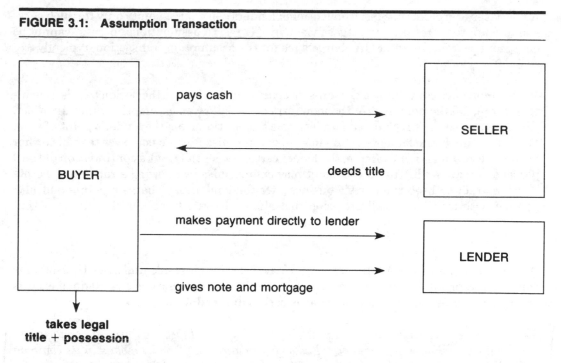

an existing mortgage and agrees to be personally liable for payment of the mortgage. This includes personal liability for the loan balance including any deficiency judgments if the loan is defaulted and the property foreclosed. A buyer taking title to property "subject to" a mortgage is not personally liable for payment of the note. In the event of default and foreclosure of the property the buyer could lose his or her equity in the property but would not be liable for a deficiency judgment.

Mechanics of Assumptions

There are essentially two types of assumption transactions: with and without a due-on-sale clause. In the latter instance, *the lender has no choice but to permit the assumption* provided the buyer qualifies. On conventional loan instruments (nongovernmental), however, the new borrower must meet the lender's underwriting qualifications so that the loan's security is not threatened. In these cases, the lender will perform the necessary credit checks and charge the buyer accordingly. However, the interest rate on the old note remains the same. FHA or VA loans are examples of assumable loans because their loan documents do not contain due-on-sale clauses. If a purchaser assumes an FHA loan and subsequently defaults on it, the property is sold at foreclosure and the original borrower is not pursued to make up any deficiency since it is paid from the FHA insurance. This is not always the case in a VA assumption. In a VA assumption, therefore, the seller should get a "release of liability," which releases the original borrower of liability if there is a deficiency. When a release of liability is requested, the VA will look into the creditworthiness of the buyer.

Simply illustrated, a seller has a $50,000 30-year mortgage at 9 percent interest. Five years later the seller wants to sell her home for $75,000. Assuming the mortgage, a buyer takes over the $402.32 monthly PI payments on the principal balance, now paid down to $47,950. At closing the borrower pays the seller $27,050: $75,000 minus $47,950 for the balance due on the purchase price; in addition the borrower pays the fees due the lender for services and credit checks. Conventional lenders can charge points only for such services and not to increase the mortgage yield. In VA or FHA assumptions "points" cannot be charged; however, VA and FHA charge a fee for the assumption transaction, typically $50 to $150.

With a mortgage containing a due-on-sale clause, the lender has the option to raise the interest rate, charge points, alter the loan term or not allow an assumption at all. In effect, the DOS clause has precluded an undesirable transaction from the lender's point of view. What remains is the lender's willingness to compromise lest the borrower take his or her business elsewhere. For example, the lender certainly doesn't want a continuation of the 9 percent mortgage illustrated above but may compromise by allowing a rate 1 or 2 points below market to keep the party's business. Or the lender may charge 5 points and 11½ percent with a five-year call provision that allows the rate to be raised again after that period.

Assumability and the DOS Clause.   We have seen that residential sales transactions can succeed or fail on the basis of whether a seller's senior mortgage is assumable. It is therefore meaningful to examine what is assumable and what is not.

Technically, all mortgages are "assumable" if the buyer qualifies. However, some mortgages can be altered while others cannot. Thus what "assumability" really means in its common sense is a mortgage that can be assumed by a buyer with its original terms left intact.

In this context, a mortgage is assumable (transferable without alteration) if it does not contain a due-on-sale clause. That is the simple rule. Two examples of assumable mortgages are FHA and VA mortgages previously mentioned, neither of which contains the DOS clause. A third example is the conventional mortgage generally issued before 1975, when the DOS clause began to appear.

On the other hand, a mortgage *with* a DOS clause may or may not be assumable without alteration, depending on the individual lender. Essentially, the DOS clause gives a lender the legal option or prerogative to alter a loan's terms if a new borrower takes over payments. The lender may decide not to change the terms, but he or she has the option to do so.

FNMA Article 17.   Shown below is the standard due-on-sale clause found in most mortgage note instruments used today: a clause worded by Fannie Mae (FNMA) and integrated into its standard forms.

> **17. Transfer of the Property; Assumption.** If all or any part of the Property or an interest therein is sold or transferred by Borrower without Lender's prior written consent, excluding (a) the creation of a lien or encumbrance subordinate to this Deed of Trust, (b) the creation of a purchase money security interest for household appliances, (c) a transfer by devise, descent or by operation of law upon the death of a joint tenant or (d) the grant of any leasehold interest of three years or less not containing an option to purchase, Lender may, at Lender's option, declare all the sums secured by this Deed of Trust to be immediately due and payable. Lender shall have waived such option to accelerate if, prior to the sale or transfer, Lender and the person to whom the Property is to be sold or transferred reach agreement in writing that the

credit of such person is satisfactory to Lender and that the interest payable on the sums secured by this Deed of Trust shall be at such rate Lender shall request. If Lender has waived the option to accelerate provided in this paragraph 17, and if Borrower's successor in interest has executed a written assumption agreement accepted in writing by Lender, Lender shall release Borrower from all obligations under this Deed of Trust and the Note.

If Lender exercises such option to accelerate, Lender shall mail Borrower notice of acceleration in accordance with paragraph 14 hereof. Such notice shall provide a period of not less than 30 days from the date the notice is mailed within which Borrower may pay the sums declared due. If Borrower fails to pay such sums prior to the expiration of such period, Lender may, without further notice or demand on Borrower, invoke any remedies permitted by paragraph 18 hereof.

In our context, the important part of this clause is the phrase "the interest payable on the sums secured by this Deed of Trust shall be at such rate as the Lender shall request." In short, the loan can be accelerated in full unless the lender and borrower come to written agreement about the terms of the assumption.

Other Characteristics and Considerations of Assumptions

The Broker's Liability.   Whether or not a mortgage is fully assumable, or whether a DOS clause is in fact enforceable, is strictly a matter for a seller or buyer's legal counsel to determine—not a real estate broker. Any broker who advises a buyer or seller that an assumption is okay or acceptable is courting serious legal liability should a lender accelerate the loan or foreclose. Similarly, a broker who states that a lender will not accelerate on a DOS clause can be sued if a principal party is damaged as a result of a false statement. For those reasons, real estate brokers should not offer legal advice regarding DOS clauses nor should brokers attempt to interpret varying types of clauses.

The Seller's Liability.   Contrary to common opinion, the seller may remain primarily liable for mortgage payments should the buyer/assumptor default on a mortgage whose terms remain unchanged. In this case the lender can seek legal recourse with the seller as well as the buyer if the buyer defaults. This continued seller's liability is released only by a specific document called a substitution agreement (also called novation or release of liability) granted by the mortgagee after certain conditions have been met. Similarly, the seller's release of liability from VA or FHA loans requires that very specific conditions and requirements be met. A VA or FHA release of liability may take up to six months. To safeguard the seller, both buyer and seller should agree in writing within the sales agreement that the release of liability has been ordered and will be signed when received by both parties.

The Mortgage Balance.   The remaining balance on an assumable mortgage in large part determines the attractiveness of the assumption transaction. If the mortgage has a very low remaining balance, significant new financing at much higher rates will probably be required. Contrarily, a low-rate mortgage with a large remaining balance represents a good buyer opportunity.

SELF-QUIZ: ASSUMPTIONS

1. Why do sellers favor assumption as a financing technique?

2. A silent assumption is not a legal transaction. True or false?

3. A lender cannot alter the term of a conventional fixed-rate mortgage unless a new borrower has bought the secured property. True or false?

4. Liability of legal title remains with the seller even though a buyer has assumed the seller's mortgage. True or false?

5. A fully assumable mortgage still entails a vigorous credit check of the buyer. True or false?

6. Due-on-sale clauses do not prevent assumptions from taking place; they merely give lenders an option to alter the assumed loan's terms. True or false?

ANSWERS TO SELF-QUIZ: ASSUMPTIONS

1. They can typically obtain a higher price if the buyer's obtainable financing is cheaper.

2. False. The silent assumption is not inherently illegal. It is vulnerable, however, to the lender accelerating the underlying mortgage should it contain a DOS clause.

3. Generally true, unless the loan contains a call provision.

4. False. Title transfers to the buyer in an assumption. The seller may remain liable for the *senior mortgage payments,* however, should the buyer default.

5. True. The lender has the legal right to ensure that the security of his/her loan is not jeopardized.

6. True.

THE PURCHASE-MONEY MORTGAGE (PMM)

A purchase-money mortgage is a mortgage loan given to the buyer by the seller as part of the property's purchase price. In professional vernacular, a purchase-money mortgage, or trust deed, is financing that is "carried back" by the seller as part of the purchase price. The PMM note is also referred to as "paper" carried back, or simply a "seller's first, second, third, or fourth mortgage or trust deed."

Distinctions and Comparisons in Terminology

A purchase-money mortgage is *not* a "conventional mortgage" or "mortgage note." Terminology such as "conventional mortgage" or "mortgage loan" commonly refers to loans issued by third-party institutional lenders. PMMs are distinct from these loans in that they are granted by the homeseller as part of the sales transaction.

A PMM is *not* an "equity loan." An equity loan is a third party's loan to a homeowner, collateralized by the equity in the property. The seller can do as he or she wishes with the proceeds from the equity loan. By contrast, the PMM is secured by the home equity but is loaned by the seller to the buyer and does not entail a cash transaction.

Types of Purchase-Money Mortgages

Purchase-money mortgages are categorized by lien priority and the status of the seller's underlying mortgage. In terms of lien priority, there are senior lien PMMs and junior lien PMMs. Among the junior PMMs, there are simple "seconds" or "thirds" and what is called the wraparound.

Senior Lien PMMs.   A senior lien PMM is a seller's loan to a buyer issued in the absence of any underlying debt on the property. Any senior mortgage previously recorded on the property has been paid off, and the new PMM takes first priority. For example, a seller owning his home free and clear sells the property for $75,000 by taking a $20,000 down payment and carrying back a senior PMM for $55,000.

Senior lien PMMs are less common than junior PMMs and cannot usually take place in conjunction with an assumption since lenders will not permit a loss of priority in their underlying mortgages.

"Simple" Seconds (or 3rds or 4ths).   The most common form of purchase-money mortgage is the "simple second," where the seller fills any gap in the financing needed by the buyer. In these cases the buyer has either assumed the seller's loan or has obtained senior mortgage financing from another lender for the major portion of the purchase price. The seller then "fills the gap" between the senior mortgage and the down payment with a simple second-lien PMM. For example, if a $75,000 home has a $50,000 assumable mortgage and the buyer puts $15,000 down, the seller may carry back a $10,000 PMM second to make up the difference. As stated earlier, an assumption plus the simple second is typically the cheapest form of financing a buyer can obtain.

Wraparounds.   The third type of purchase-money mortgage is a junior-lien PMM where the seller *retains* the underlying senior mortgage and carries back a note which typically encompasses both the amount of the underlying mortgage and any additional financing needed. In effect, this junior note "wraps" the old mortgage balance with the new financing needed. For example, if Anita sells a $75,000 home with a $50,000 underlying mortgage and a $15,000 down payment, she carries back a junior wraparound note for $60,000 and continues payments on the underlying mortgage. (A full examination of wraparounds follows in the next chapter.)

FIGURE 3.2:   Purchase-Money Mortgage Types

SENIOR PMMS

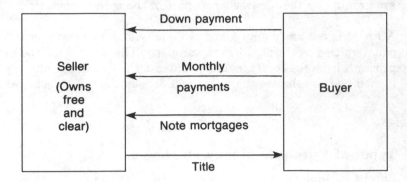

SIMPLE JUNIOR PMMS (2NDS, 3RDS, 4THS)

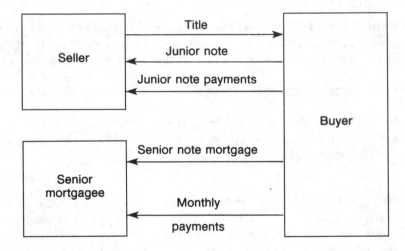

WRAPAROUNDS

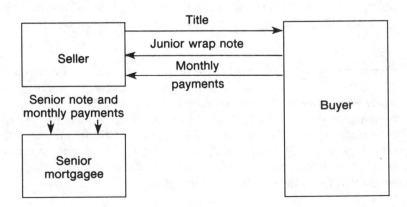

To review the types of purchase-money mortgages:

- Senior-lien PMMs,
- Simple junior PMMs,
- Wraparounds.

Figure 3.2 shows the workings of each.

Key Characteristics of PMMs

The major reasons for the popularity of PMMs are simplicity and versatility. The PMM is a straightforward note and mortgage security document executed as an IOU between buyer and seller. Few restrictions govern what the seller may grant in terms of the amount, the interest rate, the type of payment, the frequency of payments, and so on. The PMM can accommodate virtually any financing structure the principal parties agree upon. However, most PMMs do have the following characteristics:

Form of Payment.   The PMM may be an interest-only loan with a balloon payment, particularly the "simple second." As the amount of the PMM increases, such as with a senior-lien PMM, amortizing payments become more common. Payments are almost always monthly.

Loan Term.   PMM financing is typically short-term, ranging from two to ten years. The average term is five years, after which the loan balance is refinanced on a more permanent basis.

Priority.   As presented, PMMs can have senior or junior lien priority status.

Interest Rates.   The interest rates on PMMs run 1 or more percent below market, making the home more affordable and salable.

Loan Source.   The homeseller.

Legal Title.   In all purchase-money mortgage transactions, title is passed to the buyer (lien theory states) as opposed to the title remaining with the seller. This contrasts with the contract-for-deed transaction, where title remains with the seller until the terms and conditions of the contract are met.

SELF-QUIZ: PURCHASE-MONEY MORTGAGES

1. Senior-lien purchase-money mortgages are always for a greater amount of the purchase price than junior-lien PMMs. True or false?

2. Senior PMMs are vulnerable to due-on-sale clauses in the seller's underlying mortgage. True or false?

3. Why can a homeseller charge a lower interest rate on a loan than an institution?

4. How does a "simple second" differ from a wraparound?

5. A homeowner is selling his home for $80,000 and needs $15,000 down. He will carry back financing, interest only, for 11 percent. What are the borrower's monthly payments on a senior PMM? What are the borrower's payments on a simple second if a $50,000 senior loan is obtained elsewhere? What are the borrower's payments on an interest-only wraparound?

ANSWERS TO SELF-QUIZ: PURCHASE-MONEY MORTGAGES

1. False. Wrap notes are often larger in amount.
2. False. No senior note underlies a senior PMM.
3. Because the homeseller does not have to pay for sources of funds.
4. The wraparound lender retains the underlying mortgage.
5. Senior PMM: $80,000 − $15,000 = $65,000 × .11 = $7,150 ÷ 12 = $595.83
   Simple Second: $80,000 − $15,000 − $50,000 = $15,000 × .11 = $1,650 ÷ 12 = $137.50
   Wraparound: $595.83 (same calculation as the senior PMM above)

Key Legal Considerations and Pitfalls to Avoid in PMMs

As PMMs have become popular, so has the American penchant for the civil lawsuit. Thus the pitfalls in PMM financing increase every day, both in number and in kind. The cause of legal problems can often be traced to a failure to use standard forms and employ knowledgeable attorneys. But in many cases the lawsuits happen despite the use of competent experts.

What can be done to minimize exposure to litigation? The cardinal precaution is to have competent legal and financial experts representing the principal parties involved in the transactions. Second, brokers must be intimately aware of what issues can cause trouble so that a safe course can be navigated.

The purpose of this section is to highlight some important legal issues relating to PMM functioning. The discussion is far from exhaustive, however, and readers should seek further information on these legal considerations as they apply locally. No legal opinion or legal advice is offered here, and the author disclaims responsibility for the veracity or legality of anything said about legal matters.

The legal considerations that seem to cause the most trouble are:

1. the broker's investment-counselor liability,
2. the broker's disclosure responsibilities to buyers and sellers regarding financing,
3. default considerations and over-financing,
4. the enforceability of balloon payments and the balloon problem in general.

The Broker's Investment-Counselor Liability.   A very confusing controversy exists over the agent's role in developing financial packages for buyers and sellers. The role definition becomes controversial as soon as the broker's activities in qualification and loan structure are construed as "investment advice."

This issue presents innumerable problems. The definition of "investment advice" is extremely vague. Ever since real estate brokerage began, for example, practitioners have analyzed and forecasted—and talked about—appreciation rates. A broker tells a buyer that his forecast of appreciation for a property is ten percent per year. Is that investment advice? Is that investment advice that has in fact *been rendered?* A ten percent appreciation rate may be investment data, but did the broker tell the buyer to purchase, based on that information? Better yet, was a suggestion to make the investment implied? Were there any witnesses to the statement who would testify that it was indeed given?

Cases do go to court. For example, a buyer's balloon note comes due and he or she can't refinance. So the buyer sues the broker for claiming that interest rates would come down. Whether rates went up or down, the practitioner must go to court.

How is this type of lawsuit avoided? First, the defined roles of the broker and the investment counselor are based on fine-line distinctions. The main distinction is that the investment counselor *recommends* what clients should do with their money, whereas the broker is limited to *providing information* to clients so that they can make up their own minds.

Given the above generalization, licensees can reduce their chances of problems by avoiding statements that direct the client to do anything. For example, instead of saying "I think you should . . . ," stress that "I can provide information, but it's your decision."

A second way to avoid the investment-counselor problem is to *avoid straightforward statements about the future* or about a money transaction. For example, note the kinds of phraseology that can be grounds for a lawsuit.

- "I think interest rates will come down."
- "Prices will definitely go up."
- "A 12½ percent PMM rate is a good rate to offer."
- "This house is a solid investment that will appreciate."

Neither you nor any investment counselor knows what's going to happen in the future because there are too many events that can occur. For example, a home *may* appreciate 15 percent, but it's hardly a good investment if the buyer loses his job and cannot make the payments.

Thus there are two rules: (1) avoid the word "will," and (2) always hedge investment-type remarks with language like the following:

memorize

- "Interest rates may come down, but then again they may not. No one can be certain."
- "Prices may go up since they have in the past. But there's no guarantee."
- "12½ percent PMM rates are common."
- "Many homes can be good investments due to appreciation."

Equivocal language avoids "the investment-counselor role" as does letting the client make his or her own decision.

The Broker's Disclosure Responsibilities.   Real estate practitioners have a clear obligation to disclose to buyers and sellers the terms and meanings of financing packages that they have helped structure. Disclosure includes such items as the dollar amounts involved in the transaction, the interest rate, other fees and payments, balloon payments and what they are, and so forth. To be safe, the disclosures should be exhaustive as well as explanatory. For example, state not just that a balloon payment of X amount will be due in Y years but what happens if the payment is not made. As a rule, one cannot tell buyers and sellers enough about what happens in a financing arrangement.

The issue of brokers' disclosure in noninstitutional financing recently became a national debate revolving around Truth-in-Lending Laws and Regulation Z. The debate was centered on whether a broker could or should be construed as an "arranger of credit" in a seller financing situation. If so, the broker would be subject to the extensive disclosure requirements of Regulation Z. A recent ruling on the issue said that brokers do not fall into the "arranger of credit" category and are not subject to Regulation Z provisions.

Despite this, practitioners must be conscientious in making disclosures to the principal parties. Going one step further, brokers may be held liable for nondisclosure when disclosures *were* made and the principal did not understand what was being disclosed. Thus in addition to disclosure, make sure the disclosure is understood.

Following is a list of items that institutional lenders must disclose under Regulation Z. Brokers would be well-advised to disclose such items themselves in a PMM transaction:

1. the total dollars charged for interest,
2. the annual percentage rate,
3. the amortization schedule (if applicable),
4. the amount and due date of a balloon payment,
5. when the loan period begins and when payments are due,
6. charges for late payments, prepayments,
7. all security interests in the transactions,
8. the total amount of the credit extended,
9. the price and down payment.

Default Considerations Including Buyer Default

Default is the nightmare in any financing transaction, and in real estate the losses can be heavy. When parties are in default, no one is necessarily exempted from the court proceedings, including the broker or agent. For that reason, default is a critical professional issue.

For any of several reasons, buyers may default on loan obligations the broker took part in structuring, such as a PMM second. Here are ways to prepare for such a possibility.

1. Have the contract clearly and thoroughly set forth what constitutes default and what is to be done in the event of default.
2. Make sure there are provisions defining a grace provision for late payments.
3. Make sure all parties understand what redemption period may be involved upon default and what redemption is.
4. Have adequate provisions set forth in the sales contract for default/foreclosure/ power of sale proceedings, and make sure the parties understand such provisions.

Increasingly, brokers are being sued by defaulting parties for damages resulting from "overfinancing." The allegation is that the broker allowed (or convinced) the buyer to borrow too much money, therefore the broker was a contributing cause to the default. Without question, it's a case the defaulting party can win.

To avoid the problems and liability of overfinancing, practitioners should observe prudent lending standards in financial qualification. Underwriting ratios exist for good reason—people have bills other than housing. The specific quantity of the ratios, for example, the 28 percent PITI-to-gross-income ratio, means that other bills tend to be 72 percent of income. Thus, following the ratios as closely as possible is the best way to avoid overfinancing and default.

DISCUSSION QUESTIONS

1. When can "overfinancing" be the broker's liability?

2. What is the best way to minimize the liability of a broker acting as an investment counselor?

3. How is it that a broker can be sued if a buyer defaults on a PMM loan?

4. What are three ways to minimize the risk of a balloon default?

4

Wraparound Purchase-Money Mortgages

In the previous chapter we examined two popular financing methods: assumptions and purchase-money mortgages. In this chapter we will look at another very popular purchase-money mortgage: the wraparound. A junior lien debt instrument, the wraparound mortgage is the financing choice among homesellers who wish to involve themselves in financing as an investment. More than any other financing method, the wraparound offers the homeseller potentially high-yield real estate income investment.

In this chapter we will analyze the fundamentals of wraparounds: what they are, how they work and their key characteristics. We will illustrate wraparound mechanics and reinforce the initial presentation with questions and exercises. Then we will take a closer look at wraparounds as investments and how they can yield attractive returns on the home-seller's equitable interest in the property. Concluding the chapter will be exercises to test your ability to analyze and identify the investment yields of hypothetical wraparound investments.

LEARNING OBJECTIVES

When you have completed this chapter, you will be able to:

1. define wraparounds and distinguish their unique position among the family of purchase-money mortgages,
2. identify the major financial characteristics of wraparounds in terms of lien priority, transfer of title, the loan's term, type of payments, etc.,
3. understand how wraparounds are affected by due-on-sale clauses,
4. understand how wraparounds work as income investments for the homeseller, and
5. calculate a seller's investment yield on a given wraparound.

DEFINITION AND MECHANICS

A wraparound purchase-money mortgage is a *junior lien carried back by the homeseller for an amount usually equal to the purchase price of the property minus the buyer's down payment.* The unique feature of the wraparound is that while the seller conveys title to the buyer, he or she *retains* the primary obligation for payment of the underlying senior mortgage. In effect, then, the seller has "wrapped" together the new financing needed by the buyer with the remaining balance of the underlying loan, all into a single loan. Once the wraparound has been executed, the buyer makes periodic payments to the seller, and the seller continues to make payments on the senior loan to the senior mortgagee. The homeseller in this case has opted to keep the senior loan instead of allowing the buyer to assume it. Figure 4.1 summarizes the wraparound transaction.

As illustrated in Figure 4.1, there are two lenders and two borrowers in the wraparound, as the seller is both lender and borrower. The seller receives the down payment and monthly payments from the buyer and in turn makes the monthly payments on the senior note to the original lender. Figure 4.2 demonstrates a hypothetical wraparound transaction in dollars and cents.

As shown, the seller prices the property at $100,000 and receives $15,000 down. The wrap note, for the price less the down payment, is $85,000, interest only at 13 percent. Thus the buyer makes monthly payments to the seller of $920.83.

The seller originally obtained a fixed-rate 30-year mortgage for $50,000 at 10 percent interest. Thus he continues payments of $438.79 to the senior mortgagee. On a cash basis, this wraparound produces a net monthly income of $482.04 to the seller ($920.83 income minus $438.79 paid to the lender).

Note that because this wraparound is interest-only it will have a balloon payment due after a predetermined time period. At that time the note will either be rolled over, extended or retired through refinancing.

Case Study Exercise: Wraparounds

A homeseller prices her property at $80,000 and requires 20 percent down. She has an underlying loan that was originally issued for $45,000 on a 25-year term for 9½ percent interest. The seller executes a wraparound with a buyer for 12½ percent interest on an interest-only note. What is the seller's approximate net monthly income?

Solution to Case Study: Wraparounds

Wrap note = $80,000 − $16,000, or $64,000
Monthly payment on wrap = ($64,000 × 12½ percent) ÷ 12 = $667
Monthly PI payment on underlying senior = $393
Seller's net income = $667 − $393 = $274

To be precise, the seller's principal payment in the $393 PI payment must be subtracted out of the equation because principal repayments are not part of interest income and expense.

FIGURE 4.1:   The Wraparound Purchase-Money Mortgage

MECHANICS

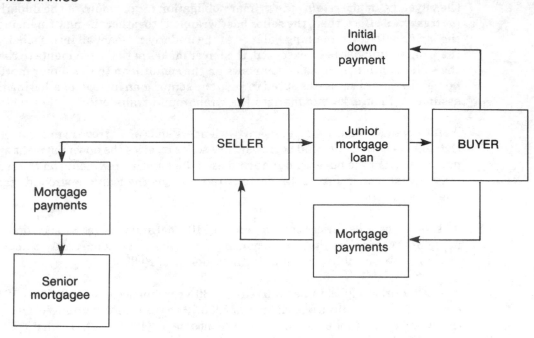

LIEN PRIORITY

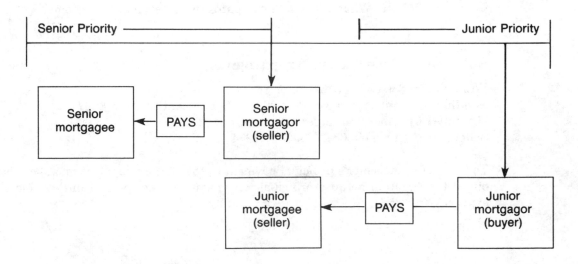

FIGURE 4.2:   The Wraparound Illustrated

Price: $100,000
Down: $15,000
Wrap note: $85,000, interest only
Wrap rate: 13%
Junior loan payments: $920.83

Senior note: $50,000
                     30 years, 3 years old

Senior loan rate: 10%
Senior loan payments: $438.79

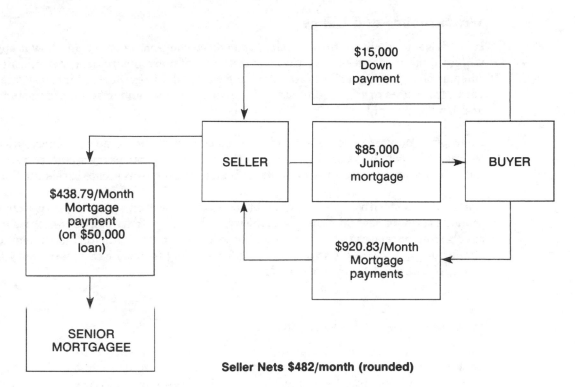

Seller Nets $482/month (rounded)

KEY CHARACTERISTICS OF WRAPAROUNDS

As the purchase-money mortgage carried back by a private loan source—the seller—the wraparound can be an extremely flexible debt instrument. It can be structured for any amount and can be interest-only with a balloon or amortized over any loan term. Payments can be monthly, quarterly or annually. The interest rate is negotiated between the principal parties and can have any range. Further, the rate can be fixed, variable or preset to increase or decrease periodically over the loan term. In short, the wraparound can be flexibly adapted to the cash and income objectives of the seller within the credit limitations of the buyer.

A typical wraparound is an interest-only loan with a three- to five-year balloon, at 1 to 4 percentage points below conventional market rates. Wraparounds are almost always junior liens that accompany the transfer of title to the buyer.

Wraparounds and Due-on-Sale Clauses

Although a wraparound mortgage does not entail an assumption, the transaction *is a transfer of legal interest in property*—which makes the wraparound and underlying senior mortgage vulnerable to any due-on-sale clause in the seller's mortgage documents. In other words the lender may accelerate the seller's senior mortgage, if the seller executes a silent or otherwise unauthorized wraparound over any senior loan containing a DOS clause. To protect themselves from silent wraparound loans, senior lenders may try to detect them by monitoring the property for changes such as: recording of liens on the title, new name of the insured or new address for the mortgagee.

Wraparounds and Usury

It is advisable to obtain professional legal advice concerning usury and how it applies to wraparound mortgages under the circumstances of a given case. In general, usury is defined as charging higher interest rates than the legal maximum. The interest rate ceiling varies from state to state. Some states have no usury laws, and in some circumstances federal laws will apply.

A wraparound mortgage issued and received as part of the home's purchase price is not technically a loan but a credit sale. Thus the wraparound can carry an interest rate nominally in excess of a state's usury limits and can yield an effective rate exceeding that limit.

If a wraparound with a balloon payment comes due, however, and both parties agree to extend the term for several more years, the wraparound mortgage can be construed as a loan that no longer relates to the home sale but exists as a pure financing instrument, or loan. Extension of a wraparound's term (in effect, rolling it over) can create usury liability when its interest rate exceeds the legal limit.

Wraparounds and Taxation

The income tax impact of wraparounds on the buyer is identical to any other home financing arrangement—the buyer's interest payments are deductible. The seller/junior mortgagee, on the other hand, must declare all interest payments received from the buyer as ordinary income. In turn, the interest portions of the monthly payments on the seller's underlying senior mortgage are deductible.

THE WRAPAROUND AS AN INVESTMENT

Among contemporary residential financing methods, the wraparound mortgage stands out as the most attractive alternative for the homeseller in terms of investment potential. Whereas conventional financing is best for a seller desiring cash, or liquidated equity, the wraparound can yield substantial return on equity that the seller elects to retain in the sold property.

For example, a seller who sells a $150,000 home with a $100,000 underlying mortgage balance will receive $50,000 cash after retiring the mortgage balance under a conventional mortgage. The $50,000 can then be used for a subsequent home purchase or other investment. If the seller agrees to sell for 10 percent down with a wraparound, the seller liquidates only $15,000 of his or her equity and keeps the remainder in the property as an investment. In this case, the seller prefers the investment potential of a wraparound to liquidating the equity for cash. Presumably there is an advantage to doing this that outweighs the benefit of having the cash in hand—which is what we will analyze in this section. First, let's look at what we mean by the wraparound as an investment.

Investment Yield of Wraparounds

The attractiveness of an investment, in real estate or elsewhere, is largely determined by the investment's yield or potential yield to the investor. In simple terms, yield is what the investor earns on the amount of money or equity invested: If a $10,000 certificate of deposit carries a 10 percent (noncompounded) interest rate, its yield is 10 percent or $1,000 on an annual basis because that is what the bank pays the investor for the use of the deposit. Conventionally, an investment's yield can be stated quantitatively as a dollar amount generated from the investment over a period of time or as a percentage of the original investment that is generated in an annual period. In either case, the concept of yield is one of the most basic measurements of an investment's attractiveness because it pinpoints exactly what the investor gets back in return for his or her investment. Note, however, that precise calculation of investment yield is a very complex and intricate process that is not attempted here. Only a generalized approximation of investment yield will result from the following formulas and calculations. Thus the yields derived should not be construed as being precise to the dollar.

The Investment Yield Formula

The percentage yield of an investment can be derived by doing this formula:

$$\text{Yield (\% Return)} = \frac{\text{Net Income per Year}}{\text{Investment Principal}} \quad \text{or simply} \quad R = \frac{I}{P}$$

To analyze the investment potential of a wraparound mortgage, it is necessary to enter the seller's *net income* and investment *principal* into the equation to derive its yield. Once an investment yield is known as a percent, the seller can compare the wraparound with yields on other investments. This key comparison of yields tells the seller just how attractive his or her prospective wraparound will be and tells whether it should be undertaken or not.

Net Income of a Wraparound

The net income the seller receives on a wraparound is *the interest paid to the seller by the buyer over a time period minus the interest the seller pays on the underlying mortgage over the same period.* It is important to remember that only interest paid or received is used to derive net income, *not* payments or receipts of loan *principal.* Principal payments made or received by the seller must be factored out of the calculation of net income because repayment of a loan balance does not constitute income. Thus from our equation for I, or net income, we have:

$$\text{interest received} - \text{interest paid} = I \text{ (net income)}$$

To be conventional, the quantity "I" should be expressed as an annual amount to derive the annual yield of the investment. Thus we have:

$$I = \text{annual interest received} - \text{annual interest paid}$$

The Investment Principal in the Wraparound.   The seller's principal amount invested (or not liquidated) in the wraparound is equal to the balance of the wraparound note minus the balance of the underlying senior mortgage. Also known as the seller's equity, this amount comprises the denominator of our yield equation and completes it:

$$\text{Yield} = \frac{\text{annual interest received} - \text{annual interest paid}}{\text{wraparound balance} - \text{senior mortgage balance}}$$

A Sample Yield Derivation.   Using the foregoing formula, we can derive the yield of a hypothetical wraparound as follows. Assume a $100,000 sale price on a home with 10 percent down and an interest-only wrap note for 12 percent. Assume further that the seller has an interest-only senior loan of $60,000 at 9½ percent. The seller's annual yield on this investment would be:

$$\text{Yield} = \frac{(12\% \times \$90,000) - (9\tfrac{1}{2}\% \times \$60,000)}{\$90,000 - \$60,000}$$

$$\text{Yield} = \frac{\$10,800 - \$5,700}{\$30,000}$$

$$\text{Yield} = \frac{\$\,5,100}{\$30,000}$$

$$\text{Yield} = .17 = 17\%$$

This wraparound offers a potential yield of 17 percent—substantially greater than conventional certificates of deposit. Wraparounds generally produce greater yield than the purchase-money mortgages. Because the seller is able to "use" $60,000 of borrowed funds at a cost of only 9½ percent, the seller earns 2½ percent on the $60,000 (12 percent − 9½ percent) plus an even 12 percent on the $30,000 for a yield of 17 percent overall. If this were strictly a purchase-money mortgage transaction, the seller would gain exactly the rate charged to the buyer: 12 percent. Thus this wraparound yields an extra 5 percent above a purchase-money mortgage.

Investment Yield of Amortized Wraparound Loans

In many cases, a seller will carry back an amortized wraparound note from the buyer to give the buyer a chance to increase his or her equity in the property. Even more commonly the seller's underlying note will be an amortized loan to the senior mortgagee. In either case payments to either the seller or senior mortgagee will contain portions of principal. To determine the yield on a wraparound containing amortized loans, the principal portions of the payments must be taken out of the net income calculation, and the constantly changing equity amount, for general purposes, must be averaged over the annual period.

In the previous example, we looked at a $90,000, 12 percent wraparound note. What happens if this becomes an amortized loan over a 15-year amortization period instead of interest only? Assume the senior loan was issued five years ago for $64,034 on a 25-year amortization schedule at the same 9½ percent interest rate. The loan amount after 5 years is $60,000.

To complete the yield calculation with these amortized loans, we first determine net income by taking out the principal payments. Then we must determine the *average* equity the seller retained in the investment over a given annual period. With those figures we can return to the original equation to find investment yield.

Taking Out the Principal Payments.   The calculation for isolating the interest payments from total annual principal and interest payments is:

$$\text{PI payments} \times 12 - \text{change in principal balance} = \text{interest paid}$$

For our illustration, the PI payments on the wraparound loan are $1,080.16 per month. After the first year the principal balance (from loan progress charts) drops from $90,000 to $87,750; hence $2,250 in principal was paid. Thus, from the above equation, the seller received $1,080.16 × 12, or $12,961.92. Subtracting the $2,250 in principal paid, we calculate that the interest paid totalled $10,711.92.

Going through the same steps on the seller's loan: The seller paid $6,716 principal and interest during the year, of which $1,024 was principal. Thus the seller paid $6,716 − $1,024 = $5,692 in interest during the year. Thus the seller's net income was $10,712 − $5,692, or $5,020. This is the net income figure to use in the original yield formula.

Averaging the Seller's Equity.   With amortized wraparound loans, the seller's equity will fluctuate depending on the age and amortization rate of either the wrap loan or the senior loan.

The seller's equity increases as the senior loan is paid off and decreases as the wraparound loan is paid off. The changing level of equity in turn affects the seller's investment yield—hence the need to identify the average equity held by the seller during a given year.

For our purposes the seller's equity is the average principal balance of the wraparound note minus the average principal balance of the senior loan. The average principal balance of either loan is found using the equation:

$$\text{Average Balance} = \frac{\text{beginning balance} + \text{ending balance}}{2}$$

Returning to our illustration, we note that the $90,000 wraparound note dropped to $87,750 after the first year. Thus the average balance over the year was

$$\frac{\$90,000 + \$87,750}{2} = \$88,875 \text{ average balance}$$

Similarly, the senior note during the year dropped $1,024 from $60,000 down to $58,976. Its average balance was thus

$$\frac{\$60,000 + \$58,976}{2} = \$59,488$$

The seller's average equity over the year is thus $88,875 − $59,488, or $29,387. Returning to the original yield equation, we can see that the seller's yield on the amortized wraparound is

$$\frac{\$\ 5,020}{\$29,387} = 17.08 \text{ percent}$$

Note that although the yield changes only slightly between the interest-only wraparound (17 percent) and amortized wraparound in this example (17.08 percent), the yield can vary substantially in actual situations.

SELF-QUIZ: WRAPAROUNDS

1. One limitation to wraparound loans is that they must have fixed interest rates and payment schedules. True or false?

2. Wraparounds can be flexibly structured by sellers to have either junior or senior lien priority. True or false?

3. FHA and VA senior loans provide sellers with excellent opportunities to structure wraparounds. True or false?

4. Generally speaking, wraparound loans are not subject to state usury laws. Why is this?

5. The interest the seller receives from a wraparound loan is taxed as interest income. True or false?

6. A wraparound loan is ideal for a seller needing maximum cash for a subsequent home purchase. True or false?

7. Why is the yield on a wraparound potentially greater than the yield on a senior purchase-money mortgage?

8. As the seller's equity in a wraparound investment decreases, the seller's yield will increase. True or false?

9. Suppose a seller entered into a wraparound agreement and one year later decided to pay off half his underlying loan balance. What effect would the prepayment have on the seller's wraparound investment yield?

10. Calculate the seller's first-year yield on the following wraparound, given the following:

Price: $95,000   Senior loan: $60,000 at 9¼% for 20 years,
Down: $15,000   amortized.
Wrap note: 11½% interest-only   Loan is 6 years old.

11. From Exercise 10, calculate the seller's yield in the sixth year of the wraparound loan agreement. (The seller's mortgage at the beginning of the sixth wraparound year is 11 years old.) What is the effect of the seller's amortized loan on investment yield between year one and year six?

ANSWERS TO SELF-QUIZ: WRAPAROUNDS

1. False

2. False. Wraparounds carried back by sellers are always junior liens.

3. True, because neither will contain due-on-sale clauses.

4. Because technically wraparound transactions are credit sales, not loans. Therefore they are not subject to usury laws.

5. False. The income (net) is taxed as ordinary income.

6. False. A seller wanting maximum cash should get the buyer to obtain permanent conventional financing.

7. Because the seller makes money on the senior loan over and above the interest rate on the note.

8. True.

9. The yield would decrease, since the seller's equity increased.

10. a. Net income = ($80,000 × 11½%) − ([$549.53 × 12] − $1860)
$$= \$9,200 - (\$6,594 - \$1,860)$$
$$= \$4,466.$$

   b. Average equity = $80,000 − $\dfrac{\$51,660 + \$49,800}{2}$
$$= \$80,000 - \$50,730$$
$$= \$29,270$$

   c. Yield after one year = $\dfrac{\$4,466}{\$29,270}$
$$= 15.258\%$$

11. a. Net income = ($80,000 $\times$ 11½%) − ($549.53 $\times$ 12) − $3,000 principal paid

                                                            on eleventh year

                = $9,200 − ($6,594.36 − $3,000) = $5,605.64

   b. Average equity = $80,000 $- \dfrac{\$40,200 + \$37,200}{2}$

                        = $80,000 − $38,700 = $41,300

   c. Yield after year 6 $= \dfrac{\$\ 5,606}{\$41,300}$

                           = 13.57%

The amortized loan reduces the yield as the loan is being paid off more rapidly, thereby increasing the seller's equity. As the seller's equity increases, the yield on equity drops (even though net income itself is increasing).

5

Contracts for Deed

In Chapters 3 and 4 we examined the fundamentals of two important seller-financing mechanisms: purchase-money mortgages coupled with assumptions and the wraparound. The third major form of seller-financing to become popular recently is the contract for deed (CFD) or land contract. Like its two relatives CFD financing offers homebuyers a cheaper way to finance properties in time of high interest rates and scarce conventional mortgage money. In addition, the CFD often enables the homeseller to complete an otherwise difficult or conventionally unacceptable sales transaction. As CFDs can be very flexible, the principal parties to the sale can negotiate terms and rates that are satisfactory to individual needs as opposed to institutional standards.

On the other side of the ledger, however, land contracts are controversial sale instruments that are often frowned upon within the brokerage and lending communities. As we will discuss later in this chapter, land contracts are unique documents among the roster of financing alternatives, and they carry with them unique pitfalls and dangers for buyers and sellers.

In this chapter we will look at the advantages and disadvantages of CFDs as well as the CFD's financial mechanics. It should be expressly stated, however, that this presentation of contracts for deed does not advocate specific legal positions, nor does it attempt to present all possible considerations that might be wisely included in the land contract. State laws vary widely on land contracts and it is extremely important to have legal counsel represent each principal *before and during* its execution. This will ensure that local laws are addressed and that the roles of broker and attorney are kept in their proper place. It is solely the role of the attorney to structure the specific language of the contract—not the real estate agent, or in this case, the author.

LEARNING OBJECTIVES

When you have completed this chapter you will be able to:

1. describe the basic mechanics of the contract for deed and the ways it differs from other seller financing techniques,
2. explain the unique advantages and potential disadvantages as well as the key characteristics of the land contract,
3. discuss the major legal considerations that must be made clear in the CFD, and
4. understand how the CFD is affected by due-on-sale clauses.

WHAT IS A CFD?

A contract for deed is a method of transferring title to real property wherein the seller (vendor) is paid principal and interest, or interest only, by the buyer (vendee) for a specific period of time. Under the contract for deed, the seller holds legal title to the property during the contract term and the buyer is granted equitable title and possession. At the end of the loan term the balance of principal and unpaid interest are paid to the seller, who then deeds the property to the buyer.

A CFD is also known as a land contract, conditional sale contract, agreement for deed, contract sale, article sale, land installment contract, contract of sale.

MECHANICS OF THE CFD

In practical terms the contract for deed is a contractual set of provisions and conditions between a homeseller and homebuyer that, when satisfied, entitle the buyer to the property's deed. In other words, it represents a situation where the seller says, "Okay, if you do this and this, and pay me this and that, then at the end of so and so years, I'll give you title to the property. In the meantime, you can move in so long as you do such and such." Briefly, that is all the contract for deed is. The parties agree to certain conditions and payments, the buyer moves in, and the seller holds title to the property; all goes well if the conditions are met and the money is paid. The money the buyer owes the seller over the contract period represents a form of junior financing. If the loan is recorded, the CFD becomes a bona fide junior lien.

Often, however, CFDs are not recorded.

Recording versus not recording a contract sale has become a sensitive legal issue with some states requiring it and others remaining silent on the issue. The act of recording a contract sale makes the transaction visible to the lender, who can in turn declare the transaction to be a violation of the due-on-sale clause. Then, as with PMMs and wraparounds, the lender may accelerate any underlying mortgage the seller may have.

In addition to holding title, the seller retains the senior mortgage on the property and carries back the second junior loan as set forth in the agreement. Thus the seller retains liability for payment of the senior loan. *There is no assumption involved in the CFD transaction.* Because there is no separate collateral pledge (such as a mortgage) or other promissory note, the contract for deed instrument becomes both a financing and sale document that stands on its own without a mortgage or note.

Figure 5.1 depicts how the CFD works in its most fundamental form. Note that in a CFD transaction the seller is called a *vendor* and the buyer is called a *vendee*. This terminology is unique to contract sales and will be used throughout the remainder of this chapter. The vendor (seller) retains both the title to the property and the senior mortgage; the vendee (buyer) is given equitable title (possession of the property) and a junior loan. The term of the loan is pre-established, usually three to five years, and the vendee makes payments directly to the vendor. These payments can be directed toward principal and interest or be interest-only, depending on the agreement. Out of such proceeds, the vendor will continue to make payments on the senior mortgage.

Satisfaction of the CFD usually calls for refinancing payment at the end of the term for the outstanding balance of the junior loan. Theoretically, by the end of the contract's term, the vendee will have accumulated enough additional funds to be able to obtain permanent financing. Such financing must be arranged prior to the end of the term so that when the maturity date arrives, the vendee will be able to pay off the junior loan entirely and record the first-priority new senior loan. In turn, the vendor (or his or her escrow agent) will deliver clear title to the vendee and extinguish the CFD.

Listed below are the key mechanics of the contract for deed.

1. The CFD is an all-inclusive legal contract—it does not require execution of separate mortgage or note instruments.
2. The CFD provides for *junior loan* financing; the senior loan remains in existence.
3. The CFD provides that the seller, or vendor, retains title until the contract has been satisfied; title does not transfer with possession at the closing.

The CFD and the Wraparound

In terms of financial mechanics, the CFD is the wraparound mortgage. In effect, the vendor's retaining the senior mortgage sets up the same financial mechanics as a wraparound. In addition, the vendor may enjoy the investment advantage of arbitrage—the spread between higher interest rate payments received and lower rate payments paid. With a wraparound, however, title is transferred at the closing. This aspect alone creates numerous legal differences between the wraparound and the CFD, particularly with regard to default and foreclosure procedures, which will be discussed later in this chapter.

A Sample CFD

The following example illustrates the financial mechanics of a CFD. Assume the following data:

Price: $120,000
Down: 10 percent
CFD loan: Balance owed at 11½ percent, interest only, to be refinanced in 4 years.
Senior loan: $70,000 originally, at 9 percent, amortized for 30 years, five years old.

With this data,

1. the vendee pays the vendor 10 percent down, or $12,000,
2. the vendee pays the vendor $12,420/year ($108,000 × 11½ percent),
3. the vendor continues payments to the senior mortgagee of $563.24/month,

FIGURE 5.1:   The Contract for Deed

During the Contract Term:

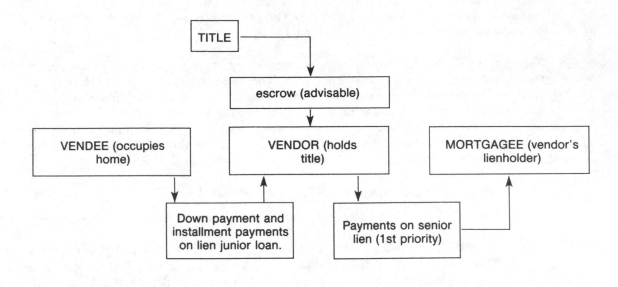

At End of Contract Term:

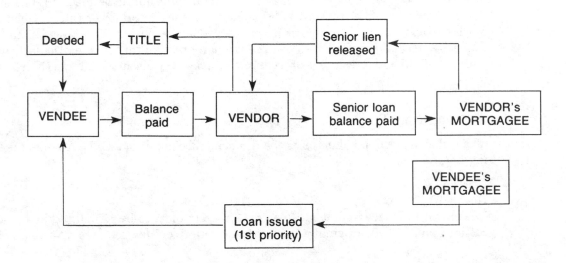

4. At the end of four years:
   a. the vendee obtains other financing for $108,000 and pays off the vendor in full,
   b. the vendor pays off the balance of the senior loan, a total amount of $63,700,
   c. the senior mortgagee releases the senior lien, and the vendor delivers clear title to the vendee.

INVESTMENT POTENTIAL OF THE CFD

The CFD offers the homeseller an investment opportunity with a yield identical to that of a wraparound because the financial mechanics are the same. Briefly reviewing the CFD's investment potential from our illustration, the vendor's yield is approximated as follows:

1. The vendor's senior mortgage balance went from $67,130 at the beginning of the first year of the CFD to $63,700 at the end of the CFD term. The average balance was thus $65,415 ($67,130 + $63,700 ÷ 2).
2. The vendor pays $563.24/month or $6,759 (rounded) PI per year. Because the loan balance was paid down $3,430 over the four years, the vendor paid an average principal amount of $857 per year. This must be subtracted from the annual PI amount to ascertain the vendor's interest expense per year. This equals $6,759 − $857, or $5,902.
3. The vendor's interest income is $12,420 per year. The vendor's net income is $12,420 − $5,902, or $6,518/year.
4. The vendor's average equity was $108,000 owed minus his average debt balance of $65,415 or $42,585 ($108,000 − $65,415).
5. The vendor's average annual yield was $6,518 ÷ $42,585, or 15.3 percent.

As you can see, the CFD, like the wraparound, can present an attractive investment opportunity for the homeseller over and above the purchase-money mortgage. Whether to do a CFD or a wraparound as an investment therefore depends on the seller's decision to retain or convey title—a decision with its own set of complexities.

Qualitative Aspects of CFDs

Loan Terms. CFDs are most often used when unfavorable economic conditions make conventional financing very difficult for the average buyer. Typically, CFDs are short-term financing alternatives designed to make transactions possible under temporary terms—until economic circumstances improve for permanent financing. Accordingly, the typical terms of the CFD loan include a lower-than-usual down payment, a below-market interest rate, and more lenient underwriting ratios. Usually the loan payments are interest-only, and the loan term 3 to 5 years with a balloon payment due at maturity. However, a CFD could be written for a ten-year term or longer and provide for amortization of the loan balance. Title to the property is always retained by the seller, although the use of title escrows has become popular as a safeguard for the vendee during the CFD loan term. The vendor's loan to the vendee may or may not be recorded, as discussed further in the next section.

The "All-Inclusiveness" of the CFD. As mentioned previously, CFD transactions do not involve a mortgage or promissory note, only the contract itself. Therefore the CFD document must be all-inclusive; that is, it must contain each and every point of agreement between vendee and vendor. Because a CFD is a complicated and important document, a real estate attorney's advice or aid should be used in preparing the document.

LEGAL CONSIDERATIONS

The CFD agreement must address many important points in order to be complete and workable. These questions, listed below, have the potential to cause legal difficulties unless they are handled carefully. See the sample contract for deed at the end of this chapter.

Rights of ownership and the pledge of collateral
Conditions of purchase
Default and recourse
Vendor's and vendee's responsibilities
The escrow option
Improvement of the property and new liens against it
Contract satisfaction and delivery of deed
Vendors title insurance
Property description
Existing mortgage information
Insurance clause
Rights of tenants
Payment under a contract for deed
Mortgage clause
Provision for deed
Recording of contract for deed
Judgments and the contract for deed
Default and foreclosure
Loss of payment under the contract
Foreclosure
Strict foreclosure

Rights of Ownership and Pledge of Collateral

In the CFD legal title to the property rests with the vendor until contract obligations are met. At the same time, the vendee enjoys actual possession of the property, or equitable title, provided that no default occurs. These are standard provisions that are set forth in all CFDs in language that has become fairly conventional.

Because the CFD does not entail a legal transfer of title, no mortgage is pledged as collateral for security against default. Rather, the collateral pledged is, in effect, a down payment that can be forfeited upon default.

Remember that the vendor's ownership of title should be confirmed by a title insurance policy.

Conditions of Purchase

Obviously all CFDs must contain the price of the property and the down payment to be received and acknowledged by the vendor. It is also important to expressly state the terms and provisions for the financing arrangements. Such terms include:

1. the principal balance to be financed by the vendor,
2. the form of repayment, whether interest-only payments with a balloon, principal and interest payments that fully amortize the loan, or principal and interest payments with a balloon,
3. the term of the loan, including the date the loan is fully payable (balloon) or the date the loan should be fully amortized,
4. when, where and to whom the periodic payments should be made,
5. the annual interest rate of the loan.

The CFD should also state whether or not the vendee can prepay all or any part of his or her loan and whether any penalty would result. In addition, if the loan can be prepaid in full, the CFD should indicate when the vendee is entitled to the deed (immediately? in a week? after inspecting the property?).

Default and Recourse

Perhaps the most important area in which the CFD should be clear and precise is the one regarding default and recourse. Provisions for each party's legal recourse if the other defaults set forth the powers that each party possesses to protect his or her interests.

Default.   The CFD should first set forth exactly what constitutes default by either party to the agreement. Several actions certainly signal a default, such as the vendee's failure to make a payment or the vendor's failure to pay on the underlying senior mortgage. For the vendor's protection, the CFD should state that the buyer's failure to comply with any contractual responsibilities or obligations constitutes default. But none of this language is sufficiently specific.

There must be a reasonable *measure* against which a default can be determined. To illustrate, let's look at several ways a vendee could default. He or she could make a late payment, damage the property, fail to make the balloon payment, fail to pay taxes, fail to maintain adequate insurance or fail to pay the insurance premiums. In any of the examples, a default may have occurred—or may not have. The vendee may have paid seven days late, but how long a grace period is allowed? The vendee's children may have destroyed the carpeting, but is that a default? The vendee may not be able to procure financing until three weeks after the due date of the balloon. Is that a default? What is "adequate" insurance; or how late can a tax payment be made before a default clearly exists?

Many CFDs fail to clarify the foregoing issues; clarification is more or less left to the vendor's discretion or the court's opinion. As a rule, however, the more specific an agreement can be, the better off are the parties to it.

Whether or not the other items are given a quantitative measure, the vendee's loan payment schedule should include a specified grace period based on the payment's postmark or date of hand delivery. Late payments are the most common form of default, and exactly *when* the late payment becomes a default should be specified. In addition, the CFD should include some provision that the vendee will receive a delinquency notice prior to default and forfeiture.

Protection against default is not solely the vendor's concern. The vendee can incur damages if the vendor defaults on his or her obligations. The vendor's principal exposure to default is failure to pay on the senior mortgage. To guard against that, the CFD should provide that a default on the senior loan triggers an assumption of the senior loan by the vendee (given lender approval) or other similar remedy. Further, the CFD contract can require the vendor to arrange with his or her mortgagee that a notice of default be sent to the vendee if the vendor defaults on the senior loan.

Legal Recourse.   Like default, legal recourse must be explicit and clear. An example might illustrate: A vendee is three weeks late on the monthly payment, and default is stipulated to be two weeks. Would it be reasonable to evict the family? If so, how much time should they be given to vacate? Is the vendor entitled to the down payment *and* the balance of the loan, or just the loan, or the difference between the market value and the senior loan, or what? When does the vendor collect? Does the vendee get a redemption period to make the payment after the default has occurred? What if the vendee has added and paid for a new bathroom? Can the vendor legally claim the value of the improvement as well as the original property value?

As explicitly as possible, the CFD contract should state the vendor's cancellation powers, including what property and/or property value can be repossessed or recovered, and when.

It is common to include in the CFD a redemption period that grows longer in proportion to the vendee's current equity. The following table illustrates a sample redemption schedule:

Less than 20 percent equity	30 days forfeiture
Between 20 percent and 30 percent equity	60 days forfeiture
Between 30 and 50 percent equity	120 days forfeiture
50 percent or more equity	180 days forfeiture

Obviously in a more complex setting a redemption period determines precisely what part of the property's value the vendor can legally reclaim. In some states, the recourse consists of a forfeiture of the down payment, loss of any equity paid in or built up from appreciation and possession of the property. In other cases, specific performance of the contract can be litigated. This means that the vendee must fulfill all obligations of the contract, including full payment of the loan. In some areas it is also possible that the vendor can sue only for the balance owed on the junior loan less the balance he or she currently owes on the senior loan. In any case, the forfeiture powers may be limited by state laws and should be left to local attorneys to interpret.

Vendor's and Vendee's Responsibilities

A CFD contract should set forth the respective responsibilities of the vendor and vendee, with special emphasis on those of the vendee. Only two vendor responsibilities need to be stated in the contract: vendors must acknowledge payments by receipt and they must faithfully make payments on the underlying senior mortgage.

The contract should expressly state three primary responsibilities of the vendee:

1. maintaining the property in satisfactory condition,
2. paying real estate taxes (vendor may prefer to pay taxes, which should be so stated),
3. maintaining and paying for adequate insurance (vendor may want to maintain insurance at his or her cost, which should be so stated).

Escrow

The use of an escrow agent and escrow account is a well-advised practice to ensure that transactions occur smoothly during the contract term. Usually the escrow is used for the deposit of tax and insurance payments made by the vendee and often for the money debt payments as well. The escrow agent can also hold title and institute title delivery or default proceedings in accordance with the stipulations in the agreement. In addition, to avoid the vendor's failure to pay the senior loan, the escrow agent can be used to disperse the senior loan payments from the vendee's monthly payment.

Two considerations should be explicit in the CFD contract when opting for the use of an escrow. The first is clear and complete instructions as to how the escrow is to operate. Second, it is a common and advisable practice to indemnify all escrow parties—who have acted in good faith and without fault—against loss, damages, expenses or liabilities arising out of the provisions of the agreement.

Improvement of Property and New Liens Against It

A complete CFD will address the issue of the resident vendee making improvements on the property and the possibility of recording new liens against the property for construction or financing of the improvements.

Specifically, the contract should address three considerations. First, can the vendee make improvements at all without the vendor's permission? Second, if so permitted, should the vendee be allowed to have new liens placed against the property? And third, how are the costs of the improvement to be handled if the vendee defaults on the contract?

The contract should specify how an improvement should be handled if the vendee defaults. The contract should state who is liable for debts incurred on any approved improvements and how such debts would be paid.

Contract Satisfaction and Delivery of Deed

The CFD agreement should set forth the terms and conditions that once and for all satisfy the contract requirements for delivery of the deed. In addition, it should clearly identify exactly what kind of deed will be delivered.

Most agreements also provide that the delivery of the deed is evidence or proof that the contract has been satisfied.

The closing of the agreement should of course be properly recorded.

Vendor's Title Insurance

A prerequisite to executing a CFD is making sure the vendor in fact has bona fide title to deliver. This is best evidenced by a title insurance policy. If the vendor has no title insurance, or other title evidence, the sale process should be halted. Since the contract for deed calls for delivery of title to the vendee upon satisfaction of the contract's terms, title insurance becomes the vendee's guarantee that delivery of good title can be done.

If the title is clear for delivery—as it usually is if it has been insured—the next safeguard is to ensure that the title *remains* deliverable throughout the contract period.

Specifically, title insurance assures that

1. the vendor has title subject only to stated exceptions,
2. the vendor has the right to sell his or her interest in the property,
3. the vendee has a right to a deed in the event the vendor declares bankruptcy or otherwise defaults, so long as the vendee continues to make payments and occupy the premises,
4. the vendee will receive all rights to the property that are paid for.

Equally important, title insurance also insures that the CFD contract itself is validly drawn and executed and is subsequently defensible. In many instances, vendors or their heirs have claimed that a contract for deed was invalid. Title insurance in these cases protects the vendor insofar as the insurer will defend the contract against these claims. Further, if the claims prove valid, or if title is later found to be defective, or if the contract is held to be unenforceable, the title insurer will compensate the vendee for any loss incurred.

In summary, title insurance gives legitimacy to the vendor's selling proposition as well as protecting the vendee against unforeseen contingencies that may arise. As such contingencies are very possible, obtaining title insurance is a prerequisite to entering into a CFD.

CFDs and Due-on-Sale Clauses

We have seen in previous chapters that other seller-financing transactions are vulnerable to DOS clauses in the seller's underlying senior mortgage. Such clauses impose the lender's right to foreclose the mortgage should a transfer of interest in the property occur.

With CFD transactions, however, it is not so clear-cut whether in fact a transfer has taken place. The vendor under a CFD retains the title over the contract term and issues a title to the vendee *only if* certain conditions are met. The vendee holds no mortgage during the term and has little or no leverage upon a default. So who really owns the property? And if ownership is in question, how can the lender say interests have been transferred upon the execution of the contract?

Until recently the foregoing argument held its own against the lender's protestation that CFDs are little different than PMM sales. Presently, however, it has been generally ruled that CFD sales *do* constitute sufficient transfer of interest to warrant defensible use of the DOS clause. Since both principal parties assume themselves that a sale has taken place—unless something goes wrong—and since a transfer of equitable interest has in fact taken place, the DOS clause may be legitimately used.

This general consensus led to another practice: concealing the transaction from the lender altogether—and the CFD was the best device for this. Since the vendor had greater powers to remedy default in a CFD as opposed to a wraparound, it wasn't so critical to record the junior loan. In turn, if nothing was recorded, how would the lender find out a sale had taken place?

The CFD proved very effective in concealing DOS-vulnerable transactions. However risky, this device made it very difficult to discover the unrecorded sale. At this point we can see one reason why vendors disallow property improvements. If not paid for in cash, the improvement could be vulnerable to a mechanic's lien, which the builder would record. Once recorded, the lien gives evidence—potentially to the bank—that something is going on with the secured property. Moreover, the mechanic's lien or any vendee loan on the improvement would take priority over the CFD loan since the latter was never recorded. Thus it is not difficult to see why the vendor often prohibits property improvements. Overall, the practice of executing home sales via CFDs for the purpose of concealing the transaction from the senior mortgagee is a risky business indeed.

SELF-QUIZ: CFDs

1. Describe two reasons CFD transactions are controversial.

2. CFDs are all-inclusive contracts. How does the term "all-inclusive" distinguish the CFD from a wraparound?

3. What is arbitrage?

4. a. Why would a vendee want to see the vendor's title insurance policy?

   b. Why would the vendee want to use a title escrow?

5. The vendor as well as the vendee can default on a CFD. What is the primary way a vendor can default and how can the vendee protect himself/herself against it?

6. In a CFD arrangement, who pays taxes and property maintenance costs?

7. Why would CFDs become popular during recessionary periods?

8. We have seen that CFDs provide that the seller retain legal title. What are two potential *disadvantages* of retaining title?

FIGURE 5.2:   Sample Contract for Deed

CONTRACT FOR DEED

THIS CONTRACT, entered into   **between**

hereinafter referred to as "Seller", and

hereinafter referred to as "Buyer",

WITNESSETH: That in consideration of the mutual covenants herein contained, Seller agrees to sell and convey, and Buyer agrees to purchase upon the following terms and conditions, all that certain property, hereinafter called "said property", situate in the County of _____, State of _____, and described as follows, to-wit:

Order No. ....

The purchase price of said property which Buyer agrees to pay is the sum of

($) DOLLARS, payable as follows:

All payments under this contract shall be made to

_____, _____, hereinafter called "Escrow agent", which Escrow agent is hereby authorized to receive the above payments and to receipt therefor.

All taxes, interest on special assessments, utility charges, rents, premiums for fire and extended coverage insurance, and interest on existing mortgages and contracts of sale have been prorated and settled.

Buyer shall pay all taxes, special assessments and utility charges now and hereafter assessed against said property.

Buyer shall keep the buildings erected, and to be erected upon said property, insured against fire and other hazards in the amount of the reasonable insurable value thereof, in insurance companies to be approved by Seller, for the mutual benefit and protection of the parties hereto, and to place the policy or policies representing the fire and extended coverage insurance and evidence of the payment of premiums thereon with Escrow agent, to be held by it or a mortgagee.

Buyer agrees to maintain said premises and all improvements thereon in good repair, to permit no waste thereof, and to take the same care thereof that a prudent owner would take.

Buyer hereby agrees that he has examined the deed herein agreed to be furnished by Seller and the preliminary report for title insurance or has caused the same to be examined for him by his attorney and from such examination has found the title to said property satisfactory, and hereby agrees that when he has performed or complied with all of the terms and conditions of this contract and is entitled to receive said deed, he will accept said deed and the title to said property as the same is shown by the policy of title insurance.

Buyer may enter into possession of said property and continue in such possession for and during the life of this contract.

Seller agrees to make, execute and acknowledge forthwith a deed granting and conveying said property to Buyer, free and clear of all encumbrances as of the date of this contract, except as herein provided, and subject to any restrictions of record, reservations in State or Federal patents, and zoning ordinances of any municipality or county, and to place said deed and a copy of this contract in escrow with Escrow agent and to deliver to Buyer a policy of title insurance insuring Buyer as vendee under this contract. Escrow agent is hereby authorized and directed to deliver said deed to Buyer upon payment of the purchase price in accordance with the terms of this contract.

FIGURE 5.2:   Continued

Seller and Buyer, and each of them, promise to pay promptly and to indemnify and hold harmless Escrow agent against all costs, damages, attorney's fees, expenses and liabilities which, in good faith and without fault on its part, it may incur or sustain in connection with this agreement and in connection with any court action arising out of this contract.

In the event Buyer fails to pay the interest or principal on any mortgage or contract above mentioned, or any taxes or the interest or principal of any special assessment or fire and extended coverage insurance premiums, as the same shall become due, then it shall be lawful for Seller to pay the same, and the amount so paid shall be a lien on said property and shall be added to the amount due Seller under this contract, and shall thereafter bear interest at the rate of eight per cent (8%) per annum until paid.

It is expressly understood and agreed that each and every thing to be performed by Buyer under the terms of this contract shall be considered to be a condition. Upon any default on the part of Buyer of any of the terms, conditions or covenants herein contained, Seller may, at his sole option, either (1) forfeit and terminate this contract, in which event Seller shall declare this contract forfeited, and all rights of Buyer hereunder shall thereupon cease and terminate and all sums of money paid hereunder shall be forefeited to and retained by Seller as liquidated damages, and Buyer shall immediately deliver to Seller peaceful possession of said premises, and Seller may forthwith re-enter said premises and remove all persons therefrom, and withdraw from escrow forthwith the deed hereinabove provided for, or (2) Seller may treat this contract as continuing, and may enforce the same either by specific performance or other appropriate remedy. Waiver of one or more defaults by Seller shall not constitute a bar to declare future default or defaults, nor shall an election to treat the contract as continuing constitute a bar upon the occurrence of future default or defaults, to again elect as to the remedy. The affidavit of Seller that default has occurred shall be sufficient evidence of default for Escrow agent to deliver the deed to Seller.

If any suit shall be brought by either party to enforce or cancel this contract, the prevailing party to said suit shall be entitled to recover all costs and expenses necessarily incurred by him in connection therewith, including a reasonable attorney's fee to be fixed by the court.

It is mutually agreed by and between the parties hereto that time shall be of the essence of this contract, and that all covenants and agreements herein contained shall extend to and be binding upon the heirs, administrators, executors, successors and assigns of the respective parties hereto.

IN WITNESS WHEREOF, the parties hereto have executed these presents the day and year first above written.

---   ---

---   ---

---   ---

       SELLER   BUYER

STATE OF _____ }
COUNTY OF _____ } ss.

   This instrument was acknowledged before me this   day of   19   ,
by _____

My Commission Expires: _____

                                            NOTARY PUBLIC

STATE OF _____ }
COUNTY OF _____ } ss.

   This instrument was acknowledged before me this   day of   19   ,
by _____

My Commission Expires: _____

                                            NOTARY PUBLIC

Assume the information provided below for a hypothetical transaction and answer questions 9 and 10.

Price: $105,000
Down: $10,000
Senior mortgage: $60,000 originally, at 9¼ percent amortized over 25 years.
    Presently 7 years old.
CFD note: Interest-only with a 5-year balloon

9. What interest rate must the vendor charge on the CFD loan to obtain an average yield of 18.5 percent over the 5-year period?

    Hint one: Use the vendor's average senior loan balance over the 5-year period.
    Hint two: Assume the vendor's yearly principal payments were equal amounts.

10. What is the vendor's equity after five years if the property appreciates 25 percent?

ANSWERS TO SELF-QUIZ: CFDs

1. a. Because legal recourse for default is done via breach of contract suit rather than through foreclosure law. This creates more opportunity for the vendor to receive compensation disproportionate to actual loss. In addition, redemption and grace periods may be much more stringent.

    b. Because they are the best instruments for concealing transactions from the senior mortgagee.

2. CFDs do not involve separate promissory notes or mortgage investments. All terms and conditions are written in the sale document.

3. The point spread between interest rates on loans receivable versus interest rates on loans payable.

4. a. To ensure that the vendor has deliverable title.

    b. So the title will not be disturbed (or transferred) during the CFD loan period.

5. The vendor can default on the senior mortgage. The vendee can protect himself/herself by requiring that notice be provided by such default and that default triggers a new financing arrangement, such as an assumption.

6. Such conditions are not pre-established; who pays for what must be stipulated in the agreement.

7. Because vendor's underwriting standards are likely to be more lenient than those of institutional lenders.

8. One disadvantage is having to repossess the property upon default—since the vendor still owns it. This could be very inconvenient if the vendor has moved some distance away from the property. Another disadvantage is that the vendor could suffer property damages in excess of the vendee's down payment. If the vendee defaults, the vendor will suffer a net loss in having to both repair and resell the property.

9. a. The vendor's balance went from $53,940 down to $46,560.
    The average balance was thus *$50,250.*
    The average principal paid each year was ($53,940 − $46,560) ÷ 5, or *$1,476.*

b. The vendor's average equity was ($95,000 − $50,250), or *$44,750*.

c. The vendor's monthly payment is $514 (rounded), or $6,168/year. Taking out principal payments, the vendor's average interest expense was ($6,168 − $1,476), or *$4,692*.

d. To yield 18.5 percent annually on $44,750 average equity, the vendor must *net* 18.5 percent × $44,750, or *$8,279* per year.

e. To net $8,279 with expenses of $4,692, the vendor must have interest income from the vendee of $8,279 + $4,692 or $12,971.

f. To receive $12,971 on an interest-only loan of $95,000, the vendor must charge ($12,971) ÷ ($95,000), or 13.65 percent.

10. After five years the vendor's equity is ($95,000 − $46,460), or $48,440. Appreciation only affects the vendee's equity, not the vendor's.

6

Adjustable Mortgage Loans and Adjustable-Rate Mortgages

This chapter is an examination of the adjustable mortgage loan (AML) authorized by the Federal Home Loan Bank Board (FHLBB) for *federally chartered* savings and loan associations, and the similar adjustable-rate mortgage (ARM), recently authorized by the Office of the Comptroller of the Currency (OCC) for *nationally chartered* banks. This chapter does not cover authorized or unauthorized adjustable-rate mortgages issued by state-chartered banks, state-chartered savings and loan associations, or other mortgage lenders, including the homeseller.

In 1981 five percent of new loans were ARMs. This grew to two-thirds of loans originated in 1984 when it was thought that adjustable loans might supplant fixed-rate loans. However, with declining interest rates, the market share of ARMs fell to 50 percent in 1985. While its share of the mortgage market will fluctuate as interest rates change, the ARM has become a permanent fixture of the mortgage market. In the early 1980s ARMs were still evolving and earned a bad reputation because they were unregulated and because borrowers were unaware of the pitfalls of the new loans. When fixed-rate loans were 13 percent, it was not uncommon for lenders to quote a first-year ARM rate as low as 6 or 7 percent. When the loans were adjusted in the second year, borrowers would find themselves paying almost the same rate as a fixed-rate mortgage, with provisions in the loan for the rate to increase even higher in future years. More recently, interest rate caps, payment caps and other protections have been added, and regulations to standardize the loans have been passed by Congress. These have helped protect the borrower as adjustable loans continue to evolve.

Because of the likelihood of change and the magnitude of the ARM itself, active real estate practitioners should stay abreast of new evolutions of adjustable loans as they occur.

The term ARM can refer to an entire family of adjustable-rate loans, or it can refer to a specific adjustable-rate loan. The purpose of this chapter is, therefore, twofold: first, to introduce characteristics and provisions of ARMs that, by authorization, refer to *all* types of ARMs issued by nationally chartered banks and savings and loans; second, to focus on the major type of ARM—the senior priority ARM with no special provisions such as graduated payment schedules.

LEARNING OBJECTIVES

In addition to becoming familiar with the essential components of ARMs, how they work and the legal provisions that routinely accompany them, you will learn to

1. calculate interest rate changes on the basis of index movements,
2. derive monthly payment, the new principal balance, and the new loan term as a result of an interest rate change,
3. understand the qualitative essentials of an ARM,
4. be familiar with indexing of interest rates and what indexes are used,
5. understand "payment capped" ARMs and their potential pitfalls,
6. compare OCC adjustable-rate mortgage restrictions with FHLBB adjustable mortgage loan restrictions,
7. be familiar with the ARM provisions regarding disclosure, notification, prepayments, negative amortization and due-on-sale clauses, and
8. be aware of the role the secondary mortgage market will play in the development and standardization of ARMs.

WHAT ARE ARMs AND AMLs?

In the spring of 1981 both the Federal Home Loan Bank Board (FHLBB) and the Office of the Comptroller of the Currency (OCC) issued authorizations for adjustable-rate mortgages. These two landmark authorizations set forth the rules and regulations permitting nationally or federally chartered banks and savings and loan associations to issue, purchase or otherwise deal with adjustable-rate mortgage loans on one- to four-family residential dwellings.

The ARM and AML authorizations supersede previous regulations defining and authorizing variable-rate mortgages (VRMs) and renegotiable-rate mortgages (RRMs). Both VRMs and RRMs are, in effect, included within the provisions of the AML and ARM authorizations, but as of July 31, 1981, they can no longer be called RRMs or VRMs nor can they be authorized in their pre-AML/ARM form.

Adjustable Mortgage Loan (AML) is the name for adjustable mortgages authorized by FHLBB for federally chartered savings and loan associations.

Adjustable-Rate Mortgage (ARM) is the name for adjustable-rate mortgages authorized by OCC for national banks.

An AML/ARM is any mortgage loan secured by a one- to four-family dwelling that provides for periodic interest rate adjustments by the lender.

An AML/ARM can be a junior lien or a senior lien and can have widely different structures. For example, AML/ARMs can be for ten years or for 30 years. They can have varying payment schedules and special features such as graduated payment provisions, balloon payments or provisions for pledged accounts. But in every case, the loan is an

AML or ARM if it is secured by a one- to four-family residential property and allows for interest rate changes.

Authorizations

The adjustable-rate mortgage and the adjustable mortgage loan effectively return lending authority back to the lender as opposed to federal government regulations. The two authorizations permitted interest rates to be established by the marketplace rather than the government. In effect, the federal government got out of regulating interest rates, leaving that responsibility to the lender.

Intent or Purpose of ARMs and AMLs.   Both ARM and AML programs have four common purposes, or intents:

- to give lenders an incentive to make mortgage loans,
- to provide a means of responding to housing demand,
- to allow the market rather than government to regulate interest rates, and
- to keep mortgage interest rates in synchronization with the lender's cost of funds (i.e., to keep loan rates above deposit interest rates).

Loan Provisions of ARMs and AMLs.   Both ARM and AML loans have the following major characteristics in common.

- They provide for adjustable interest rates that are tied to an economic index. Movements in the index periodically trigger proportionate movements in the loan's interest rate.
- Increases or decreases in the interest rate are implemented by adjusting the *monthly payment,* the *principal balance* or the *loan term.*
- Increases in the index *may* trigger interest rate increases—at the lender's option. Decreases in the index (greater than the minimum) *must* trigger a decrease in the interest rate—the lender has no option.
- Advance notification of 30 to 45 days is required prior to an interest rate change.
- Fees cannot be charged for changing rates.
- Any part of the outstanding loan balance can be prepaid at any time without penalty, with the exception of the initial payment period on an ARM when prepayment may carry a penalty.
- The loans can be recast upon assumption, and due-on-sale clauses are enforceable.
- Within limits, negative amortization is allowed (an increasing loan balance).
- Extensive disclosure is required of the lender to the borrower for the latter's education and protection.

ESSENTIALS OF THE AML AND ARM: AN IN-DEPTH EXAMINATION

Although the AML or ARM may at first appear complicated, the loan reduces to three essential phases:

- the interest rate's relationship to the index movement,
- the resulting change in the interest rate as the index goes up or down, and
- the implementation of the change through adjustments to principal, monthly payment or loan term.

Everything else about ARMs and AMLs is related to these three steps, whether it be restrictions, refinements, requirements or specific calculations.

The Index

The most distinctive feature of the adjustable-rate mortgage is its interest rate tie-in to a financial index. As the index moves, so does the mortgagor's interest rate, at periodic rate-adjustment intervals.

National Banks.   The index rule for national banks calls for one of the three following indexes to be used (note that each index must be beyond the control of any individual lender, must be verifiable by the borrower and must reflect the *cost of funds* made available to the lender):

1. the monthly average of weekly average auction rates on U.S. Treasury bills with a maturity of six months (from *Federal Reserve Bulletin*),
2. the monthly average yield on U.S. Treasury securities adjusted to a constant maturity of three years (from *Federal Reserve Bulletin*), and
3. the monthly average contract interest rate charged by all lenders on mortgage loans for previously occupied homes (from the Federal Home Loan Bank Board's *Journal* and FHLBB mid-month news releases).

Identifying the Index Value.   The OCC authorized two methods for using the indexes in determining periodic interest rate changes. One method is to select the initial index value and subsequently to use the most recently available change in the index. For example, at the beginning of the loan period, a most recently available index value might be 13.50. The 13.50 would then become the *base index value* for the loan. If at the time for notifying the borrower of a rate change, the most recently available value of the index had become 13.80, the new value of 13.80 would be applied to the interest-rate-change calculations.

The other authorized method for using the index is the moving average method. In this method the loan's original index value is the *average* of the index's values over a period prior to the loan's closing that is equivalent to the future interest change periods of the loan. Subsequent index changes are the average of all index movements during each interest adjustment period. As this method is more complex and uncommon, this chapter will focus solely on the nonaveraged method of measuring the index change.

Relationship Between Index and Interest Rate.   The relationship between the index and the mortgage interest rate is *direct and identical*. If the index increases 5 basis points (.05 percent), the interest rate increases 5 basis points. If the index decreases 15 basis points, the interest rate decreases 15 basis points, and so on. Thus, if an ARM's interest rate is 14 percent, and its financial index decreases .5 percent, the interest rate on the loan becomes 13.5 percent.

Federal Savings and Loan Associations.   The index ruling for savings and loans made by the FHLBB did not mandate that any specific index be used. It specified only that the index meet two requirements:

- It must be easily verifiable by the borrower.
- It must be beyond the control of the lender.

The FHLBB index ruling gave federal savings and loans unprecedented flexibility. It also responded specifically to two issues: First, the index could reflect the lender's cost of funds; second, unlike those of national banks, savings and loan indexes could be regional and thus sensitive to more local economic conditions. It has been estimated that there are 15 to 20 indexes that meet FHLBB requirements. If lenders intend to sell these mortgages to the secondary market, however, their choice of indexes is much more restricted.

Among indexes likely to be used more frequently, besides the three indexes stipulated for national banks, are:

- the FHLBB average cost of funds to FSLIC savings and loan institutions,
- three-month T-bill rates, and
- the monthly average yield on treasury securities adjusted to constant maturities of one, two, three or five years.

Although much latitude exists in what index may be selected, practicality and the forces of the market will restrict wide discrepancies. For example, an index such as three-month T-bill rates may be too volatile for borrowers to accept.

Under the authorization, federal savings and loans may also employ moving average index values as well as latest available values.

Finally, whatever index is selected *must be used for the duration of a particular loan,* even though a different loan made by the same lender can be tied to a different index. The exception to this occurs only when the index ceases to exist during the loan term.

Margins

Lenders add a few percentage points, called "margin," to the index rate to determine the rate they will charge on the ARM. While the margin will be constant over the life of the loan, it can differ from one lender to another. The borrower should look at both the index

---

TABLE 6.1: Comparison of Major ARM Indices in Recent Years

Year	6-Mo. T-Bill	1-Yr. Treasury	3-Yr. Treasury	5-Yr. Treasury	National Median Cost of Funds
1981 June	13.95	14.86	14.29	13.95	10.79
Dec	11.47	12.85	13.66	13.60	11.58
1982 June	12.31	14.07	14.48	14.43	11.38
Dec	8.23	8.91	9.88	10.22	10.43
1983 June	8.89	9.66	10.32	10.63	9.54
Dec	9.14	10.11	11.13	11.54	9.90
1984 June	10.55	12.08	13.18	13.48	9.67
Dec	8.36	9.33	10.56	11.07	9.92
1985 June	7.16	7.80	9.05	9.60	8.95
Dec	7.09	7.67	8.40	8.73	8.48
1986 June	6.28	6.73	7.41	7.64	7.95
Dec	5.53	5.87	6.43	6.67	7.33

The choice of index is a significant factor in determining how much the payment changes will be on an ARM. The table above shows that the size of the rate change varies between indices.

and margin when comparing plans. Loan plans with lower margins are usually used with higher indexes.

$$\text{Index Interest Rate} + \text{Margin} = \text{Loan Rate}$$

This is referred to as the full-indexed interest rate.

Discounts

Initial ARM rates that are lower than the sum of the index and margin are offered by some lenders. These are called discounted rates and are often combined with higher initial loan fees (points) and much higher interest rates when the discount period expires. A lender may use the lower initial interest rate in qualifying a borrower for a loan. The borrower must consider carefully whether he or she will be able to afford the higher payments in later years when the discount expires and the rate is adjusted higher.

DISCUSSION QUESTIONS

1. True or false: An ARM or AML can have varying rates of interest, varying loan terms, graduated payment features and can be issued by any mortgage lender.

2. What are three reasons AML and ARM-type loans were authorized?

3. If an index for an ARM moves up 50 basis points, the interest rate for the ARM must move up 50 basis points. True or false?

4. At periodic intervals, the ARM's interest rate is increased or decreased according to the movement of an index. What are the three ways an increase or decrease in the rate is charged to the borrower?

5. What are the two restrictions on federal S&Ls in selecting an ARM index?

ANSWERS

1. False. AMLs and ARMs can have varying terms, but they can be issued only by federally chartered S&Ls or nationally chartered banks respectively.

2. • To give lenders an incentive to make mortgage loans profitable
   • To respond to housing demand
   • To deregulate interest rates

3. False. It is the lender's option to raise the rate. If the index goes down, he or she *must* lower the rate.

4. By adjusting the monthly payment, the principal loan balance or the loan term.

5. • The index must be verifiable.
   • The index must be beyond the control of the lender.

The Interest Rate Adjustment

The adjustment in the interest rate is determined by movement in the selected index, the provisions in the loan that structure the rate movement and the restrictions for all AML/ARM loans established by the OCC and FHLBB. *Do not confuse interest rate adjustments with payment adjustments*—they are two distinctly different things that can occur independently of each other.

There are two important aspects to interest rate changes: how much and how often the rate can change. These considerations are summarized in Figure 6.1.

Interest Rate Change Provisions.   There is no explicit rate change frequency for federal savings and loans. However, since they are required to give a 30- to 45-day notification of rate changes, savings and loans are effectively precluded from making rate adjustments more frequently than once a month. From a practical point of view, rate adjustments are likely to occur every six months.

Both banks and savings and loans can extend the initial adjustment period. This allows lenders to synchronize rate adjustment for groups or pools of loans, which in turn facilitates sales to the secondary markets.

The national bank limit on single adjustments (5 percent) is to encourage lenders to make adjustments at least every two and one-half years. The carryover provision lessens the impact of this interest change ceiling by allowing interest increases in excess of the one percent or five percent ceiling to be carried over to the next period, so long as reductions in the rate do not negate the carryover.

FIGURE 6.1: Interest Rate Changes

	NATIONAL BANKS	FEDERAL SAVINGS AND LOANS
Frequency	• No more often than every six months, except initial period	• As often as every month, except for initial period
Amount	• Maximum of 1 percent per six-month period; no single adjustment greater than 5 percent	• No rate change limits required, though limitations are likely to be set by individual lenders.
	• No overall limit to rate change over the entire loan term.	• Minimum movements may be established.
	• Minimum index movements to change interest rate may be established, but must apply for ups and downs equally.	
	• Upward rate adjustments based on index movement are optional at the lender's discretion.	
Carryover	• Index movements that aren't applied to a rate change *may* be carried over to the next adjustment period. Decreases not applied *must* be carried over to the next period.	• Not provided for by FHLBB; the assumption as a result is that savings and loans that do not use portions of a rate change *cannot* carry them over into the next term.

For example, if the ceiling is one percent and during one period the rate moves 1.25 percent, the .25 percent cannot be applied to the current rate but may be carried over into the next period. Thus, if the interest increased another .75 percent in the next period, the second rate adjustment would be the .75 percent plus the .25 percent carried over, or 1.00 percent total change. If the index decreased, the .25 percent decrease would *have to be* applied to the interest rate during the second adjustment period.

It is important to note that the index chosen and the subsequent interest rate movements have nothing to do with the initial interest rate established by the lender. In fact, nothing in the AML or ARM sets restrictions on where the initial interest rate is set; only that it subsequently must bear a direct relationship to index movements.

The FHLBB sets no limit on interest rate changes, with the expectation that the lender will act prudently in setting such limitations. However, overly frequent changes in the rate can present administrative nightmares for lenders. For example, monthly rate changes on every mortgage together with notification requirements would create more overhead costs for the lender than any income that could possibly result from those changes.

ARM loan programs without a per-period rate change ceiling also could be asking for serious problems. On most loans a 1 percent interest rate change increases the monthly payment about 7 percent. If a volatile index were selected that swung upwards 2 percent during an annual period, the 14 percent payment increase could be very burdensome for the borrower, and, in marginal instances, could trigger loan default.

Should savings and loan associations establish rate change ceilings—which they are likely to do—the ceiling on the upward change *does not* have to be the same amount as the downward change maximum. For example, a program might stipulate a maximum upward rate change of 1.50 percent and a downward maximum of 2 percent.

SELF-QUIZ: ARMs AND AMLs

Several interest-rate-change exercises based on index movements follow. Complete each exercise before reviewing the answers.

1. Initial interest rate of 13.75 percent set by Washington National Bank. Rate to be adjusted every six months on the basis of an index's latest available figure. Initial index value 14.45. Index during first six months moved to 15.85. What is the new interest rate?

2. In the above data, .40 percent was carried over into the next period. During that period, the index moved from 16.50 to 15.00. What was the new interest rate?

3. Initial interest rate 14.5 percent set by Chicago National Bank. Rate to be adjusted every three years on the basis of six-month T-bills. The initial index value was 14.00 percent. After three years the index had moved to 19.25 percent. What was the new interest rate?

ANSWERS TO SELF-QUIZ: ARMs AND AMLs

1. New interest rate is 14.75, since the interest change ceiling per period is 1 percent. To arrive at this, you identify the change in the index, 15.85 minus 14.45, which is 1.40. As discussed, national banks may increase the rate by only 1 percent in a six-month period.

2. New interest rate is figured thus: 40 percent carried over, less 1.5 percent decrease in index, equals .90 percent decrease in interest rate, or 13.85 percent.

3. New interest rate is 19.5 percent, because of the 5 percent single-rate-adjustment maximum.

Implementation of the Interest Rate Adjustment

Implementation is the process of converting changes in rates into changes in dollar amounts that the borrower owes. This change in money amounts can take the form of increases or decreases in monthly payments, or it can be accomplished by changing the loan term or the amortization rate.

The details of implementation are subject to guidelines set down by the authorizing agencies. Figure 6.2 summarizes these requirements, and the following sections examine each process in greater depth.

Synchronization. Both regulatory authorities allow rate changes to occur *without* changes in the monthly payment. Especially in the case of savings and loans, this effectively permits the lender to add or subtract interest amounts from the loan's principal balance until the payment adjustment date. It is the lender's option whether to set up payment adjustments concurrently with the interest rate change.

FIGURE 6.2: Implementation of Interest Rate Changes

	NATIONAL BANKS	FEDERAL SAVINGS AND LOANS
Authorization	Can be implemented by changing the principal balance, loan term or the monthly payment.	
Synchronization	Interest rate changes do not have to be synchronized with payment adjustments, i.e., rate changes can occur without payment changes, thereby effectively allowing additions to principal to occur.	
Monthly Payments: Limitations on payment change amounts	Cannot exceed the amount resulting from the maximum rate change of 1 percent per six-month period, and 2.50 percent during any single period.	No stipulated limitation on the amount a payment may change from period to period. Up to the lender to establish limitations.
Limitation on payment change frequency	No more often than once every six months	No more often than once every month
Loan term limitation	No loan term can exceed 30 years.	No loan term can exceed 40 years.
Adjustments to principal and negative amortization	• Negative amortization cannot exceed the equivalent of 1 percent of the principal balance per each six months of a payment period. • Can *never* exceed 10 percent of the principal balance at the beginning of a payment period. • Payments must be adjusted at least once every five years to amortize the loan over the remaining term (which cannot exceed 30 years from closing date). Preempts state laws prohibiting the charging of interest on interest.	• No limits as to amount of negative amortization permitted. • Payments must be adjusted at least once every five years to amortize the loan over the remaining term (which cannot exceed 40 years from closing date).
Payment-capped mortgages	Must be reviewed and approved by OCC. Certain disclosures required.	Specifically permitted.

Monthly Payment Changes: Amounts and Frequency.   We have examined how the interest rate moves according to movements in the loan's index. National banks, however, have limitations on how much a monthly payment can be increased during a given period and how often the payment can be changed (no more than once every six months). Savings and loans, on the other hand, have no restrictions on how much payments can increase, and they can adjust payments as often as monthly. However, prudent savings and loan lenders will establish limitations on potential payment increases in order to make their loans attractive and accepted by the public. In addition, payment changes are not likely to happen monthly due to the administrative expense of doing so and the public's distaste for constantly changing payments.

Limitations on Adjusting the Loan Term.   The ceilings on AML and ARM loan terms are 40 and 30 years, respectively. Because ARM loans are most likely to be issued at or near the term limit, adjustments to the terms of these loans would implement only the most marginal of interest rate movements. Even for savings and loans issuing 30-year loans, a maximum ten-year extension of the loan term would accommodate an interest rate change of less than 20 basis points—which is only a slight rate change.

The role of the term extension in implementing rate changes, then, will be minor. Three possible uses for the term extension are:

1. to implement the most moderate of interest adjustments on a savings and loan 30-year loan to avoid the trouble of the payment change or principal change,
2. to provide for much shorter-term loans, such as 10- to 15-year junior loans, and
3. to cope with a drop in interest rates below 10 percent (the approximate rate at which a 10-year extension of a 30-year loan can implement a 50-basis-point rate change).

Implementation by Adjustments to Principal.   In addition to implementing interest rate changes by adjusting the monthly payment and/or the loan term, the rate can be implemented by adding or subtracting interest owed from the borrower's principal balance. Adding unpaid interest to the loan balance is negative amortization.

The lender and the borrower must be cautious when implementing interest rate changes by adding new interest costs to the loan's principal balance. Both lender and borrower can get into trouble if this practice is used to excess.

About AML and ARM Negative Amortization.   The OCC's position with regard to negative amortization is more restrictive than the FHLBB's. Both programs, however, permit a significant amount of negative amortization.

The FHLBB's AML Authorization.   The FHLBB again places the burden of prudence and responsibility on the lender and the marketplace. The AML has no legal restriction on negative amortization except that the loan must be re-amortized *at least every five years* in order to amortize the principal balance fully at the current interest rate (or less) over the remaining term of the loan (never to exceed 40 years from date of origination).

The OCC's Position.   The ARM loan can amortize negatively subject to three limitations:

1. At no time can the negative amortization exceed one percent per *six-month period* of the outstanding principal balance at the beginning of the term. For example, if a

rate adjustment period on a loan is one year and the outstanding balance on the loan at the beginning of that period is $52,000, no more than a net of two percent of negative amortization (one percent times two six-month periods) of the $52,000, or $1,040, can occur during the year.

To carry the example further, assume that a net of $1,000 was added to principal as negative amortization. During the next year, the same maximum of two percent negative amortization would hold for the new beginning principal balance of $53,000. Thus, during that period the principal balance could increase two percent of $53,000, or $1,060. And so on, until the second and third restrictions (below) come into effect.

2. At no time can negative amortization during a period exceed ten percent, regardless of the length of the period(s).

   The first restriction limits negative amortization to no more than one percent per six-month period. But what if an adjustment period were six years? Under the first limitation, this would permit a total of 12 percent negative amortization to occur (one percent times 12 six-month periods). But the second limitation would supersede the first and would limit negative amortization to ten percent regardless of the length of the adjustment period.

3. The third restriction is virtually identical to the second; that is, the amortization schedule can be adjusted only if, after every five years at minimum, the payments are adjusted to amortize the loan fully over the remaining loan term (never to exceed 30 years from origination).

For example, assume a loan of $100,000 has a 2½-year rate adjustment period, synchronized with a 2½-year payment adjustment period. Assume further that the negative amortization during the first term was $4,500, or 4½ percent; during the second period it was another 4½ percent, or $4,700. The beginning balance is within restrictions (1) and (2) since *the periodic additions never exceeded one percent per six-month increment, or ten percent overall*. However, five years have elapsed, and under the third restriction this loan would have to be fully re-amortized over the remaining term ($109,200 amortized over 25 years at the prevailing interest rate).

The Mechanics of Effecting the Rate Adjustment

Thus far we've seen that interest rate movements created by movements in a financial index are implemented by changing the monthly payment, principal balance or the loan term. These methods of implementing the interest rate changes are regulated by certain rules and restrictions set forth by the FHLBB and OCC as summarized in Figure 6.2.

Aside from rules and regulations, interest rate adjustments are implemented using the following principles and equations for the adjustment to the monthly payment, the principal balance or the loan term.

Adjustment to Monthly Payment.   The most common method of adjusting the interest rate is by changing the monthly payment, which requires finding three factors:

- new interest rate,
- remaining balance, and
- remaining term.

The new rate is derived from the index movement calculation, the remaining balance is found by using mortgage loan constants and the remaining term is the original loan term minus the age of the loan. The monthly payment is then found by the same procedure as for any other amortized mortgage.

To illustrate how to adjust the monthly payment, assume a borrower obtains a 30-year $80,000 mortgage at 13 percent. The monthly payment on this loan (PI) is $884.96. Let's assume this loan is pegged to an index with a beginning value of 11.5. If the payments were to adjust after two years and the index moved to 10.5, the new interest rate would be 12 percent. Because the loan is two years old, the remaining term is 28 years. Using loan progress charts for a 13 percent loan, the remaining balance factor of 994 times $80,000 (in thousands, $80.00) indicates that $79,520 remains unpaid on the loan. Thus:

- new interest rate = 12 percent
- remaining balance = $79,520
- remaining term = 28 years

Using the chart for the monthly payment needed to amortize a $1,000 loan, the factor for a 12 percent loan at 28 years is 10.37, which is multiplied times $79,520 (in thousands, $79.52) for the monthly payment. This product is $824.62, which is the new PI payment.

Adjusting the Loan Term.   The procedure for adjusting the loan term to effect the interest rate change is:

1. Divide the loan amount in *thousands* into the original monthly payment. This yields the monthly amortization constant.
2. Identify the new interest rate on the AML/ARM.
3. In the table, "Monthly Payment to Amortize a $1,000 Loan," select the column under the new interest rate. Go down the column until you locate the constant that is closest to the constant you found in step 1. The year associated with this constant is the new loan term. Do not, however, select a year beyond the maximum allowable loan term, which is 30 years for an ARM and 40 years for an AML from the loan's date of *origination*. For example, an AML issued five years ago cannot have a new loan term exceeding 35 years (40 years minus 5 years); an ARM that is two years old cannot have a new term in excess of 28 years (30 years minus 2 years).
4. Multiply the new constant by the remaining balance, found in a loan progress chart. This gives you the new monthly payment.

Rounding.   As mentioned previously, term adjustments play a minor role in implementing interest rate adjustments in AMLs. For our purpose, the foregoing procedure is workable assuming the new interest rates are rounded to the nearest .25 percent. In addition, the procedure yields a new monthly payment that is *approximately* the same as the previous payment—but not exactly the same.

It should also be noted that if an AML is originally issued at or near its maximum term, a term adjustment is not possible if the interest rate moves upward because the loan is already cast at its maximum term. If the index and rate move downward, the term adjustment can be used if the borrower wants his/her payments to remain approximately the same.

As an example of the term adjustment procedure, assume a $50,000 AML at 14 percent issued for a 25-year term. The PI payment is $601.89 a month. The interest rate moves down to 13½ percent after two years. Using our formula, then, we have:

1. $601.89 ÷ $\dfrac{\$50,000}{1,000}$ = 12.04 (rounded) constant
2. New rate = 13½ percent
3. From the indicated table, the nearest figure in the 13½ percent column to 12.04 is 12.08, the constant for a *twenty*-year loan. Thus *the new loan term is twenty years*.
4. The new 12.08 constant multiplied by the remaining balance (from loan progress charts) of $49,500 produces the new monthly payment of $597.96. Note that the new payment is not exactly the same as the previous payment, but close.

Note that if the loan's interest rate increases two years later, the new term of the loan cannot exceed 36 years (40-year maximum minus 4-year age of the loan).

Adjusting the Principal Balance.   The last of the three ways to implement an AML's interest rate change is to adjust the principal balance. This is done when a borrower elects to have his or her payments "capped," i.e., set at a maximum amount. If the interest rate later goes up, the additional amount owed is added to the loan balance instead of being paid right away. If the rate goes down, the overpayment is applied to a *reduction* of the loan balance if the borrower so chooses.

Monthly additions or reductions in the loan balance are calculated using the following formula:

$$\frac{\text{new rate} \times \text{remaining balance}}{12} - \text{monthly payment} = \text{monthly change}$$

Again, this formula will not produce *exact* reductions or additions-to-principal amounts, since it does not use complex compounding derivations that require new computations each month. However, the formula does reflect the basic principle involved in adjusting a loan's outstanding balance, which is:

$$\text{rate} \times \text{loan balance} = \text{interest owed per period}$$

Thus, if the borrower pays *less* than is owed per the equation, the owed amount is added to the balance, or essentially financed. If more is paid than owed, the overpayment amount is charged to the loan balance, reducing the borrower's principal.

To apply our formula, assume a $60,000, 13¾ percent amortized ARM loan is issued for 30 years. The monthly payment is $699.07. The borrower wants payments carried at the initial level and fixed should the rate go down. The loan is to have two-year adjustment periods. After two years the index moves up 50 basis points, which raises the rate .50 percent to 14¼ percent. Since the borrower's payments remain at $699.07, unpaid interest must be added to the principal balance—which by the way was slightly paid down during the first two years.

Using our formula, then, the approximate (noncompounded) monthly addition-to-principal is:

$$\frac{14\frac{1}{4}\% \times \$59,700}{12} - \$699.07 =$$

$$\$708.94 - \$699.07 = \$9.87 \text{ monthly addition-to-principal}$$

During the next two years, then, the borrower continues the original $699.07 payment, and the loan negatively amortizes $9.87 per month.

Assume now that after this second two-year period, the interest rate goes *down* one percentage point, to 13¼ percent. What is the impact on the loan balance in this instance? The new loan balance of $59,700 + ($9.87 × 24 months), or $599.37, is multiplied by the new rate of 13¼ percent and divided by 12. This is the interest owed, which is measured against what the borrower paid:

$$\frac{13.25 \times \$59,937}{12} - \$699.07 =$$

$$\frac{\$7,942}{12} - \$699.07 =$$

$$\$661.83 - \$699.07; \text{ or: } - \$37.24$$

Thus, $37.24 will be subtracted from the borrower's loan balance each month (noncompounded).

SELF-QUIZ: ARM PAYMENT ADJUSTMENTS

1. A loan is made by a national bank for $50,000 with a 30-year term. The initial interest rate is 13.00 percent, which is scheduled to adjust in two years. The payment is to adjust simultaneously and begins at $573.00. The index over the period moves from 13.00 to 15.00. What is the new monthly payment?

2. A loan is made by a federal savings and loan for $50,000 at 13.50 percent interest, with a 30-year term. The initial rate is to adjust every year, and *payments will adjust every two years*. Thus, the principal balance must be adjusted for the second year. At the end of the first year the index moves from 13.00 to 14.00, and ending the second year, it moves from 14.00 to 14.50. What is the new monthly payment after the payment adjustment date two years later?

3. A federal S&L issues a 20-year, $65,000 loan at an interest rate of 12.75 percent. The initial index is 11.50. Interest rate changes are to be implemented every 5 years by first adjusting the term, and then adjusting the monthly payment if necessary. At the end of 5 years, the index has moved up to 12.75. What is the new loan term and the new monthly payment after the rate change has been implemented?

ANSWERS TO SELF-QUIZ: ARM PAYMENT ADJUSTMENTS

1. a. To derive the new payment, multiply the new interest rate by the remaining balance times the remaining term.

   b. The interest rate moves directly with the index, i.e., it moved up 2.00 percent for a new rate of 15.00 percent.

   c. From remaining balance tables, the remaining principal on the $50,000 is $49,700.

   d. Because the maximum national bank ARM term is 30 years, the remaining term is 28 years. The monthly payment for $49,700 at 28 years at 15 percent is $631.19.

2. a. Fill in the formula for the addition-to-principal during the second year and multiply times 12 or the *annual* addition

$$\frac{(14.5\% \times \$49,850)}{12} - \$572.71 = \$602.35 - \$572.71$$
$$= \$29.64 \text{ added each month}$$
$$= \$355.68 \text{ added during year}$$

   b. For the following year, the interest rate increased .50 percent to 15 percent.

   c. The new loan balance is $49,850 + $355, or $50,206.

   d. The new loan term is 28 years.

   e. The new payment is derived using the standard procedure: 15 percent at $50,206 at 28 years = $637.62.

3. a. The monthly payment of $749.98 ÷ $65,000 yields a constant of 11.54.

   b. The new interest rate is (12.75 + 1.25) or 14 percent.

   c. On 14 percent loans, the constant nearest 11.54 is 11.72, the constant for a 40-year loan. However, this loan's maximum term cannot exceed 35 years (40 years − 5 years' age of loan or 35 years). Thus, the term is extended to 35 years, and the additional interest owed is implemented by increasing the monthly payment.

   d. The new monthly payments are: 14 percent at $60,060 remaining balance at 35 years = $706.31.

Note that these payments are less than the original payments because principal has been paid down nearly $5,000.

Payment-Capped Mortgages and the Pitfalls of Negative Amortization

It is likely that homebuyers and borrowers—particularly those who are already homeowners—will prefer fixed-payment loans. They have become accustomed to level-payment, conventional mortgages. Now that interest rates fluctuate, they want at least to hang on to the fixed-payment feature of the mortgage loan. That way they can, for the short term at least, know what their monthly costs will be. The payment increase that will come further down the line with an adjustable mortgage they want to worry about later.

These prospective homebuyers and borrowers are not financial experts and are unaware of the pitfalls that their preferences can lead them into. It is advisable to keep the borrower informed about the problems a level-payment adjustable mortgage can create.

In this section we will look at payment-capped mortgages, how they work and the hazards they create for borrower and lender alike.

A payment-capped adjustable mortgage is simply an *AML or ARM that sets a maximum monthly payment over one or several rate adjustment periods.* In many cases, the payment on the loan can be the initial monthly payment set at closing, which will amortize the balance over the loan term at the beginning rate of interest. The loan then provides that no increases will be made on this payment until some time in the future, say two and one-half years or five years. (Payment-capped loans usually have longer payment adjustment periods than non-payment-capped loans.)

With payment-capping, once the payment limit is reached, all subsequent interest rate changes within the payment adjustment period are implemented via adjustments to the principal balance. When the interest rate increases beyond the rate at which the principal is paid down every month, negative amortization results. It is this specific occurrence—negative amortization in a payment-capped mortgage—that triggers the problems discussed here. Were there never negative amortization, everything would be fine. But in inflationary times negative amortization is very probable, so let's look at what can happen when it occurs.

The FHLBB's AML authorization permits payment-capped loan programs and, again, gives the responsibility back to the lender for setting prudent limitations on these types of loans. The payment-capped AML, however, must comply with the rules and regulations for all AMLs. Therefore, these loans must be re-amortized every five years, so that any negative amortization accrued on the outstanding balance is built back into the monthly payment to fully retire the loan over its remaining period. Other than that, there is no AML regulation on the limit of negative amortization that can occur.

The OCC took a more restrictive position in its ARM authorization with respect to negative amortization and payment-capped mortgages. As we know, its regulatory limit on negative amortization is one percent of the principal balance per six-month adjustment period, never to exceed ten percent of the balance for any five-year period. The ARM, like the AML, must be re-amortized every five years to retire the loan fully. Thus, a payment-capped loan that accrued more than, for example, ten percent negative amortization in less than five years would have to be "uncapped" at that point and the monthly payment readjusted—regardless of the payment-cap provisions.

The OCC also went one step further. In its ARM authorization, it stipulated that any payment-capped program currently in effect is subject to review and re-approval and that any future payment-capped programs must be reviewed and approved in advance.

The Pitfalls of the Payment-Capped Mortgage.   The serious concerns of government regulators and prudent lenders with respect to payment-capped mortgages are not unfounded. These concerns principally relate to these issues:

1. affordability once the payment is finally adjusted, and
2. the risk and possible consequences of the high loan-to-value ratio.

Affordability When Payment Is Adjusted.   The homebuyer's "pay more later" attitude can mean problems, particularly if his or her income is stable and fixed. What can happen is simply that the borrower won't be able to afford long-forestalled payment adjustments once they are made.

Nonaffordability occurs because not only do rises in the interest rate increase the (deferred) costs of the loan, but over long payment adjustment periods, interest amounts added to principal early on can compound and recompound to significant degrees.

For example, take a $75,000, 30-year loan with a five-year payment adjustment period that has its rate adjusted once each year. If the first-year interest moves from 14 percent to 15 percent, the one percent added to the principal during the second year (assuming the index stays high) is about $750. This amount, compounded for four years at 15 percent, grows to about $1,300, or almost double the original amount.

A more elaborate example might illustrate better how a principal balance can grow, even within the limitations prescribed by the AML regulation. Let's continue with the preceding example and assume the interest increases one percent per year for five years. Remember, the level payments are set to retire the loan at 14 percent. As Table 6.2 shows, the balance rises more dramatically every year; after five years, the borrower owes an additional $7,757.

Let's look now at the borrower's new monthly payment. The new interest rate of 18 percent applied to the balance of $82,757 for the remaining term of 25 years leaves our borrower with a monthly payment of $1,256. Since the original payment was $889/month (rounded), the mortgage payment has increased 40 percent or about 10 percent per year over the period of negative amortization.

The question that arises now is simple: Can the borrower afford the new payment? What if the scenario had been worse? Has the family increased its income at the rate of ten percent to keep up with the compounded negative amortization?

According to the FHLBB regulations, it is up to the lender to establish meaningful limitations on the amount of negative amortization that should be allowed without a payment adjustment. As a rule of thumb, given current interest rates and loan amounts, *a one percent increase in the interest rate* in a single period *increases the borrower's monthly payment by seven percent* on a noncompounded basis. Thus, for purposes of projecting housing costs, an interest increase of more than two percent in a year will increase the amount owed by 14 percent. Because this rate exceeds inflation, particularly if left to compound for several years, it is reasonable to assume that affordability problems may result with stable-income borrowers. Assuming their incomes increased at a more moderate rate of eight percent per year, a 15 to 20 percent affordability gap could easily result after the second or third year.

TABLE 6.2:   Negative Amortization

	Balance	Interest Rate	Negative Amortization
Year 1	$75,000	14%	
Year 2	$74,850	15%	$ 559
Year 3	$75,409	16%	$1,379
Year 4	$76,788	17%	$2,386
Year 5	$79,174	18%	$3,583
Year 6	$82,757	18%	

In sum, there is an affordability pitfall that can occur when payment adjustment periods are extended well beyond the period of rate adjustments. The comfort of the level payment can be illusory when the realities of compounded interest are realized in the new monthly payment.

The Risk of High Loan-to-Value Ratios.   When payment-capped mortgages cause negative amortization, the loan-to-value ratio on a home can rise significantly. In market areas where appreciation rates have slackened, a rising loan-to-value ratio can:

1. increase the risk of default because the borrower's equity has eroded and payment of the mortgage depends solely on income and other assets,
2. create a negative worth situation where, upon sale of the home, the seller actually owes more than he or she receives from the sale proceeds, or
3. reduce the ability of the lender to recover the funds receivable as a result of (2).

No one stands to gain from a situation that goes from being excessively risky to being an outright default. The homeowner loses equity and the lender loses assets. Although not specifically required, raising the original down payment on any payment-capped loan can help hedge against the pitfall of high loan-to-value ratios. Prudence dictates that the longer the payment adjustment period, the higher the down payment and/or income requirements should be. It is also wise for the borrower desiring a payment-capped mortgage to obtain mortgage insurance on at least the top 20 percent of the loan.

EXAMINATION OF OTHER PROVISIONS AND REQUIREMENTS OF AMLs AND ARMs

In addition to the index, interest adjustment and rate implementation provisions of the AML and ARM authorizations, there are several other important regulations and provisions (summarized in Figure 6.3) that apply to adjustable mortgages. They are:

1. federal preemption,
2. due-on-sale clauses and assumption,
3. prepayment privileges,
4. fee restrictions,
5. notification requirements, and
6. disclosure requirements.

Federal Preemption

Although written simply and concisely, the federal preemption provisions in the ARM and AML authorizations raise complex questions and do *not* stand as across-the-board preemptions of state laws that can affect adjustable loans. What follows is a discussion of what federal preemption actually means.

The general intent of the federal preemption provision is to preempt state laws and regulations that *limit, prohibit* or *restrict* federally or nationally chartered savings and loans and banks from structuring, purchasing or participating in, or otherwise dealing in adjustable mortgage loans as authorized, including state laws that prohibit or restrict:

- use of an index,
- adjustments to interest,
- adjustments to term,
- adjustments to monthly payment, and
- adjustments to principal.

With regard to adjustments to principal, also preempted are prohibitions or restrictions regarding negative amortization and charging interest on interest.

State usury laws are also preempted *unless the state re-enacted its usury law* for first-lien residential mortgages before April 1, 1983. The laws of states that have recently revised their usury laws on such mortgages *may not be preempted.*

FIGURE 6.3: Other Requirements

PROVISION	OCC's ARM	FHLBB's AML
Federal preemption	ARM authorization preempts state laws restricting the issuance of ARM loans.	AML authorization preempts state laws restricting the issuance of AML loans.
Due-on-sale clauses and assumption	ARM authorization makes due-on-sale clauses enforceable, and loan terms can be reset upon assumption.	AML authorization makes due-on-sale clauses enforceable, and loan terms can be reset upon assumption.
Notification disclosures	Borrowers must be notified 30 to 45 days in advance of upcoming interest rate changes.	Borrowers must be notified at least 25 days in advance of upcoming payment changes.
Prepayments	ARM loans can be prepaid without penalty at any time after 30 days before the first rate adjustment.	AML loans permit any degree of prepayment of the principal balance without penalty.
Fees	Fees may not be charged for making periodic interest rate changes.	Fees may not be charged for making periodic interest rate adjustments.
Other disclosures (e.g., truth-in-lending)	The following items must be disclosed at the time of loan application or when ARM availability is announced by the institution:	How the AML works must be explained.
	explanation of the ARM and how it works,	Key loan terms must be summarized and implementation of rate changes explained.
	the index used and where it is available for the borrower's review,	
	a current ten-year history of the index's values,	Truth-in-lending factors must be disclosed (upon consummation of the loan agreement).
	how and when interest rates will change and be implemented, including an explanation of negative amortization if it occurs,	Historic example must be given of how mortgage payments would have changed over the past 15 years using the index or formula on which interest rate changes are based.
	what fees will be charged.	

State banks and state thrift institutions are not covered by federal preemption statutes. As a rule, inclusion in the preemption is strictly a function of the institution's charter, whether state or national. Mortgage bankers are not exempted from state laws.

State laws that have an impact on AMLs and ARMs but do not restrict or prohibit federal lenders from making or dealing with such loans remain in force, unpreempted. Such laws would include recording laws, foreclosure laws, tax laws, the Uniform Commercial Code, and any other law that does not represent a restriction or prohibition.

Due-on-Sale Clauses and Assumption

Both ARM and AML authorizations stipulate that a federally chartered savings and loan or bank may, at its discretion, enforce the due-on-sale clause. This provision is self-explanatory, the only condition being that in order for the loan to be called due, the due-on-sale clause must be written into the loan agreement. The terms and conditions for a loan's assumption are matters to be determined between the lender and borrower. It is the lender's prerogative, subject to such negotiations, to require that new terms be established for any loan upon its assumption.

Prepayment Privileges

As stated in the notification requirements, prepayment without penalty is a consistent feature of the adjustable-rate mortgage. The one exception to this feature is that national bank ARMs may impose prepayment penalties prior to the first rate change notification. This is to lower the risk involved in offering an ARM with fewer rate increases and longer adjustment periods.

Fee Restrictions

Fees for the normal servicing of AMLs and ARMs are not allowed. No charge, for example, may be imposed for changing the interest rate or payment amount, or for complying with disclosure and notification requirements. Costs may be incurred by the borrower, however, if he or she causes disruption in the normal servicing of the loan, as in the case of an assumption. In such a case assumption fees may be charged, although possible appraisal costs must be borne by the lender.

Notification Requirements

Both banks and savings and loans are required to provide the borrower advance notification of any payment or interest rate changes.

ARM Disclosure Requirements

Federal law requires the lender to provide the borrower with extensive ARM loan information at the time of the loan application. See Figure 6.3 for specific disclosure requirements.

Conversion of ARMs

Some ARMs may contain a clause that allows the borrower to convert the ARM to a fixed-rate mortgage during time periods designated in the mortgage. If the mortgage is converted, the new rate is usually set at the current market rate for fixed-rate mortgages. There may be a special fee for exercising the conversion option. Also, the interest rate or loan origination costs may be higher for an ARM with a conversion option. Convertible mortgages have become popular because they offer the advantage of lower initial interest rates as well as the chance to convert to fixed-rate mortgages if interest rates drop. Their popularity is further enhanced now that FNMA and FHLMC both purchase convertible ARMs.

Comparing ARMs

ARMs are complex loans making it difficult to compare loan plans between lenders. Here are the features that should be considered when comparing loan plans:

- the annual percentage rate,
- the annual rate adjustment cap,
- the life rate cap,
- the minimum rate,
- the index used,
- the historical movement of the index,
- the margin,
- the frequency of rate adjustments,
- the option to convert at a fixed rate, and
- the conversion charge.

DISCUSSION QUESTIONS

1. If interest rates were rising and you as a homeowner wanted to pay off your mortgage as soon as possible, would you want a payment-capped adjustable mortgage? Why or why not?

   What if rates were falling? Would you want a cap then?

2. Why must ARMs be recategorized every five years?

3. If a state's laws prohibit charging interest on interest, can a mortgage banker in that state issue a payment-capped adjustable mortgage?

4. A bank must notify an ARM borrower of the fees it will charge for periodically adjusting the borrower's payments. True or false?

5. Why do you suppose there are no prepayment charges on AMLs?

7

Graduated Payment Mortgages and Graduated Payment Adjustable Mortgages

In 1974 new developments were brewing in the Department of Housing and Urban Development. Housing was becoming less and less affordable, and HUD decided early on to do something about it. The first idea was to add a graduated payment feature to conventional fixed-rate fixed-payment mortgages to enhance affordability. Then, under Section 245 of the National Housing Act, the graduated payment mortgage, or GPM, was authorized as a conventional loan fully insurable by the Federal Housing Authority (FHA).

The graduated payment mortgage, familiarly known as the FHA 245, thus became one of the forerunners—and grandfathers—of the many alternative financing instruments that prevail in today's financing market.

In the broadest sense, the GPM is a conventional mortgage that has a graduated payment period during which time the initial monthly payments are less than the amount needed to amortize the loan. Over the graduation period, these payments increase until, at some point, they are sufficient to amortize the loan over the remaining term. Most important, in practice, the prospective homebuyer is qualified by the lender based on the initially reduced monthly payment. The homebuying family is, therefore, more likely to qualify for a given home purchase based on the smaller monthly payments of the initial payment period. That, in a nutshell, is the purpose and value of the GPM.

During the middle and late 1970s, the GPM gained wide popularity as an approach to amortizing the conventional loan, particularly because of its acceptance by VA, FHA and the secondary mortgage market. Millions of mortgage loan dollars flowed to the homebuyer under various GPM plans, and the graduated payment feature of the mortgage loan proved successful.

112

Toward the end of the decade, however, problems with the conventional fixed-rate mortgage arose. Lenders had fixed-rate, low-yielding mortgages, but interest rates were rapidly escalating in the market. To survive, the institutional lender had to ease out fixed-rate mortgages with or without graduated features as quickly as possible. Because interest rates on deposits as well as loans had become volatile, only loan instruments with very short terms or adjustable interest rates could assure lenders that their loan proceeds would safely exceed the high cost of deposit interest. To replace the fixed-rate loan, the adjustable mortgage loan (AML) emerged. The AML represented the lender's only solution to dealing with the roller-coaster ride that banking and finance had become in the 1980s.

Today the commotion about the inevitable switch-over from fixed- to adjustable-rate mortgages continues. Many borrowers still resist the uncertainty of the variable rate, but then they face either a much more costly and shorter-term fixed-rate loan or no institutional mortgage at all.

Despite the various conflicts in the market between lender and borrower, consumer demand for housing finance and lenders' desire to accommodate such demand persist. It is not surprising then that one form of the fixed-rate mortgage that was beneficial to the buyer—the graduated payment—had reemerged. In July 1981, the Federal Home Loan Bank Board (FHLB) authorized that the graduated payment feature of a fixed-rate loan could now accompany the conventional loan's replacement, the AML. The result: the graduated payment adjustable mortgage loan (GPAML).

The GPAML became more acceptable to lenders after the February 1982 announcement by FNMA of its various GPAML purchase programs. With the assurance that the GPAMLs are salable in the secondary markets, the lender is less reluctant to originate a new type of loan. Thus the GPAML is now a full-fledged member of the institutional lender's alternative product line.

During the second half of the 1980s the inflation rate was greatly reduced and interest rates for mortgages also fell. The lower interest rates allowed more borrowers to qualify for loans, which decreased the need for using GPMs. The lower inflation rate decreased future salary raises for borrowers thus making a GPM loan more risky. As long as inflation and interest rates remain at moderate levels the popularity of this type of financing will be low.

The GPAMLs discussed in this chapter are those that have been authorized by the Federal Home Loan Bank Board for federally chartered savings and loan associations. GPAMLs associated with other agencies or institutions are not covered in this chapter.

In the sections that follow, we will take a close, in-depth look at the GPM, particularly FHA 245s and the GPAML. We will examine regulations that govern their use and how they work in practice. In addition, we will look at types of graduated payment loans that have been adopted by secondary market loan purchasers.

LEARNING OBJECTIVES

The section on GPMs is designed to give readers a basic working proficiency with graduated payment mortgages. When you have completed this section you will be able to:

1. describe and explain what GPMs are and how they work, including:
   a. the basic mechanics of the GPM, including graduation period, degrees of payment graduations, and payment change frequency,
   b. how GPM payments and principal balances are adjusted under various GPM plans,
   c. how to identify the GPM postgraduation payments,
   d. the latest regulations governing GPMs,
2. discuss five FHA 245 GPM plans currently in use and the borrower qualification standards that apply to them, and
3. discuss the major legal considerations that affect GPMs.

After the section on GPAMLs, you will be able to:

1. define and describe the basic concept and working mechanism of GPAMLs, including:
   a. the graduation rate,
   b. the graduation period,
   c. the graduated payment change frequency,
   d. how interest rates are adjusted per index movement,
   e. how interest rate adjustments are implemented,
   f. the major regulations and limitations of adjustable loans,
2. ascertain what type of buyers are most suitable for a GPAML,
3. understand a generalized loan amortization scenario in terms of monthly payments and remaining loan balance on a GPAML, and
4. describe to a prospective buyer the general characteristics of FNMA-purchasable GPAMLs.

WHAT IS THE GPM?

The graduated payment mortgage is essentially a modified way of paying off the traditional, fixed-rate conventional mortgage. The GPM is defined formally as a conventional mortgage instrument with scheduled payments *that begin at a lower level than those for a comparable-level payment fixed-rate mortgage and that rise during a payment graduation period to a predetermined point whereafter such payments remain constant.* The graduation period, the degree and frequency of payment increases and the interest rate are set at the time the loan is originated. Thus, the standard GPM will always be originated as a conventional fixed-rate, fixed-term mortgage instrument with a beginning monthly payment that is insufficient to amortize the loan. Over the payment graduation period at successive intervals, the borrower's payments are increased by a preselected percent until they reach a point at the end of the graduation period when the amount being paid each month is equal to the amount needed to retire the remaining loan balance over the remaining term.

Figure 7.1 shows the numbers that result from adapting a $50,000 conventional mortgage for 30 years at 15¼ percent interest to a GPM payment plan. Under this plan the borrower's initial monthly payment on the loan is set to increase 7½ percent every *successive year* for five years. Thus the initial payment of $503.68 increases to $541.46 the second year; to $582.06 the third year, and so on until the beginning of the sixth year. At that time the graduation period ends, and the loan's payments remain constant at $723.14 until the entire loan is paid off. Interestingly enough, the $723.14 is the exact amount necessary to amortize the remaining balance at the 15¼ percent interest rate for the remaining 25 years. Note also that in the monthly payment section the conventional fixed-level

FIGURE 7.1: The Graduated Payment Mortgage (GPM)

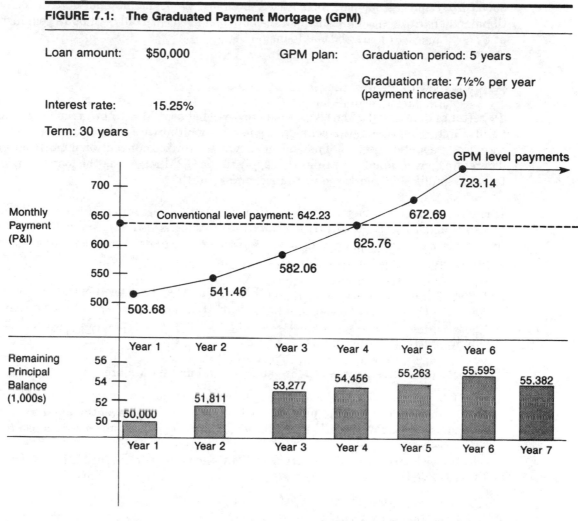

Loan amount: $50,000

GPM plan: Graduation period: 5 years

Graduation rate: 7½% per year (payment increase)

Interest rate: 15.25%

Term: 30 years

monthly payment for the loan is $642.23. Only after the fourth year do the GPM payments "catch up" to the conventional monthly payments. However, the GPM payments after the fifth year remain about $80 *greater* than the conventional payment for the remainder of the loan term, in contrast to the cheaper GPM payments the first five years.

The bottom half of Figure 7.1 illustrates the inevitable result of the conventional GPM: negative amortization. Because the borrower's payment is *less than the amounts owed, the unpaid difference is tacked onto the loan's principal balance.* For example, during the first year the borrower owes 15¼ percent interest on $50,000, which is about $7,625 per year uncompounded. The $503.68 payment, however, covers only about $6,044 of that. Thus, an uncompounded amount of $1,580 is unpaid. Adding to that amount the monthly compounded interest, a total of $1,811 is left unpaid during the first year. Therefore, that amount is added to the principal, which you can see is $51,811 at the beginning of the second year. This process of adding interest onto principal continues through the graduation period each year until the end of the fifth year. Once the payment moves up to $723.10, this loan's balance begins to amortize positively. In the 25 years of the remaining loan term, the $723.14 monthly payment will reduce the principal balance outstanding to zero.

Note that although this GPM borrower will incur almost $6,000 of negative amortization during the first five years, he or she will be qualified for the loan based on the reduced

$503.68 payment as opposed to the fixed-level $642.23 payment. Therefore, by conventional underwriting standards, a qualified borrower need earn only $21,500 a year instead of $27,500 a year for the $50,000 loan.

GPM Regulations

To better understand GPMs, let's quickly review what a GPM is from a regulatory standpoint. First, the GPM is not technically a new loan authorization but rather a newly authorized, graduated method of paying an already authorized conventional mortgage loan. Therefore conventional loan rules still apply to the GPM regarding the loan term, loan-to-value limitations, mortgage insurance, and so forth.

It is also important to note that the various regulations regarding GPMs that follow in this section *apply only to FHA GPMs and GPMs that are issued by federally chartered savings and loan associations.* Lending institutions operating under a state charter are subject to state laws and may not be able to issue GPMs.

The second thing to understand about GPMs is that they have been authorized autonomously by two federal agencies, HUD and the FHLB. Thus there are two separately authorized GPMs: HUD's FHA 245 GPM and FHLB's conventional GPM, with each group having its own set of rules.

The major difference between "245s" and conventional GPMs are:

1. The FHA's are FHA-insured and the conventionals are not.
2. Under FHA, a specific plan must be adopted; under conventional GPM regulations, any GPM variation may be adopted so long as certain restrictions are followed.
3. As with level-payment mortgages, FHA and conventional regulations vary as to the maximum loan amount and the loan-to-value requirements.

FHLB's Conventional GPM Regulations.   The major regulations governing conventional GPMs are the following:

- By definition, the GPM's payment levels, graduation period, and frequency of payment changes are fixed at the time the loan is originated. Such terms cannot be altered subsequently.
- It is no longer required that lenders disclose to GPM borrowers a comparison of payments between a GPM and a conventional mortgage.
- The maximum graduation period is ten years. The rules limiting the degree of payment increases and frequency of increases have been abolished.
- The maximum loan is 30 years.

FHA 245 GPM Regulations.   FHA 245 regulations require that specific GPM specifications be adopted for FHA qualification, as opposed to various limits or ranges stipulated for conventional GPMs by FHLB. The five FHA plans are:

Plan I: Monthly payments increase 2½ percent each year for five years.
Plan II: Monthly payments increase 5 percent each year for five years.
Plan III: Monthly payments increase 7½ percent each year for five years.

Plan IV: Monthly payments increase 2 percent each year for ten years.

Plan V: Monthly payments increase 3 percent each year for ten years.

The following are applicable to these FHA 245 GPM plans:

1. Payment increases can only occur annually. During the year the payments are fixed.
2. The participant must be the owner and occupant of the mortgaged property; it must be a single-family dwelling unit.
3. The term of the loan is limited to 30 years or ¾ of the remaining economic life of the property, whichever is less.
4. Mortgagors with existing conventional loans cannot convert to a GPM by refinancing. However, GPM mortgagors can convert to a level-payment mortgage at any time.
5. Other credit underwriting and administrative requirements for GPMs are identical to other FHA-insured loans and must comply with FHA Section 203(b) or Section 234(c).
6. The maximum loan amount for any FHA GPM is 97 percent of the appraised value of the property or the maximum FHA loan amount for a local area, whichever is less.

Note that the maximum loan amount for FHA is also construed as being *inclusive* of negative amortization. Thus, if negative amortization were projected to be $3,000 in an area where the FHA loan maximum was $72,000, then the *initial* loan maximum would be $69,000, not $72,000. Requirements for FHA loan plans frequently change. It is best to call an approved FHA lender or the FHA office nearest you about the current guidelines or requirements pertaining to specific loan programs.

Negative Amortization and the FHA 245s

The five GPM plans set forth by FHA are a good basis for close analysis of how negative amortization in GPMs occurs. Each 245 plan authorized amortizes negatively in varying degrees, depending on the degree of annual payment escalation and the number of years in the graduation term. The actual amount of negative amortization that occurs in any plan is, however, known down to the penny because everything is predetermined at loan origination.

Briefly scanning the five plans listed above, the graduation magnitude ranges from 2 to 7½ percent annually and the period from five to ten years. The particular plan chosen ideally should be a function of borrower qualification, *particularly the anticipated rate of increase of the household's gross monthly income.* The most extreme FHA plan, and by far the most popular, is Plan III, the 7½ percent graduation for five years. More conservative borrowers would prefer either the lower graduation rate or longer terms of Plans I and IV, respectively.

In each of the plans, the actual monthly mortgage payment is set at a level so that each year the payments increase by the prescribed percent. This amount is also calculated such that at the end of the graduation period, the last graduated payment is the precise amount needed each month over the remaining term to amortize the remaining balance. In addition, at no time can any outstanding principal balance amount exceed a given loan-to-value percent. Thus, when you take into account that principal and interest are computed and partially paid every month, you can quite correctly presume that a computer is necessary to lay out the actual amortization schedule on any 245 plan.

FIGURE 7.2:   FHA Table 2

PLAN II GRADUATED PAYMENT MORTGAGE (SECTION 245) WITH INCREASING PAYMENTS FOR 5 YEARS AT 5.00 PERCENT EACH YEAR

OUTSTANDING PRINCIPAL BALANCE FACTORS
(PER THOUSAND DOLLARS OF ORIGINAL LOAN PROCEEDS)

FOR 30 YEAR MORTGAGES WITH ANNUAL CONTRACT INTEREST RATES OF

INSTALL-MENT NUMBER	15.25	15.50	15.75	16.00	16.25	16.50	16.75	17.00	17.25	17.50
1	1001.7835	1001.8104	1001.8366	1001.8622	1001.8872	1001.9116	1001.9354	1001.9587	1001.9814	1002.0037
2	1003.5896	1003.6441	1003.6973	1003.7492	1003.7999	1003.8494	1003.8978	1003.9451	1003.9913	1004.0365
3	1005.4187	1005.5015	1005.5824	1005.6613	1005.7385	1005.8139	1005.8876	1005.9597	1006.0301	1006.0990
4	1007.2711	1007.3829	1007.4922	1007.5990	1007.7034	1007.8054	1007.9052	1008.0028	1008.0983	1008.1916
5	1009.1470	1009.2886	1009.4271	1009.5625	1009.6949	1009.8243	1009.9509	1010.0748	1010.1961	1010.3148
6	1011.0467	1011.2190	1011.3874	1011.5522	1011.7133	1011.8710	1012.0252	1012.1763	1012.3241	1012.4688
7	1012.9706	1013.1742	1013.3735	1013.5684	1013.7591	1013.9458	1014.1285	1014.3074	1014.4827	1014.6543
8	1014.9189	1015.1548	1015.3856	1015.6114	1015.8326	1016.0491	1016.2611	1016.4688	1016.6723	1016.8717
9	1016.8920	1017.1609	1017.4241	1017.6818	1017.9341	1018.1813	1018.4235	1018.6608	1018.8934	1019.1214
10	1018.8902	1019.1929	1019.4893	1019.7797	1020.0642	1020.3429	1020.6160	1020.8838	1021.1464	1021.4039
11	1020.9137	1021.2512	1021.5817	1021.9056	1022.2230	1022.5342	1022.8392	1023.1384	1023.4318	1023.7197
12	1022.9630	1023.3360	1023.7016	1024.0598	1024.4111	1024.7556	1025.0934	1025.4248	1025.7501	1026.0693
13	1024.4920	1024.8925	1025.2848	1025.6693	1026.0461	1026.4156	1026.7779	1027.1333	1027.4820	1027.8241
14	1026.0405	1026.4690	1026.8888	1027.3001	1027.7033	1028.0985	1028.4860	1028.8660	1029.2388	1029.6046
15	1027.6087	1028.0660	1028.5139	1028.9527	1029.3829	1029.8045	1030.2178	1030.6232	1031.0208	1031.4110
16	1029.1968	1029.6835	1030.1603	1030.6274	1031.0852	1031.5339	1031.9739	1032.4053	1032.8285	1033.2437
17	1030.8051	1031.3220	1031.8283	1032.3244	1032.8106	1033.2872	1033.7544	1034.2127	1034.6622	1035.1032
18	1032.4338	1032.9816	1033.5182	1034.0440	1034.5593	1035.0645	1035.5598	1036.0456	1036.5222	1036.9898
19	1034.0833	1034.6626	1035.2303	1035.7865	1036.3317	1036.8663	1037.3904	1037.9046	1038.4089	1038.9039
20	1035.7536	1036.3654	1036.9648	1037.5523	1038.1282	1038.6928	1039.2466	1039.7898	1040.3228	1040.8459
21	1037.4453	1038.0902	1038.7221	1039.3416	1039.9489	1040.5445	1041.1287	1041.7018	1042.2642	1042.8162
22	1039.1584	1039.8372	1040.5025	1041.1548	1041.7943	1042.4216	1043.0370	1043.6409	1044.2335	1044.8153
23	1040.8933	1041.6068	1042.3063	1042.9921	1043.6647	1044.3246	1044.9720	1045.6074	1046.2311	1046.8435
24	1042.6502	1043.3993	1044.1337	1044.8540	1045.5605	1046.2537	1046.9340	1047.6018	1048.2574	1048.9013
25	1043.8559	1044.6318	1045.3925	1046.1384	1046.8700	1047.5878	1048.2922	1048.9835	1049.6622	1050.3287
26	1045.0769	1045.8802	1046.6678	1047.4399	1048.1973	1048.9403	1049.6693	1050.3848	1051.0872	1051.7769
27	1046.3135	1047.1448	1047.9598	1048.7589	1049.5425	1050.3113	1051.0656	1051.8059	1052.5327	1053.2462
28	1047.5657	1048.4257	1049.2698	1050.0954	1050.9060	1051.7012	1052.4815	1053.2472	1053.9989	1054.7370
29	1048.8339	1049.7232	1050.5949	1051.4497	1052.2879	1053.1102	1053.9171	1054.7089	1055.4862	1056.2495
30	1050.1182	1051.0374	1051.9385	1052.8220	1053.6886	1054.5386	1055.3727	1056.1913	1056.9949	1057.7840
31	1051.4188	1052.3686	1053.2997	1054.2127	1055.1082	1055.9867	1056.8487	1057.6947	1058.5253	1059.3409
32	1052.7359	1053.7170	1054.6788	1055.6219	1056.5470	1057.4546	1058.3452	1059.2194	1060.0777	1060.9206
33	1054.0698	1055.0828	1056.0760	1057.0499	1058.0053	1058.9427	1059.8627	1060.7657	1061.6524	1062.5232
34	1055.4206	1056.4662	1057.4915	1058.4970	1059.4834	1060.4513	1061.4013	1062.3340	1063.2498	1064.1493
35	1056.7886	1057.8675	1058.9255	1059.9633	1060.9815	1061.9807	1062.9614	1063.9244	1064.8701	1065.7990
36	1058.1740	1059.2869	1060.3785	1061.4492	1062.4999	1063.5310	1064.5433	1065.5373	1066.5137	1067.4728
37	1058.9748	1060.1125	1061.2282	1062.3226	1063.3963	1064.4501	1065.4845	1066.5002	1067.4977	1068.4776
38	1059.7857	1060.9486	1062.0890	1063.2076	1064.3049	1065.3818	1066.4389	1067.4767	1068.4959	1069.4970
39	1060.6069	1061.7956	1062.9612	1064.1044	1065.2259	1066.3264	1067.4065	1068.4670	1069.5084	1070.5313
40	1061.4386	1062.6535	1063.8448	1065.0131	1066.1593	1067.2839	1068.3877	1069.4713	1070.5354	1071.5806
41	1062.2808	1063.5225	1064.7400	1065.9340	1067.1053	1068.2546	1069.3826	1070.4899	1071.5773	1072.6453
42	1063.1338	1064.4027	1065.6469	1066.8671	1068.0641	1069.2386	1070.3913	1071.5229	1072.6341	1073.7255
43	1063.9976	1065.2943	1066.5658	1067.8127	1069.0359	1070.2362	1071.4141	1072.5706	1073.7061	1074.8214
44	1064.8723	1066.1974	1067.4967	1068.7709	1070.0209	1071.2474	1072.4512	1073.6330	1074.7935	1075.9334
45	1065.7582	1067.1122	1068.4398	1069.7419	1071.0192	1072.2726	1073.5028	1074.7106	1075.8966	1077.0615
46	1066.6553	1068.0388	1069.3953	1070.7258	1072.0311	1073.3119	1074.5691	1075.8034	1077.0155	1078.2061
47	1067.5639	1068.9774	1070.3634	1071.7229	1073.0566	1074.3655	1075.6502	1076.9116	1078.1505	1079.3674
48	1068.4840	1069.9280	1071.3442	1072.7332	1074.0961	1075.4335	1076.7465	1078.0356	1079.3018	1080.5456

FIGURE 7.2: continued

PLAN II GRADUATED PAYMENT MORTGAGE (SECTION 245)
WITH INCREASING PAYMENTS FOR 5 YEARS AT 5.00 PERCENT EACH YEAR

OUTSTANDING PRINCIPAL BALANCE FACTORS
(PER THOUSAND DOLLARS OF ORIGINAL LOAN PROCEEDS)

FOR 30 YEAR MORTGAGES WITH ANNUAL CONTRACT INTEREST RATES OF

INSTALL-MENT NUMBER	15.25	15.50	15.75	16.00	16.25	16.50	16.75	17.00	17.25	17.50
49	1068.7834	1070.2481	1071.6844	1073.0931	1074.4750	1075.8311	1077.1621	1078.4689	1079.7523	1081.0129
50	1069.0866	1070.5724	1072.0291	1073.4577	1074.8591	1076.2341	1077.5835	1078.9083	1080.2092	1081.4870
51	1069.3937	1070.9008	1072.3783	1073.8272	1075.2183	1076.6426	1078.0109	1079.3540	1080.6728	1081.9680
52	1069.7047	1071.2335	1072.7322	1074.2016	1075.6128	1077.0567	1078.4441	1079.8060	1081.1430	1082.4560
53	1070.0197	1071.5705	1073.0906	1074.5810	1076.0127	1077.4766	1078.8835	1080.2643	1081.6200	1082.9512
54	1070.3386	1071.9118	1073.4538	1074.9655	1076.4180	1077.9022	1079.3289	1080.7292	1082.1038	1083.4535
55	1070.6616	1072.2575	1073.8217	1075.3551	1076.8588	1078.3336	1079.7806	1081.2006	1082.5946	1083.9632
56	1070.9887	1072.6077	1074.1945	1075.7499	1077.2751	1078.7710	1080.2386	1081.6788	1083.0924	1084.4803
57	1071.3200	1072.9625	1074.5721	1076.1500	1077.6971	1079.2145	1080.7030	1082.1637	1083.5974	1085.0050
58	1071.6555	1073.3218	1074.9547	1076.5554	1078.1248	1079.6640	1081.1739	1082.6554	1084.1096	1085.5373
59	1071.9952	1073.6857	1075.3424	1076.9662	1078.5583	1080.1197	1081.6513	1083.1542	1084.6292	1086.0774
60	1072.3392	1074.0544	1075.7351	1077.3825	1078.9976	1080.5816	1082.1354	1083.6600	1085.1563	1086.6253
61	1072.0237	1073.7528	1075.4469	1077.1072	1078.7346	1080.3304	1081.8956	1083.4310	1084.9377	1086.4167
62	1071.7042	1073.4473	1075.1549	1076.8282	1078.4681	1080.0758	1081.6524	1083.1998	1084.7160	1086.2051
63	1071.3806	1073.1379	1074.8591	1076.5454	1078.1979	1079.8177	1081.4058	1082.9633	1084.4911	1085.9904
64	1071.0528	1072.8245	1074.5595	1076.2589	1077.9241	1079.5560	1081.1558	1082.7244	1084.2630	1085.7725
65	1070.7210	1072.5070	1074.2558	1075.9686	1077.6465	1079.2907	1080.9022	1082.4822	1084.0316	1085.5515
66	1070.3849	1072.1855	1073.9482	1075.6744	1077.3652	1079.0218	1080.6452	1082.2365	1083.7969	1085.3272
67	1070.0445	1071.8597	1073.6366	1075.3763	1077.0801	1078.7492	1080.3845	1081.9874	1083.5588	1085.0997
68	1069.6998	1071.5298	1073.3209	1075.0743	1076.7912	1078.4728	1080.1203	1081.7347	1083.3172	1084.8689
69	1069.3507	1071.1956	1073.0010	1074.7681	1076.4983	1078.1926	1079.8523	1081.4785	1083.0722	1084.6347
70	1068.9972	1070.8571	1072.6769	1074.4580	1076.2014	1077.9086	1079.5806	1081.2186	1082.8237	1084.3971
71	1068.6392	1070.5142	1072.3486	1074.1436	1075.9006	1077.6206	1079.3051	1080.9550	1082.5716	1084.1560
72	1068.2766	1070.1669	1072.0160	1073.8251	1075.5956	1077.3288	1079.0257	1080.6877	1082.3159	1083.9114
73	1067.9095	1069.8151	1071.6790	1073.5024	1075.2866	1077.0329	1078.7425	1080.4166	1082.0565	1083.6632
74	1067.5377	1069.4588	1071.3376	1073.1753	1074.9733	1076.7329	1078.4553	1080.1417	1081.7934	1083.4114
75	1067.1611	1069.0979	1070.9917	1072.8439	1074.6558	1076.4288	1078.1641	1079.8629	1081.5265	1083.1559
76	1066.7798	1068.7323	1070.6412	1072.5080	1074.3340	1076.1205	1077.8688	1079.5801	1081.2557	1082.8967
77	1066.3936	1068.3619	1070.2862	1072.1677	1074.0079	1075.8080	1077.5694	1079.2934	1080.9811	1082.6338
78	1066.0025	1067.9868	1069.9265	1071.8228	1073.6773	1075.4912	1077.2658	1079.0025	1080.7025	1082.3670
79	1065.6064	1067.6069	1069.5621	1071.4734	1073.3422	1075.1700	1076.9580	1078.7076	1080.4199	1082.0963
80	1065.2053	1067.2220	1069.1929	1071.1193	1073.0026	1074.8444	1076.6459	1078.4084	1080.1333	1081.8216
81	1064.7991	1066.8322	1068.8188	1070.7604	1072.6585	1074.5144	1076.3294	1078.1051	1079.8425	1081.5430
82	1064.3878	1066.4373	1068.4398	1070.3968	1072.3096	1074.1797	1076.0086	1077.7974	1079.5475	1081.2603
83	1063.9712	1066.0374	1068.0559	1070.0283	1071.9561	1073.8405	1075.6832	1077.4854	1079.2483	1080.9735
84	1063.5493	1065.6322	1067.6669	1069.6549	1071.5977	1073.4967	1075.3533	1077.1689	1078.9449	1080.6824
85	1063.1221	1065.2219	1067.2729	1069.2766	1071.2345	1073.1481	1075.0188	1076.8480	1078.6370	1080.3872
86	1062.6894	1064.8062	1066.8736	1068.8932	1070.8664	1072.7947	1074.6796	1076.5225	1078.3247	1080.0876
87	1062.2512	1064.3852	1066.4691	1068.5046	1070.4932	1072.4364	1074.3357	1076.1924	1078.0079	1079.7837
88	1061.8075	1063.9587	1066.0593	1068.1109	1070.0151	1072.0733	1073.9870	1075.8576	1077.6866	1079.4753
89	1061.3581	1063.5267	1065.6441	1067.7120	1069.7318	1071.7051	1073.6334	1075.5181	1077.3607	1079.1624
90	1060.9030	1063.0891	1065.2235	1067.3077	1069.3433	1071.3319	1073.2749	1075.1738	1077.0301	1078.8450
91	1060.4422	1062.6459	1064.7974	1066.8980	1068.9496	1070.9535	1072.9114	1074.8246	1076.6947	1078.5230
92	1059.9754	1062.1970	1064.3656	1066.4829	1068.5505	1070.5700	1072.5428	1074.4705	1076.3545	1078.1962
93	1059.5028	1061.7423	1063.9282	1066.0623	1068.1460	1070.1811	1072.1690	1074.1113	1076.0094	1077.7647
94	1059.0241	1061.2817	1063.4851	1065.6360	1067.7361	1069.7869	1071.7901	1073.7471	1075.6593	1077.5283
95	1058.5394	1060.8151	1063.0361	1065.2040	1067.3206	1069.3873	1071.4058	1073.3776	1075.3042	1077.1871
96	1058.0484	1060.3425	1062.5812	1064.7663	1066.8995	1068.9822	1071.0162	1073.0030	1074.9441	1076.8409

Deriving the GPM Amortization Schedule.   Since negative amortization increases a loan balance and since there are prescribed limits to a loan's LTV, *the beginning loan amount will always be less than the prescribed LTV maximum.* Thus a borrower wanting a 90 percent (LTV) NA/GPM loan, for example, on a $50,000 house could not originally borrow $45,000. The original amount would have to be an amount somewhat less than that—to be exact, the maximum original loan would be X where X equalled $45,000 minus the maximum amount of negative amortization incurred. Taking another example, assume a given loan were to negatively amortize $3,000 before it reached a maximum loan-to-value ceiling. The maximum amount of the original loan amount would then be $X -$ $3,000.

With that in mind, let's look at how to identify the initial principal amount of an FHA 245 and its various monthly payments and remaining balances.

1. Identify which plan will be adopted.
2. Identify the interest rate.
3. Identify the maximum LTV loan amount (with FHA 245s, 97 percent).
4. Identify the month where negative amortization is the greatest from Table 2 FHA 4240.2 Revised, Change 4, Appendix 3, *Outstanding Principal Balance Factors.*
5. Divide the maximum loan amount by the factor for the original loan amount. Note: the placement of decimals in the factors shown on the chart can be confusing. To perform this division, the decimal point must be moved three spaces to the left—1074.05544 becomes 1.07405544 for our purposes.
6. Multiply the original loan amount (in 1,000s) by each yearly factor in Table 3 *Factors for Computing Monthly Installment to Principal and Interest,* Appendix 1, FHA 4240.2, Revised, Change 4.
7. For the mortgage insurance premiums, multiply the original loan amount by the factors in Table 4, Appendix 2 of FHA 4240.21, Revised, Change 4.

Let's take an example and go through these steps one by one. On the following pages are the FHA 4240 tables we'll need to make the various calculations. Assume Plan II GPM and that the loan is for a residence valued at $72,000. The interest rate on this loan will be 15.50 percent (step 2). From step 3 to step 7:

3. The maximum FHA LTV of 97 percent allows for a loan on this property of $69,480. We'll round the figure to $69,800.
4. To identify the month when maximum amortization occurs, refer to Figure 7.2, FHA Table 2, under the 15.50 percent interest rate column. The point of maximum negative amortization on the loan, which in our case is $69,800, occurs in the 60th month (underlined), and our factor is 1074.0544.
5. To derive the *original* loan amount, divide the maximum loan amount, $69,800, by 1.0740544 (the factor divided by 1,000). The result, $64,987, is the original loan amount for a Plan II GPM for a $72,000 home at 15½ percent interest for 30 years.
6. To identify the monthly payments for this loan, refer to Figure 7.3, FHA Table 3. The factors found under 15.50 percent interest when multiplied by the original loan amount of $64,987 (in 1,000s) yield the monthly payment for each year of the graduation period and the final payment for the remaining loan term. Multiplying these factors, we get:

Year 1: $721.76	Year 4: $835.53
Year 2: $757.85	Year 5: $877.31
Year 3: $795.75	Years 6–30: $921.18

FIGURE 7.3: FHA Table 3

PLAN II GRADUATED PAYMENT MORTGAGE (SECTION 245)
WITH INCREASING PAYMENTS FOF 5 YEARS AT 5.00 PERCENT EACH YEAR

MONTHLY INSTALLMENT PER THOUSAND DOLLARS OF ORIGINAL LOAN PROCEEDS

FOR 30 YEAR MORTGAGES WITH ANNUAL CONTRACT INTEREST RATES OF

YEAR	15.25	15.50	15.75	16.00	16.25	16.50	16.75	17.00	17.25	17.50
1	10.9248	11.1063	11.2884	11.4712	11.6545	11.8384	12.0229	12.2080	12.3936	12.5797
2	11.4711	11.6616	11.8528	12.0447	12.2372	12.4304	12.6241	12.8184	13.0133	13.2087
3	12.0446	12.2447	12.4455	12.6470	12.8491	13.0519	13.2553	13.4593	13.6639	13.8691
4	12.6469	12.8569	13.0678	13.2793	13.4915	13.7045	13.9180	14.1323	14.3471	14.5626
5	13.2792	13.4998	13.7211	13.9433	14.1661	14.3897	14.6140	14.8389	15.0645	15.2907
REMAINING PMTS	13.9432	14.1748	14.4072	14.6404	14.8744	15.1092	15.3446	15.5808	15.8177	16.0552

You can verify on your own that these payments do in fact escalate each year by 5 percent and that $921.18 per month at 15½ percent will retire the remaining balance ($69,800) in the remaining 25 years.

7. To calculate the required mortgage insurance premiums, refer to Figure 7.4, FHA Table 4. As in step 6, multiply the factors provided by the original amount (in 1,000s) for each year in the 15½ percent interest rate column.

The process illustrated is what is necessary to qualify prospective GPM borrowers and, equally important, to be able to tell them what their monthly payments will be. As such, the process of deriving the loan amount and amortization schedule is significant in actual practice. Although many firms have computer programs for GPMs, we have demonstrated that it can be done with a calculator and three FHA tables from FHA's 4240.2 Rev. Change 4.

SELF-QUIZ: GPMs

1. Below is a set of facts for a GPM loan transaction. Using FHA Plan II tables provided (in Figures 7.2, 7.3 and 7.4), derive the original loan amount and the monthly payments for the first six years. Complete the calculations before looking at the answers.

   Home value: $64,500

   Interest rate: 15.75 percent

   Maximum loan amount: _____

   Original loan amount: _____

   Monthly payments:

       Year 1_____

       Year 2_____

       Year 3_____

       Year 4_____

       Year 5_____

       Years 6–30_____

2. Again using Plan II 245 tables (in Figures 7.2, 7.3 and 7.4), fill in the data in the blanks below.

   Home value: $56,500

   Interest rate: 15.25 percent

   Maximum loan amount: _____

   Original loan amount: _____

   Monthly payments:

       Year 1 PI _____   (principal, interest)

       Year 2 PI _____

       Year 3 PI _____

       Year 4 PI _____

       Year 5 PI _____

       Year 6 PI _____

FIGURE 7.4: FHA Table 4

PLAN II GRADUATED PAYMENT MORTGAGE (SECTION 245) WITH INCREASING PAYMENTS FOR 5 YEARS AT 5.00 PERCENT EACH YEAR

MONTHLY MORTGAGE INSURANCE PREMIUM FACTORS
(PER THOUSAND DOLLARS OF ORIGINAL LOAN PROCEEDS)

FOR 30 YEAR MORTGAGES WITH ANNUAL CONTRACT INTEREST RATES OF

PREMIUM YEAR	15.25	15.50	15.75	16.00	16.25	16.50	16.75	17.00	17.25	17.50
1	.4209	.4210	.4211	.4211	.4212	.4213	.4213	.4214	.4214	.4215
2	.4299	.4301	.4303	.4305	.4308	.4310	.4312	.4314	.4316	.4318
3	.4373	.4377	.4381	.4384	.4338	.4391	.4395	.4398	.4402	.4405
4	.4428	.4433	.4439	.4444	.4449	.4453	.4458	.4463	.4467	.4472
5	.4459	.4466	.4472	.4478	.4434	.4491	.4496	.4502	.4508	.4514
6	.4461	.4468	.4475	.4482	.4430	.4496	.4503	.4510	.4516	.4523
7	.4442	.4451	.4459	.4467	.4474	.4482	.4489	.4496	.4503	.4510
8	.4421	.4430	.4439	.4448	.4456	.4465	.4473	.4480	.4488	.4496
9	.4397	.4407	.4416	.4426	.4435	.4444	.4453	.4462	.4470	.4478
10	.4368	.4379	.4390	.4400	.4410	.4420	.4430	.4439	.4449	.4458
11	.4335	.4347	.4359	.4370	.4331	.4392	.4403	.4413	.4423	.4433
12	.4296	.4309	.4322	.4335	.4347	.4359	.4371	.4382	.4393	.4404
13	.4251	.4265	.4280	.4293	.4307	.4320	.4333	.4345	.4357	.4369
14	.4198	.4214	.4230	.4245	.4259	.4274	.4288	.4301	.4315	.4328
15	.4137	.4155	.4171	.4188	.4204	.4220	.4235	.4250	.4264	.4279
16	.4066	.4085	.4103	.4121	.4139	.4156	.4172	.4189	.4204	.4220
17	.3984	.4004	.4024	.4043	.4052	.4080	.4098	.4116	.4133	.4150
18	.3888	.3909	.3930	.3951	.3972	.3992	.4011	.4030	.4049	.4067
19	.3776	.3799	.3821	.3844	.3856	.3887	.3908	.3929	.3949	.3969
20	.3645	.3670	.3694	.3718	.3741	.3764	.3786	.3809	.3830	.3852
21	.3494	.3520	.3545	.3570	.3535	.3619	.3643	.3666	.3689	.3712
22	.3317	.3344	.3371	.3397	.3423	.3448	.3473	.3498	.3522	.3546
23	.3112	.3140	.3167	.3194	.3220	.3247	.3273	.3298	.3323	.3348
24	.2873	.2901	.2929	.2956	.2933	.3009	.3036	.3062	.3088	.3113
25	.2596	.2623	.2650	.2677	.2704	.2730	.2756	.2782	.2808	.2833
26	.2272	.2298	.2324	.2350	.2376	.2401	.2426	.2451	.2476	.2501
27	.1896	.1920	.1943	.1967	.1930	.2013	.2036	.2059	.2082	.2105
28	.1458	.1478	.1498	.1517	.1537	.1556	.1576	.1595	.1615	.1634
29	.0949	.0963	.0977	.0991	.1004	.1018	.1032	.1046	.1060	.1073
30	.0356	.0362	.0367	.0373	.0379	.0384	.0390	.0396	.0401	.0407

ANSWERS TO SELF-QUIZ: GPMs

1. Maximum loan amount = $64,500 × 97 percent = $62,565

   Original loan amount = $58,160 ($62,565 ÷ 1.0757351) [Use Figure 7.2, FHA Table 2]

   Monthly payments: [Use Figure 7.3, FHA Table 3]
   Year 1 = $656.51
   Year 2 = $689.37
   Year 3 = $723.80
   Year 4 = $760.03
   Year 5 = $798.01
   Years 6–30 = $837.91

2. Maximum loan amount = $54,805

   Original loan amount = $51,107 ($54,805 ÷ 1.0723392) [Use Figure 7.2, FHA Table 2]

   Monthly payments: [Use Figure 7.3, FHA Table 3]
   Year 1 PI = $558.26
   Year 2 PI = $586.18
   Year 3 PI = $615.47
   Year 4 PI = $646.26
   Year 5 PI = $678.58
   Year 6 PI = $712.50

WHAT IS THE GPAML?

On July 22, 1981 the Federal Home Loan Bank Board authorized federally chartered savings and loan associations to issue, purchase or otherwise deal with GPAMLs on one- to four-family residential dwellings. Use of GPAML instruments by such institutions is preemptive of any conflicting state law.

A graduated payment adjustable mortgage loan is an adjustable mortgage loan on which the initial scheduled monthly payment amount is insufficient to fully amortize the loan. In short, the GPAML is simply an AML with a graduated payment feature.

To fully understand the nature and characteristics of GPAMLs we need only look at the federal authorization for the graduated payment feature of GPAMLs. Other than the graduated payment feature, *the GPAML operates like any other AML and is at all times subject to the rules and regulations governing AMLs.*

By federal authorization the graduated payment structure of GPAMLs *must be such that scheduled payments increase over a period of time not to exceed ten years, whereafter the monthly payments must have risen to a level that is sufficient to amortize the remaining balance of the loan over its remaining term at the interest rate in effect at that time.* In other words, payments may graduate upwards for a period not exceeding ten years after which all remaining payment adjustments must be sufficient in amount to amortize the loan.

The ten-year re-amortization requirement is the only restriction placed on the graduate payment feature of GPAMLs. Needless to say, the FHLBB exercises its intention to provide maximum flexibility to the lender in structuring GPAML loans. In addition, previous regulations placing limitations on the graduation rate and frequency of payment changes have been eliminated. Only the ten-year rule remains in effect.

Let's look at an illustration to see how the graduated payment authorization works. Assume we have a $67,000 AML loan for 30 years with an initial interest rate of 16 percent. The beginning PI payments on this loan without a GP feature would be $901.

With the graduated payment feature—a plan providing for 7½ percent annual payment increases for five years—we have the following payment schedule (assume no index/interest rate change):

Original loan: $67,000   rate: 16 percent   term: 30 years
GP: 7½ percent annual increase for 5 years

Year 1: $709.65/month (PI)   Year 4: $881.60/month
Year 2: $762.88/month   Year 5: $947.72/month
Year 3: $820.09/month   Year 6: $1,018.80/month for the remaining
                                        term, assuming no rate change

Note from the payment schedule that the first year's payments of $709.65 are almost $200 below the amount needed to amortize the loan. Note also that the monthly payments increase about 7½ percent each year until the sixth year, after which payments would remain constant at $1,018.80, assuming no interest rate change occurred. The $1,018.80 is the payment amount necessary to amortize the remaining balance of the original loan over the remaining 25 years of the term.

GPs and Negative Amortization

Like its GPM counterpart, the GPAML entails negative amortization. This can be shown by using the figures from our last example. On a nongraduated loan of $67,000 at 16 percent for 30 years, the borrower owes $901 for the first monthly payment. However, he or she pays only $709.65 under the graduated payment plan. Therefore, the difference of $191.35 is added onto the principal balance of $67,000, and at the beginning of the second month, the borrower owes $67,191.35. The process of adding unpaid interest onto the principal continues throughout the graduation period until the monthly payment is finally adjusted to amortize the loan for the remaining loan term. The remaining balance on the $67,000 loan at the end of years one through five are:

Original loan: $67,000   rate: 16 percent   term: 30 years

Remaining Balances
End of Year 1: $69,373.25
        Year 2: $71,167.60
        Year 3: $73,183.56
        Year 4: $74,400.40
        Year 5: $74,972.59

Now the loan balance has increased from $67,000 to $74,972.59, an increase of almost $8,000. In addition, using mortgage tables you can confirm that the sixth year monthly PI payment of $1,018.80 is the exact amount needed to amortize the balance of $74,972 over its remaining term of 25 years.

Flexibility of the GP Authorization.   The only regulatory constraint on the graduated payment period is that after ten years the payments must be reset at a level sufficient to amortize the loan. The regulation implicitly allows considerable flexibility in structuring GPAMLs. The graduation period itself may be three years, five years, eight years or anything not exceeding ten years. In addition, there is no constraint on the frequency of payment increases, the amount of payment increases or the amount of negative amortization. Thus a GP plan could call for annual increases, quarterly increases, increases every three years, two years, five years or even monthly. The amount of the payment increases can be any percent up to the point where a payment becomes sufficient to amortize the loan. The resulting negative amortization from these plans is likewise without regulatory limitation. The graduated payment plan is negotiable between the lender and borrower, subject only to the condition that the negotiated agreements be explicitly spelled out in the mortgage contract.

In essence, the liberalized GP regulations for GPAMLs shift the burden of prudent lending practices back to the lender and away from the government. That is not to say, however, that regulatory authorities will ignore imprudent loan structures. An example of a poorly structured loan is a GPAML with monthly payment increases—a very troublesome and costly program to administer. A more obvious example would be a loan structure with steep increases in monthly payments every year or two. The key is that payment increases do not exceed the increases in the borrower's income because that only invites default and foreclosure. A good GPAML will have its periodic and overall payment increases in proportion with the borrower's periodic and overall income increase potential.

GP Regulations in Review.   The following list summarizes the major regulations governing how GPs may operate.

1. The maximum allowable graduation period is ten years. Previous regulations establishing limits on payment increase amounts and how often payments can be graduated have been eliminated. In all practicality, however, GP periods will be at least of one year's duration or longer.
2. There is no limitation on the amount of negative amortization that can occur. If the loan-to-value ratio at the loan's origination was in compliance with regulations, then future compliance is assumed by regulatory authorities. The applicable LTV regulations state that there can be an 80, 80 to 90, or over-90 percent LTV ratio on the loan, given that certain security measures, such as additional mortgage insurance, are taken. A negative amortization ceiling is not mandated. But in practice lenders and the secondary markets are likely to set their own negative amortization ceilings.
3. By federal preemption ruling, additions of unpaid interest to a borrower's principal balance do *not* constitute a new advance of credit or loaned funds, and the first lien status of the loan as a whole thereby remains intact. This ruling followed from a controversial argument that an addition to principal, say two years after a loan's origination, could be construed as a new loan instead of an increase in the original loan because payment of funds owed was deferred. What if, for example, a new loan was recorded as an encumbrance between the period of the first lien and a subsequent addition to principal? Which would have lien priority, the intervening loan or the following principal addition? For GPAMLs authorized by FHLBB, such additions have *first* lien priority. (The issue, however, has not been conclusively decided.)
4. Federal preemption rulings allow interest to be charged on interest, which happens in GPs when negative amortization occurs.

The Underlying AML Component of GPAMLs

To understand GPAMLs, one must understand the GP authorization and how it works, and the underlying AML instrument and how it works. The GPAML is then merely a fusion of the two operating in tandem fashion. We have just examined the GP feature of GPAMLs. In Chapter 6 we learned the fundamentals of AMLs. Figure 7.5 recaps how the AMLs work.

From the diagram, we see that the AML's interest rate moves with the index, and such rate movements are implemented by changing the monthly payment, the principal balance or the loan term. In the context of GPAMLs, the one critical limitation is that the monthly payments *must be adjusted at least once every five years to amortize the remaining principal balance over the remaining term, a term that can never exceed 40 years from the date of origination.* In effect, then, this is the limitation that exists for negative amortization in a GPAML.

Although the regulations for the graduated payment loans stipulate ten years as the maximum negative amortization period, in fact the maximum period for GPAMLs is five years.

The GPAML: A Combination of the GP and the AML

When you put a graduated payment feature on top of an AML you can end up with a very complex loan or a simple loan, depending on how the two fit together. The key variables involved here are:

1. the length of the graduation periods,
2. the length of the interest rate adjustment periods,
3. the length of the payment adjustment periods, and
4. whether any payment caps are involved.

FIGURE 7.5:   The Adjustable Mortgage Loan

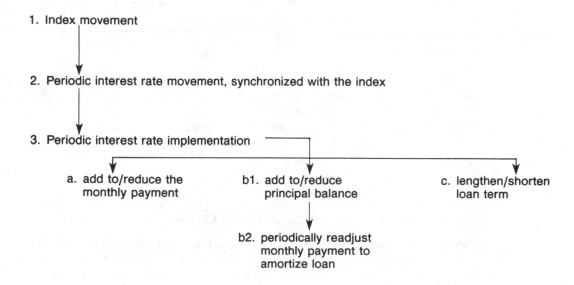

1. Index movement

2. Periodic interest rate movement, synchronized with the index

3. Periodic interest rate implementation

    a. add to/reduce the monthly payment

    b1. add to/reduce principal balance

    b2. periodically readjust monthly payment to amortize loan

    c. lengthen/shorten loan term

Figure 7.6 depicts the three possible types of GPAMLs. At its simplest, a GPAML, like Type 1, has no rate change whatsoever within the graduation period. Such a loan has a standard GP period, at the end of which the new index reading is taken, and the rate and payments changed.

A slightly more complex GPAML, Type 2, has interest rate changes during the graduation period synchronized with the GP's payment change periods. Thus at each interval, both the rate change and the GP increase are calculated into the new monthly payment.

Type 3 is a very complex GPAML with rate changes occurring more frequently than GP payment increases. In this loan, unpaid interest is added to (or subtracted from) the principal balance as a result of rate changes in addition to negative amortization resulting from GP increases. Because of this loan's complexity and unattractiveness to the borrower, it is not likely to find actual use.

GPAML Mechanics

To examine the mechanics of the GPAML, let's take the simplest GPAML structure, Type 1, where no rate change occurs within the entire graduation period. With this loan structure there are essentially two variations: GPAMLs with a payment cap and GPAMLs without a cap.

Without a payment cap, the GPAML in question works as follows.

1. The initial interest rate is established, along with the index value.
2. The graduation periods are defined and the rates of payment increases are established.
3. The rate adjustment periods and payment adjustment periods are coincident but do not occur during the GP period.
4. Loan payments begin and proceed through the GP period, increasing by the set percentage established with unpaid interest added onto principal.
5. At the end of the GP period, the remaining balance is identified along with the new interest rate per the latest available index reading.
6. The remaining loan balance is then *re-amortized* at the *new rate* over the *remaining loan period* for the second adjustment period. For each subsequent rate and payment adjustment period the same procedure takes place. Since both rate and payment adjustment dates are in synchronization, there is no further negative amortization.

With a payment cap on this GPAML, steps one to five would still occur. However, if the new payment level after the graduation period exceeded the cap, the payment would be raised to the cap limit and the remainder added onto principal as negative amortization during the second rate adjustment period. By regulation, this loan would be re-amortized after the five-year limitation unless payments did in fact become self-amortizing before five years.

Advantages and Disadvantages of GPAMLs

The advantage of opting for GPAML over conventional financing is that, as a result of the reduced monthly payments, a borrower can either obtain a larger loan than his or her financial capability would otherwise allow or can enjoy smaller early payments.

FIGURE 7.6:   GPAML Types

GPAML TYPE 1: NO RATE CHANGE IN GP PERIOD

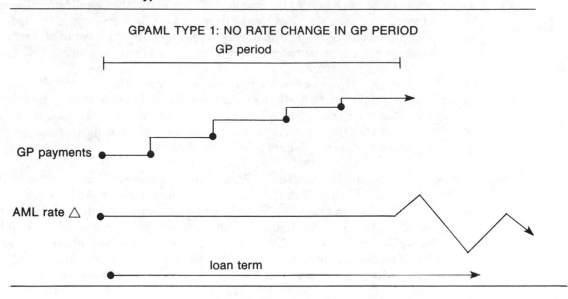

GPAML TYPE 2: RATE CHANGES IN SYNC WITH GP PAYMENT CHANGES DURING GP PERIOD

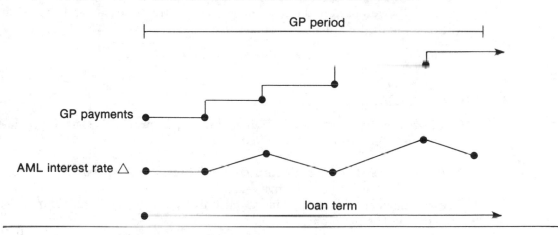

GPAML TYPE 3: RATE CHANGES OUT OF SYNC WITH GP PAYMENT CHANGES DURING GP PERIOD

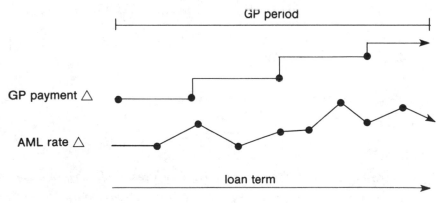

Negative amortization = GP △ s ± interest rate changes

However, the borrower's income must increase commensurately with the monthly payment graduations of the GPAML. Should this not occur, the benefit of reduced housing payments will be distinctly offset by the potential for financially burdensome payments after the graduation period. This is the big "plus and minus" aspect of all graduated payment loans. What might be today's plus could be tomorrow's minus.

Another important feature of graduated payment loans is that, as a result of the negative amortization compounding itself, the total amount of interest paid over the loan's life will be greater than on a loan without a graduation feature. This fact should be considered when opting for the GPAML, as the lesser initial cost will be made up in the overall cost of the loan, albeit in cheaper dollars paid in the future.

For many borrowers, the fact that GPAMLs are permanent financing can in itself be a nerve-settling advantage. With the absence of balloon notes, risks inherent to unknown sellers, and short-term loans, the GPAML can be a creative yet dependable financing alternative. To be fair to "seller-financing" alternatives, however, it should be noted that the GPAML is not a remedy for high interest rates or even a method that truly reduces interest rates. The initial interest rate on a GPAML is up to the individual lender to establish—and as such it can be a market, plus-market, or below-market rate.

In general terms, the various advantages and disadvantages of GPAMLs when weighed together argue that its ideal mortgagor is a younger family with income growth potential, yet a family who prefers the safer, more conservative alternative of financing long-term with the institutional lender.

SELF-QUIZ: GPAMLs

Complete the exercises below by filling in the blanks provided. The answers follow the exercise. (You will need to refer to loan constant tables.)

A 30-year GPAML is originated at 16 percent interest for $67,000. Its initial index reading is 14. The graduation period is five years and payments increase 7½ percent annually. The rate and payment change periods are also five years. The payments and remaining balance during the period are as follows:

	Monthly Payment	*Remaining Balance* (End year)
Year 1	$709.65	$69,373
2	$762.88	$71,467
3	$820.09	$73,183
4	$881.60	$74,400
5	$947.72	$74,972

1. If at the beginning of the sixth year the index reads 14, the new monthly payments will be _____.

2. If at the beginning of the sixth year the index reads 13, the new monthly payments will be _____.

3. Assume a 7½ percent annual payment cap exists on the GPAML, and that the index at year six reads 16. The new monthly payment for year 6 will then be (a) _____, and (b) _____ will be added onto the balance each month. At the end of the sixth year, *without* compounding the addition monthly, the remaining balance will be (c) _____.

ANSWERS TO SELF-QUIZ: GPAMLs

1. $1,018.84 (Amortizes $74,972 at 16 percent at 25 years)

2. $960.39 (Amortizes $74,972 at 15 percent at 25 years)

3. a. $1,018.80 (7½ percent increase over $947.72)

   b. $119.20 ($1,138 amortizes $74,972 at 18 percent at 25 years. Because the borrower only pays $1,018.80, the remainder is added to the balance each month.)

   c. $76,402 ($119.20 × 12 + $74,972)

8

Growing Equity Mortgages

In recent years hosts of new mortgages have emerged to reduce the cost of high interest rates for homebuyers. By and large these loans lowered monthly mortgage payments as much as possible—either by below-market-rate "interest only" loans or by graduated payment loans having negative amortization whereby unpaid sums were added to the borrower's outstanding loan balance. In many instances such "lower-cost" loans were not lower-cost but higher-cost loans which were "cheaper" during the first few years.

On the one hand, these mortgages did achieve their objective of making housing initially more affordable. On the other hand, homeowners found themselves in a situation of never paying off the principal balance of their loans. At the end of a five-year period, for example, the homeowner owed about as much as he or she did when the loan was originated. Thus in terms of total interest dollars being paid to own a home, the cost-saving loans in fact were more costly than ever. With interest-only loans and GPMs, more interest dollars had to be paid since the principal balance remained outstanding.

Lately, this trend has begun to reverse itself. Many homeowners don't just want "low-cost" home payments ad infinitum—they want to own their home. At the least, they want financing that generates greater equity buildup. The result is the development of amortized loans that generate equity much more rapidly. This chapter presents three types of growing equity loans: the GEM, biweekly loan, and 15-year loan.

LEARNING OBJECTIVES

When you have completed the chapter, you will be able to

1. explain the basic mechanics of growing equity mortgages,
2. highlight the benefits of these loans in terms of their overall interest-saving characteristics and accelerated equity buildup, and
3. perform preliminary GEM borrower qualification.

WHAT IS A GEM?

Introduced in 1981, the GEM (sometimes called a rapid payoff mortgage) is an accelerated-term mortgage with a variable monthly payment feature. In short, the GEM begins as a conventional fixed-rate mortgage, but payments on the loan increase according to an agreed-upon schedule or index. The additional monthly payment amounts are applied directly to the principal balance. Because the amount of principal payment increases every year, the loan can usually be retired in less than 15 years, depending on how much the payments are increased.

The Growing Equity Mortgage, or GEM, has as its underlying goal the accelerated accumulation of home equity for the borrower; in other words, home ownership in less time and for fewer interest dollars. The GEM achieves its goal through gradually increasing equity payments on a long-term loan resulting in the loan's early retirement.

Key Characteristics of the GEM

In general, growing- or increasing-equity mortgage loans are fixed-rate or variable rate mortgage loans with a pre-established term and interest rate that have the added feature of additional principal reduction above and beyond what the straight amortization schedule ordinarily requires. In other words, the increasing-equity-type loan is no more than a conventional loan with a graduated prepayment feature built into the payment schedule.

For example, the prepayment feature can be integrated into the loan by increasing the borrower's payments four percent each year over the original principal and interest (PI) amount. The additional four percent is applied *directly to principal reduction* during the year. In the second year, for example, the payments would be 104 percent of the original PI payment, and the four percent excess payment goes to pay down the principal. In the third year, the payments are increased to four percent over the second year's payments, and the new, larger principal prepayments reduce the outstanding balance at about twice the rate of the second year's principal paydown. This process speeds up equity payments at an ever-increasing rate until finally the loan is entirely (pre-) paid in 10 to 15 years depending on the rate, amount and term of the original loan.

Similar GEM-type loans achieve equivalent results using the same mechanics but with slightly different terms. Some forms may tie the increased payment amount to an economic index; for example, annual payment increases might be set at 75 percent of the Consumer Price Index. If the index were to go down, such a loan might stipulate no change in monthly payments whatsoever. Still other accelerated-equity mortgages could increase payments at a rate the borrower chooses or feels comfortable with. Still others may provide that the extra equity payment be *optional;* for example, if a ten percent increase plan becomes difficult for the borrower in the fourth year, the borrower could elect to cancel any increase, or in fact lower the payments to an affordable level (still at or above the original PI amount).

Regardless, then, of the specific terms or quantities of the accelerated-equity payments, we may define the GEM as a conventional amortized mortgage loan with some form of built-in prepayment feature.

The essential characteristic of a GEM-type loan is implicit in our definition: the borrower enjoys accelerated equity buildup on a graduated basis. Thus, GEMs compare favorably with interest-only loans, which have the advantage of minimizing the monthly payment, but leave the borrower with the full, unpaid original balance of the loan several years later.

A second characteristic of GEM-type loans is that the borrower pays fewer total interest dollars over the life of the loan. Thus the GEM carries the inflation-fighting benefit from the standpoint of total loan costs. Depending on the loan's specific provisions, GEM borrowers may pay only one-half to one-third the total interest dollars that a conventional loan borrower might pay in 25–30 years. (This will be further examined in subsequent sections.) Such large savings are achieved by the reduced amount of time that the principal balance remains outstanding.

Two other aspects of GEM-type loans are beneficial to prospective borrowers. First, the lender knows his or her money will be coming back in half the time required by a 30-year mortgage, and so may be willing to reduce the interest rate below the level charged for 30-year fixed-rate loans.

Second, because the borrower's initial payments on a GEM loan are based on a 25- to 30-year amortization schedule, the borrower can be qualified at a lower initial payment level than with short-term fixed-rate loans, whose payments directly correspond to the loan term. Hence more buyers can qualify for the GEM.

Take for comparison a $70,000, 13 percent loan as a 15-year fixed-rate loan and as a 25-year GEM. The initial monthly PI payment on the 15-year loan is $885.67 and the GEM, $789.49. If the PI debt ratio used is 27 percent, the borrower would have to make $3,870 per month to qualify for the 15-year loan, whereas the borrower would have to make only $3,280 per month to qualify for the GEM loan. If lenders are in fact using constant debt ratios for both types of loans, this income qualification difference is quite substantially in favor of the GEM-type loan.

A prerequisite for GEM-type loans is that the borrower should plausibly demonstrate an increasing income potential. Like graduated-payment mortgages, GEMs require more and more from the borrower's pocketbook each year, and the borrower should be keeping pace with these increases through increased income. If homebuyers have a steady income and want rapid equity buildup, they might prefer a fixed-payment loan unless they can get a GEM with only very modest increases.

GEM Loan Mechanics Illustrated

GEM loans, though easy to understand, have fairly complicated amortization schedules that require computer calculations for such things as the borrower's annual remaining principal balance. Nevertheless, the loan's monthly payments and remaining balances can be studied by using an actual sample.

Table 8.1 illustrates a GEM loan originated for $60,000 at 13⅜ percent interest for 25 years. The monthly PI payments increase at four percent per year. Note first that payments increase at four percent each year on a compounded basis. To qualify for this loan, a borrower should earn $2,570 per month (27 percent PI ratio) and be able to demonstrate potential income increase of at least 4 percent annually.

From the remaining balance columns, note how the GEM retires the loan at an ever-increasing rate. More specifically, you can see that the GEM loan doesn't begin to retire

TABLE 8.1:   GEM Loan: $60,000 @ 13⅜% for 25 years

Year	GEM Loan: $60,000 @ 13⅜% for 25 years Payments/Month	Remaining Balance	
1	$ 694	$59,682	99.80%
2	721	59,147	98.57
3	750	58,175	96.95
4	780	56,689	94.48
5	812	54,601	91.00
6	844	51,811	86.35
7	878	48,201	80.33
8	913	43,638	72.73
9	949	37,969	63.28
10	987	31,019	51.69
11	1027	22,586	37.64
12	1067	12,439	20.73
13	1111	315	—
14	–0–	–0–	

the loan at a rapid pace until the seventh or eighth year when it really "takes off." The implication from the gradually accelerated rate of equity buildup is that, if borrowers want to live in the home for more than six years, the GEM is a good tool for equity growth.

The GEM and Conventional Fixed-Rate Mortgage: A Comparative Analysis

Table 8.2 illustrates the monthly payments and remaining balance of three loans of $60,000 for the first ten years. The first loan is a 25-year fixed-rate mortgage at the market rate of 14¼ percent. The second loan is a 12-year fixed-rate loan at 13 percent, and the third loan is the 25-year GEM loan depicted in the previous example at 13⅜ percent. (Note that the different interest rates theoretically express an approximate interest rate spread for loans of varying terms; the shorter the term, the lower the rate.) The substantial sacrifice of equity made for the lower monthly payment of the 25-year fixed-rate loan is obvious. More remarkable still is that the beginning GEM payment is less than that of the long-term 14¼ percent loan and has been obtained with a shorter-term loan.

TABLE 8.2:   Loan Comparison

Year	Monthly Payments			Remaining Balance		
	25-Yr. (14¼%)	12-Yr. (13%)	GEM (13⅜%)	25-Yr.	12-Yr.	GEM
1	$733.76	$825.00	$694.00	99.5%	96.3%	99.8%
2	733.76	825.00	721.00	99.0	92.1	98.6
3	733.76	825.00	750.00	98.4	87.3	96.9
4	733.76	825.00	780.00	97.7	81.8	94.5
5	733.76	825.00	812.00	96.9	75.6	91.0
6	733.76	825.00	844.00	96.0	68.5	86.4
7	733.76	825.00	878.00	94.9	60.4	80.3
8	733.76	825.00	913.00	93.7	51.2	72.7
9	733.76	825.00	949.00	92.3	40.8	63.3
10	733.76	825.00	987.00	90.7	28.9	51.7

Table 8.2 also illustrates the key differences between a short-term fixed-rate loan and the GEM. The former, while carrying a higher initial payment than the GEM, retires the outstanding balance much faster in the early years of the loan. The GEM loan, on the other hand, offers the lower initial payment in exchange for a slower rate of amortization than the 12-year loan. Thus, the GEM is easier to qualify for.

OTHER TYPES OF GROWING EQUITY MORTGAGES

Variations of growing equity loans that are becoming increasingly popular are the biweekly and 15-year loans.

Biweekly Mortgage

The biweekly mortgage loan was started in Canada and is now offered by lenders in the United States. This loan is similar to the standard fixed-rate loan except for the frequency of payments. Instead of making one monthly payment, the borrower makes a payment equal to one-half of the normal monthly payment every two weeks. Under this plan, the borrower will make 26 payments over a year, which is the equivalent of 13 monthly payments. For example, a borrower who would normally pay $600 a month ($7,200 a year) for a 30-year fixed-rate mortgage would pay $300 every two weeks or $7,800 (26 × $300) a year. This type of loan arrangement makes sense because most workers are paid biweekly, allowing payments to more closely match a borrower's pay periods.

Borrowers who make biweekly payments are in effect prepaying the loan. The increased equity buildup and interest cost savings with this type of loan can be substantial and can shorten the term of the loan. For example, a $70,000 loan with an interest rate of 10.5 percent would save $60,000 in interest if paid biweekly compared to a conventional 30-year loan with the same rate. The biweekly loan would also be paid off in 20½ years instead of 30 years. Table 8.3 compares the interest saving and equity buildup of this type of loan with the 15-year and conventional mortgages.

While biweekly loans have existed for several years, they were not popular with U.S. lenders for several reasons. The biweekly loan required higher loan servicing costs, expensive alterations to computer programs for processing the new loan payment schedules, and

TABLE 8.3:   Monthly Loan Payment Comparison for a $100,000 Loan

Interest Rate	30-Year Loan	15-Year Loan	Monthly Payment Difference
8.0%	$ 733.76	$ 955.65	$221.98
8.5	768.91	984.74	215.83
9.0	804.62	1,014.27	209.65
9.5	840.85	1,044.22	203.37
10.0	877.57	1,074.62	197.04
10.5	914.74	1,105.40	190.66
11.0	952.32	1,136.60	184.28
11.5	990.29	1,168.19	177.90
12.0	1,028.61	1,200.17	171.56
12.5	1,067.26	1,232.52	165.26
13.0	1,106.20	1,265.24	159.04
13.5	1,145.41	1,298.32	152.91

there was no outlet to sell the loans. This situation has changed since the Federal National Mortgage Association (FNMA) began purchasing biweekly mortgages for resale in the secondary market. Biweekly loan plans are becoming widely accepted and are more accessible to borrowers. The number of payments in a biweekly loan is greater than a conventional 30-year loan. To facilitate payment processing most lenders offering biweekly mortgages require the borrower to open a NOW account with the lender, and the mortgage payments are automatically withdrawn from the account.

15-Year Mortgage

The 15-year home mortgage was almost nonexistent a few years ago but is becoming popular with current homebuyers who want the advantages of a shortened loan term and substantial interest expense savings. This trend has increased as interest rates dropped making the short-term mortgage more affordable for borrowers. By shortening the term of the loan to 15 years the monthly loan payment increases. If the borrower can afford the larger loan payment, however, the advantages of this type of loan make it very attractive.

The 15-year mortgage is usually offered at a slightly lower interest rate since the shorter term offers less risk to the lender. This fact plus the accelerated repayment of the principal result in a lower interest cost. For example, on a $80,000 loan with a rate of 11.5 percent the total interest cost for a 30-year loan would be $205,408 while the total interest cost for a 15-year loan would be $88,336. This is an interest saving of $117,072. Table 8.4 compares the interest saving and equity buildup of this type of loan compared with the biweekly and conventional mortgages.

Another important feature of this type of loan is that while the interest savings are substantial and the loan is paid in one-half the time, the monthly loan payments for a 15-year loan are not that much larger than a 30-year loan. Table 8.3 illustrates the monthly principal and interest payments for a 30-year and 15-year fixed-rate mortgage for $100,000.

Comparison of 30-Year and 15-Year Loan Payments

Table 8.3 compares the monthly principal and interest payments for a 30-year and 15 year fixed-rate mortgage for $100,000. The difference in payment amounts between the loan plans is relatively small and decreases as the interest rate increases.

Comparison of Conventional, Biweekly and 15-Year Loans

Table 8.4 illustrates the comparison between the conventional 30-year, biweekly and 15-year loans. Summary information for each loan is listed first followed by the remaining loan balance in both dollars and as a percent of the original loan amount. This figure graphically demonstrates the rapid equity buildup and interest cost savings that are characteristic of growing equity mortgages.

It is interesting to note that when the 15-year loan is paid off, the biweekly loan has 51 percent of its balance left. In the last six years the equity buildup accelerates rapidly paying off the remaining loan balance. After 21 years both the 15-year and biweekly loans have been paid, but the 30-year loan still has a $62,306 balance (i.e., 63 percent of the original loan amount).

TABLE 8.4:   Loan Comparison of Conventional, Biweekly and 15-Year Loans

Summary Statistics	30-Year	Biweekly	15-Year
Loan Amount	$100,000	$100,000	$100,000
Rate	10%	10%	10%
No. of Payments	360	545	180
Loan Payment Amount	$878	$439	$1,075
Length of Loan	30 years	21 years	15 years
Total Loan Payments	$315,909	$239,103	$193,428
Total Interest Paid	$215,909	$139,103	$93,428
Interest Saved	$0	$76,806	$122,481

Comparison of Remaining Balances

Year	30-Year		Biweekly		15-Year	
1	$99,444	99.4%	$98,521	98.5%	$96,968	97.0%
2	98,830	98.8	96,888	96.9	93,619	93.6
3	98,151	98.2	95,083	95.1	89,919	89.9
4	97,402	97.4	93,089	93.1	85,832	85.8
5	96,574	96.6	90,885	90.9	81,317	81.3
6	95,659	95.7	88,450	88.5	76,328	76.3
7	94,648	94.7	85,759	85.8	70,818	70.8
8	93,532	93.6	82,786	82.8	64,730	64.7
9	92,300	92.3	79,501	79.5	58,005	58.0
10	90,936	90.9	75,871	75.9	50,576	50.6
11	89,431	89.4	71,860	71.9	42,369	42.3
12	87,768	87.7	67,428	67.4	33,302	33.3
13	85,932	85.9	62,531	62.5	23,286	23.3
14	83,903	83.9	57,119	57.1	12,222	12.2
15	81,661	81.7	51,140	51.1	0	0
16	79,185	79.2	44,534	44.5		
17	76,449	76.5	37,234	37.2		
18	73,427	73.4	29,167	29.2		
19	70,088	70.1	20,254	20.3		
20	66,400	66.4	10,406	10.4		
21	62,326	62.3	0	0		

The Interest Write-Off Illusion

Some people might say that GEMs are disadvantageous because they do not provide as much interest write-off as a 30-year conventional mortgage—which they don't, particularly in the second half of the loan period. However, principal payments that cannot be deducted do not present the disadvantage to the borrower that one might think. Interest payments, whether deductible or otherwise, are still dollars out of one's pocket and gone forever as a loan cost, while the dollar paid in principal is saved as equity in the property.

Consider the following illustration. A borrower has a choice between a 30-year, 15-year or biweekly loan. The loan amount is $100,000 at a rate of 10 percent and the borrower is in the 28 percent tax bracket. Table 8.5 compares the after-tax interest expense to the borrower under the three loan arrangements.

Under the 30-year loan plan the tax reduction is greater, but the after-tax cost is also greater. It is clear from the illustration that the larger interest cost associated with the standard 30-year loan more than offsets the additional tax deduction. In addition, the 15-year and biweekly loan arrangements allow the borrower to build equity more quickly and repay the entire loan much earlier.

TABLE 8.5: Comparison of After-Tax Interest Expense

Loan Plan	30-Year	Biweekly	15-Year
Total Interest Deductible	$215,910	$139,103	$ 93,428
Tax Reduction @ 28%	($ 60,455)	($ 38,949)	($ 26,160)
Interest Cost after Taxes	$155,455	$100,154	$ 67,268
After-Tax Interest Savings	0	$ 55,301	$ 88,187

SUMMARY: ADVANTAGES AND DISADVANTAGES OF GEMs

The desire of many borrowers in recent years to accelerate the equity buildup in their homes has lead to the creation of new loan plans designed to meet this objective. The GEM, biweekly and 15-year loans all increase the borrower's equity through some form of prepayment of the loan balance. The new loan plans become even more attractive when interest rates are low, enabling borrowers to afford the larger monthly payments that usually accompany these types of loans.

The GEM loan speeds equity buildup by providing for increases in the monthly loan payment. The additional payment amounts are applied entirely against the loan balance.

The biweekly loan speeds up the timing of payments by splitting the monthly payment in half and paying every two weeks. This also results in the equivalent of one extra monthly payment being made each year.

The 15-year loan reduces the length of the loan by half creating larger monthly payments that are used to pay down the loan balance.

While these loans are referred to by different names, they all can be viewed as growing equity mortgages since their effect is to increase the buildup of equity faster than a standard 30-year loan.

Advantages of growing equity loans include:

- substantial savings on interest expense,
- shorter loan term allowing the borrower to own the property free and clear sooner,
- faster equity buildup allowing the homeowner to borrow for education, medical expenses or other purposes, and
- lower interest rates and loan fees in many cases.

Disadvantages of growing equity loans include:

- higher monthly payments that may reduce the loan amount the borrower may qualify for and divert funds a borrower might use for other purposes,
- a larger down payment that may be required to reduce the amount of the monthly payment,
- reduced income tax deductions, and
- reduced possibility of an attractive assumption.

SELF-QUIZ: GEMs

From Table 8.2, calculate the total principal and total interest payments made over the ten-year period. Then, on the basis of total interest paid, total principal paid and the monthly payment levels, pick which loan you think is the best overall deal. The solutions to the first question are below.

ANSWER TO SELF-QUIZ: GEMs

	25-year Fixed	12-year Fixed	GEM
Total payments	$88,051.20	$99,000.00	$98,181.00
Total interest paid	$82,471.20	$42,660.00	$69,200.00
Total principal paid	$ 5,580.00	$56,340.00	$28,981.00

9

Buydowns

In the early 1980s mortgage rates jumped from 8 and 9 percent up to 13, 14 and 15 percent.

At such high rates, a 1982 survey disclosed, nine out of ten potential homebuyers could not afford to purchase an average home with conventional financing. Severely depressed financial conditions hurt the homebuilder perhaps more than any other group in the housing industry.

Although many new forms of "creative financing," particularly seller financing, bring relief to the resale segment of the industry, seller financing does not address the affordability problems of the *new* buyer. New homes do not have a resident seller to carry back a 12 percent note from the buyer. To make the home salable, builders turned to two basic strategies. One was to lower the price of the property; the other was to assist in the financing with programs that offer greater flexibility than outright price reductions.

The predominant new builder-financing programs are, in reality, builder-subsidized financing programs called "builder contribution" programs, or more commonly, "buydowns."

In this unit we will take a close look at buydowns and how they are used to make the purchase of a new home more feasible, as well as competitive with the purchase of a resale home. First, we will examine the general structure of a buydown, along with its various characteristics. Then we will make an in-depth analysis of various buydown programs to see specifically how they work and how they are set up.

LEARNING OBJECTIVES

After studying this chapter you will be able to

1. define and describe the basic fundamentals and characteristics of buydowns,
2. describe the financial mechanics of the buydown,

3. explain how the interest rate buydown payment affects the buyer's effective interest rate,

4. explain how the bought-down interest rate affects the buyer's mortgage qualification, and

5. explain how the buydown term will affect mortgage payments when the buydown period expires.

WHAT IS A BUYDOWN?

A buydown is any mortgage financing alternative in which a portion of a mortgage loan's payable interest is donated or loaned in advance to the mortgagee on the mortgagor's behalf for the purpose of reducing the amount of interest the mortgagor must pay on the loan for a given period of time.

Other names of a buydown include builder assistance programs, interest rate reduction mortgages, builder contribution programs.

Because a portion of the loan's interest has been paid in advance, the borrower pays less interest on the loan and, for a period of time, a lesser interest rate. That is why the term "buydown" has been adopted: the original interest rate has been effectively "bought down" for a period of time by the advance payment.

Under ordinary operating conditions, the interest advanced to the lender is escrowed, and over the buydown period an amount of that advance is drawn out each month to supplement the mortgagor's reduced monthly principal and interest (PI) payment. At the end of the buydown period, all of the escrowed interest advance will have been drawn out, after which the mortgagor's mortgage payments increase to their original, unsubsidized level. The primary feature of buydowns, however, is that the borrower *is qualified by the lender based not on the original mortgage payment but on the reduced, bought-down payment.* This in turn qualifies the buyer to purchase a more expensive house. The diagram in Figure 9.1 summarizes the structure and operation of a buydown.

Example of a Typical Buydown

Let's refer to Figure 9.2 for a simple example of how the buydown works. A buyer would like to buy a new $80,000 home just completed by the local builder. To facilitate sales, the builder is offering a buydown program which "buys down" the best available mortgage money by 2 interest points for a period of four years. The best available financing is 15 percent. Therefore the builder is offering a qualified buyer an interest subsidy for four years that will bring the buyer's mortgage payment down to whatever the payment on the loan would be at 13 percent interest instead of 15 percent interest.

Assume that the buyer puts $15,000 down and needs a $65,000 mortgage. AT 15 percent interest, the buyer obtains a 30-year mortgage with a PI payment of $822. However, under the buydown plan, the borrower only pays an amount equal to the PI payment on the $65,000 at *13 percent,* or $719, and the builder makes up the difference. In this case, the monthly subsidy is $822 minus $719, or $103. Over four years, this subsidy is $103 times 48 months, or $5,144. To put the plan into operation, the builder deposits $5,144 in escrow with the lender, who in turn draws out $103 per month to supplement the buyer's payment of $719. At the end of the four-year buydown period, the escrow is closed and the

FIGURE 9.1:   Buying Down a (15%) Mortgage

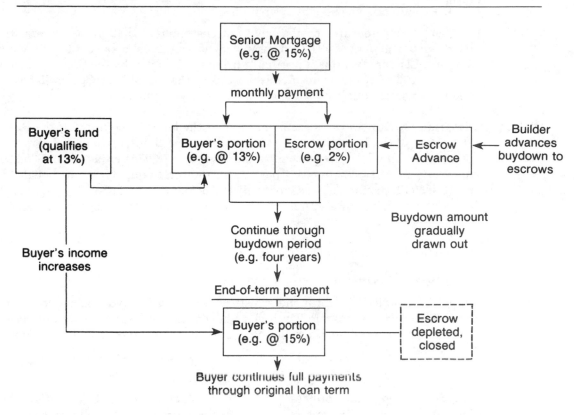

FIGURE 9.2:   A 2-Point, 4-Year Buydown

Price: $80,000
Down: $15,000
Mortgage: $65,000 @ 15%, 30 years
PI payment owed: $822

Buydown specs: 2 points, 4 years

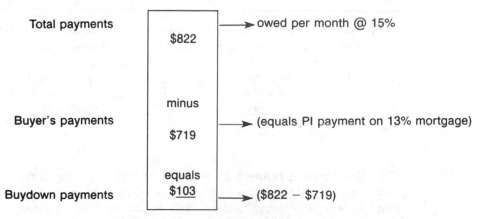

Total buydown amount = ($103/month) × (48 months) = $5,144

After 4-year buydown period, buyer pays full $822/month

borrower's payments rise to the original $822 for the remaining 26 years of the loan's term.

One attractive feature for the buydown customer is that most lenders will qualify buydown participants for the reduced payments they must make not for the actual PI loan amount. Lenders feel this is justifiable primarily because, by the time the borrower must make the full monthly payment, it is most likely that his or her income will have increased enough to safely qualify for the greater monthly payment.

Returning to our previous example, suppose the lenders require that the PI not exceed 28 percent of the household's gross monthly income. Thus, on the $65,000 mortgage of 15 percent, the family's gross income would have to be $2,935 per month, or $35,220 per year to qualify for the $822 monthly payment. However, to qualify for the bought-down payment of $719, the family need gross only $2,568 per month, or $30,816 per year. That substantial earnings differential of $4,400 can qualify more buyers for the builder's properties.

Buydown Variations

In actual practice, the form and structure of a specific buydown can vary considerably from the foregoing example. The builder, buyer, and lender all have the potential to add or subtract particular features. Following are some of the major variables encountered in actual situations.

Buydown Program Sources.   The predominant source for buydown programs is the homebuilder who offers special arrangements to promote and sell new properties. However, anyone can offer a buydown to a homebuyer, including the buyer's parents or relatives, the lender (who would convert the interest advance into a second mortgage), the seller in a resale transaction or even the buyers themselves. It doesn't matter who provides the interest buydown, so long as the various terms and conditions of the arrangement are met to the lender's satisfaction.

The Buydown Amount and Term.   The amount of interest that is advanced to lower the interest rate can vary, as can the buydown term, depending upon the builder's particular program. Some buydowns can lower the interest rate 1 percent over the entire term. Other programs may buy down the interest rate 5 points for one or two years. Still others may follow FHA or FNMA guidelines so the mortgage can be FHA-insured or sold to FNMA by the lender. The particulars of the buydown amount will always depend on the availability of buyers, the policies of local lenders, or the specific resources of the builder. Whatever the buydown amount and term quantities, however, they together determine the amount that must be escrowed and the qualification standards to be used with the buyer.

The Buydown Advance: Subsidy or Loan?   In most cases, a buydown interest advance is an outright subsidy offered to the buyer from the builder as a means of selling the builder's inventory. However, builders or lenders can arrange for the advance to be converted to a second mortgage that the buyer must repay at some given time, usually upon maturity of the buydown term. Although this latter arrangement still holds a certain attractiveness, the qualification standards must be adjusted to avoid an excessive debt burden for the buyer when the payments escalate at the end of the buydown period. If the buydown subsidy is part of the buyer's contract with the builder, the lender can hold the borrower liable for the full interest rate if the builder backs out of the deal or goes bankrupt.

The Underlying Mortgage.   The mortgage the buyer obtains under a buydown arrangement can vary in type and term. Typically, the mortgage acquired is long-term or permanent in nature, with a term ranging between 25 and 40 years. The underlying financing can be short-term, or temporary, with or without an interim call provision. Usually this mortgage is senior priority.

In addition, the mortgage can be a fixed-term, fixed-rate mortgage, or it can be an adjustable-rate mortgage with varying rates and monthly payments.

The Form of Payment.   A buydown can reduce the buyer's effective interest rate by a fixed amount over the buydown period, or it can reduce it by a different amount in any given year. A varying buydown usually takes the form of a "graduated buydown" in which the interest rate is bought down by a decreasing amount every year. For example, a "graduated" buydown with a three-year term might buy the rate down 3 points the first year, 2 points the second year, and 1 point the third year. Thus, the escrowed advance would be drawn out in successively smaller amounts. In turn, the borrower's monthly payments would increase every year by a proportionate amount. Graduated buydowns are good practice because they tend to moderate the impact of the increased payments at the end of the buydown term. Instead of a sudden 3-point increase for the buyer to absorb, the final increase is only 1 point. Usually graduated buydowns do not provide for payment escalations more often than once each year.

Custom versus FHA or FNMA Buydowns.   A builder can structure any custom-made buydown desired, where any or all of the aforementioned variables can be structured to suit the buyer. Recently, however, FHA and FNMA have developed standards for buydown programs that, if followed, could result in the buydown mortgage arrangement being either insured by FHA or purchased by Fannie Mae. Since insurability and marketability are attractive features to any lender, it is most likely that new buydown programs will follow FHA and/or FNMA guidelines.

Buydowns and the Real Estate Environment.   In an environment of high interest rates developers may have trouble selling their homes because the high interest rates will make it difficult for buyers to qualify for loans. Under these conditions the developer will be more inclined to offer buydown arrangements to assist the buyer and sell their stock of houses. If interest rates are low developers usually are able to attract enough qualified buyers without the need to offer buydowns. However, in some cases interest rates may be low, but the supply of new construction exceeds buyer demand. In this situation the developer may be forced to offer buydowns as an incentive to attract buyers.

AN IN-DEPTH LOOK AT THE BUYDOWN

In this section we will take a more detailed look at how the buydown works and how the buydown's specific terms affect buyer qualification. We will use actual figures and realistic examples followed by case exercises.

The Buydown Amount and Term and Their Effect on the Interest Rate

There are three perspectives from which to view the buydown as a financing alternative: that of the builder, the lender and the buyer. From the *builder*'s standpoint, the primary concerns are:

- How much of an interest subsidy can I afford?
- What is the minimum buydown that will attract enough buyers to move my inventory in an affordable time frame?

Any builder has a time limitation in which he must sell the newly constructed homes or face a cash shortage and construction loan maturities. Thus the builder cares most about the buydown's ability to attract buyers.

The *lender*, on the other hand, cares most about underwriting good loans that won't default. Thus the amount of the buydown advance is not as important as the buydown period. For the lender, the longer the loan term, the easier it is for the buyer to qualify for the full amount of the loan. A two-year, 6-point buydown, for example, could cause hardships when the subsidy period ended and the payments, after only two years, escalated to reflect a 6-point increase in the interest rate. Furthermore, as lenders qualify buyers based on the lower payments, a large buydown subsidy over a short time could qualify very marginal buyers who would have problems in two years when payments increased.

The *buyer*'s goals are to get maximum value for the dollars expended and to be able to afford the payments both initially and after the buydown period.

These perspectives underlie a very important fact about buydowns: *the relationship between the advanced amount and the buydown term is critical* in determining the overall attractiveness of the buydown to the builder, the lender and the buyer.

Using Table 9.1, we can understand the relationships between the buydown amount and the buydown term by first looking at how an interest rate is bought down. This process is actually quite simple. To buy down an interest rate, you first identify the beginning monthly payment for a given loan at a given rate. For example, let's use from our chart a $50,000 mortgage at 15 percent for which the monthly payment is $632. To buy down this rate, identify the number of points to be bought down and find the corresponding monthly payment. Subtract this amount from the original amount and multiply by 12 for the annual buydown cost. For example, if the 15 percent mortgage were to be bought down 2 points to 13 percent, subtract the 13 percent monthly payment of $553 from $632 and multiply by 12; or $79 multiplied by 12 for an annual buydown cost of $948. Thus, if a builder were to buy down a 30-year 15 percent mortgage of $50,000 by 2 points to 13 percent for a one-year period, the builder would deposit $948 in the buydown escrow.

TABLE 9.1: PI Monthly Payments, 30-Year Mortgage

Amount	Interest Rate						
	11%	12%	13%	14%	15%	16%	17%
$50,000	$476	$514	$553	$ 592	$ 632	$ 672	$ 712
$60,000	571	617	663	711	758	807	855
$70,000	667	720	774	829	885	941	998
$80,000	762	821	884	947	1,012	1,076	1,141
$90,000	857	926	995	1,066	1,138	1,210	1,283

To derive the buydown amount for a term greater than one year, simply multiply the annual buydown amount by the number of years in the buydown term. Thus, from our example, a 2-point buydown for the $50,000 mortgage for three years would be $948 × 3, or $2,844.

SELF-QUIZ: BUYDOWNS

1. From Table 9.1, calculate the buydown amount on a 15 percent, $90,000 mortgage for a buydown of 3 points for four years.

2. From the same table, calculate the buydown amount on a 16 percent mortgage for $80,000 that is bought down 2 points for five years.

ANSWERS TO SELF-QUIZ: BUYDOWNS

1. ($1,138 − $926) × 48 months = $10,176.

2. ($1,076 − $947) × 60 months = $7,740.

Buydown Amounts in Relation to Term and Interest Rate

For a mortgage of a given amount at a given interest rate, there is a predictable relationship between the amount of a buydown, its term, and the number of points bought down. Table 9.2 displays buydown amounts on a 15 percent mortgage for varying principal amounts, buydown periods and points bought down. The mortgage amounts presented are $50,000, $60,000, $70,000, $80,000 and $90,000. For each of these principal amounts, the table displays the buydown amount for 1, 2, 3 and 4 points bought down from 15 percent over a buydown period of one, two, three, four and five years.

For example, if a $60,000, 15 percent mortgage were to be bought down *3 points for five years,* the builder would escrow $8,460 as the buydown amount. Over the buydown term, one-sixtieth of this amount would be drawn out each month and matched to the buyer's reduced payment.

The Graduated Buydown

In the case of a graduated buydown, the monthly buydown amount increases every year while the buyer's payments correspondingly increase. For example, a four-year buydown might call for the interest rate to be bought down 4 points in the first year, 3 points in the second year, 2 points in the third year and 1 point in the fourth year. Finding the buydown costs for such a loan requires finding the cost for each year, at its own rate, and adding the results together.

SELF-QUIZ: GRADUATED AND NONGRADUATED BUYDOWNS

1. In the example just given, the nongraduated $60,000 mortgage, find the buyer's monthly payment, the escrow payment and the total monthly payment.

2. For a $70,000 loan at 15 percent with a graduated four-year buydown that decreases 1 percent per year, starting at 4 percent,

   a. what would be the *yearly* buydown amounts?

   b. what would be the *total* buydown amount?

   c. what would be the buyer's payments each year?

ANSWERS TO SELF-QUIZ: GRADUATED AND NONGRADUATED BUYDOWNS

1. The buyer's payment is identical to the monthly payment on a $60,000 mortgage at 12 percent, or $617. The escrow portion is $8,460 ÷ 60, or $141 per month. Adding those together, the total payment is $617 + $141 = $758, which is identical to the amount shown in Table 9.1 for the monthly payment on a 15 percent $60,000 mortgage.

TABLE 9.2: Buydown Costs on Selected 15 Percent Mortgages

Term		Number of points bought down			
		1 pt. (to 14%)	*2 pts. (to 13%)*	*3 pts. (to 12%)*	*4 pts. (to 11%)*
A: $50,000	1 year	480	948	1,416	1,872
	2 years	960	1,896	2,832	3,744
	3 years	1,440	2,844	4,248	5,616
	4 years	1,920	3,792	5,664	7,488
	5 years	2,400	4,740	7,080	9,360
B: $60,000	1 year	564	1,140	1,692	2,244
	2 years	1,128	2,280	3,384	4,488
	3 years	1,692	3,420	5,076	6,732
	4 years	2,256	4,560	6,768	8,976
	5 years	2,820	5,700	8,460	11,220
C: $70,000	1 year	672	1,332	1,980	2,616
	2 years	1,344	2,664	3,960	5,232
	3 years	2,016	3,996	5,940	7,848
	4 years	2,688	5,328	7,920	10,464
	5 years	3,360	6,660	9,900	13,080
D: $80,000	1 year	780	1,536	2,292	3,000
	2 years	1,560	3,072	4,584	6,000
	3 years	2,340	4,608	6,876	9,000
	4 years	3,120	6,144	9,168	12,000
	5 years	3,900	7,680	11,460	15,000
E: $90,000	1 year	864	1,716	2,544	3,372
	2 years	1,728	3,432	5,088	6,744
	3 years	2,592	5,148	7,632	10,116
	4 years	3,456	6,864	10,176	13,488
	5 years	4,320	8,580	12,720	16,860

2. a. The buydown amounts would be:

Year one (4 points, one year)	= $2,616
Year two (3 points, one year)	= $1,980
Year three (2 points, one year)	= $1,332
Year four (1 point, one year)	= $ 672

  b. Total buydown amount   = $6,600

  c. The buyer's payments would be:

Year one:	$667
Year two:	$720
Year three:	$774
Year four:	$829

If you had trouble with the exercise, use the following procedure to calculate **any** graduated buydown amount:

1. Identify the interest rate to be bought down, the mortgage amount and the monthly PI payment.

2. For each buydown year, identify that year's bought-down interest rate and monthly payment and subtract that payment from (1) above for that year's buydown amount.

3. For the total buydown amount, add each of the amounts derived in (2).

THE BUYDOWN AND BUYER QUALIFICATION

As cited earlier, one of the key benefits of a buydown is that the buyer is qualified by the lender based on the bought-down payment instead of the original mortgage PI payment amount. In principle, then, the greater the buydown in a given year, the less income the buyer must have. Given that as a rule, there must be a limit to how much an interest rate can be bought down if the same qualification standard is used. An interest rate bought down 10 points for a one-year period will create considerable hardship for a family that qualified at the bought-down rate because they must pay on 10 more interest points one year later.

Buydown Qualification Standards

The two primary standards for any mortgage qualification are:

1. the ratio between the buyer's mortgage payment and gross monthly income,
2. the buyer's total long-term debt, including housing debt, in relation to gross income.

For the purposes of our discussion, we will examine the first standard, the mortgage debt-to-income ratio. As in previous chapters, we'll assume a ratio of 28 percent.

In applying this standard to buydowns, all the lender really cares about is whether *in any given year* the buyer's mortgage debt bears that 28 percent relation to income. In other words, since the buyer's payments may not be the same from year to year during the buydown period, the key concern is whether the appropriate debt ratio will exist *at the end* of the buydown period when the full payment must be made.

The rule used in buydown qualification is that the *interest payment for each year of the buydown period should not be bought down to a greater degree than the buyer's income is expected to increase over the same period.* For example: In a two-year buydown the buyer's payments should not be bought down more than ten percent per year if that buyer's income is not expected to increase by more than 10 percent per year. That rule, if followed, will keep the buyer's debt ratio in line with changes in annual income—if not for each year in a graduated buydown, then at the end of the buydown term.

In following this rule, it is always better to structure a buydown with fewer points bought down over a longer term than with more points bought down over a shorter term. The shorter the term of a buydown, the more radical the payment increase will be at the end of the period. The longer the buydown term, the less radical the increase in monthly payments will be.

Table 9.3 shows the *percentage that a mortgage payment has been reduced* on a given buydown for a given mortgage. The table displays 30-year mortgage amounts for $50,000, $60,000, and $70,000, and for each mortgage amount, an interest rate from 13 percent to 17 percent. The various percentage figures within the table indicate the *annual decrease* in the mortgage payment amount relative to the number of points that were bought down. For example, under a $60,000 mortgage, if 3 points are bought down from an initial rate of 17 percent, the mortgage payment amount will be 16.8 percent *less* than the normal PI

TABLE 9.3: Buydown Qualification: Percent of Mortgage Payment Reduction, or Percent of Increase in Buyer's Income, Needed to Qualify for 30-Year Mortgage

Mort. Amt.	% Interest	Number of Points Bought Down				
		1 point	2 points	3 points	4 points	5 points
$50,000	from: 13%	7.0%	13.9%	20.6%	27.3%	33.6%
	14	6.6	13.2	19.6	25.8	32.1
	15	6.3	12.5	18.6	24.7	30.5
	16	5.9	11.9	17.6	23.2	29.2
	17	5.6	11.2	16.6	22.3	27.8
$60,000	from: 13%	6.9%	13.8%	20.5%	27.1%	33.6%
	14	6.7	13.2	19.6	25.8	32.1
	15	6.3	12.4	18.6	24.6	30.5
	16	5.9	11.9	17.7	23.5	29.2
	17	5.6	11.3	16.8	22.4	27.8
$70,000	from: 13%	7.0%	13.8%	20.6%	27.2%	33.7%
	14	6.6	13.1	19.5	25.8	32.1
	15	6.3	12.5	18.6	24.6	30.5
	16	6.0	11.9	17.7	23.4	29.2
	17	5.7	11.3	16.8	22.3	27.8

payment at 17 percent interest. Or, if a $50,000 mortgage of 14 percent is bought down 5 points, the mortgage payment will be reduced by 32.1 percent for each month of the buydown period.

The Payment Reduction versus the Buyer's Income Increase

As stated earlier, Table 9.3 also shows by what percent a buyer's income must increase *over the entire buydown period* to maintain a constant, safe debt ratio. For example, if a 14 percent mortgage of $50,000 is bought down 5 points on a one-year buydown period, the 32.1 percent figure is not only the amount the payment is reduced for the year but also the *percent the buyer's income must increase* during that year to be able to safely afford the full payment at the end of the term. In this example, it is obvious that a one-year, 5-point buydown will cause a burdensome debt load after 12 months have expired.

However, the table also shows the necessary income increase the buyer needs under a buydown plan that exceeds one year. This is found by dividing the percentage figure shown for any plan by the number of years in the buydown period. Thus, from our previous example, if the 14 percent mortgage for $50,000 were bought down 5 points for three years instead of one year, the buyer's income would only need to increase 32 percent divided by 3, or about 11 percent per year instead of 32 percent. Or, taking another example, if a $70,000 mortgage at 16 percent were bought down 4 points for two years, the buyer's income would need to increase 23.4 percent divided by two years or about 12 percent per year. Over this period, then, two successive 12 percent income increases would match the 24 percent increase that will occur with the mortgage payment at the end of the buydown period.

SELF-QUIZ: PAYMENT REDUCTION VERSUS INCOME INCREASE

1. A buyer projects that his income will increase about 10 percent per annum. On this basis, would he safely be able to afford the payments at the end of the buydown period on a plan that bought down a $60,000 mortgage of 17 percent by 4 points for 3 years? (Use Buyer Qualification Table.)

2. An upwardly mobile buyer would like a maximum reduction in mortgage payments over the shortest possible buydown period. Her income increase is projected to be 18 percent for the next few years. The buyer wants to borrow $50,000. If the going interest rate is 16 percent, what is the best buydown plan for this buyer in terms of the number of points bought down and the buydown term? (Use Buyer Qualification Table.)

3. A buydown plan calls for a $50,000 mortgage at 16 percent interest to be bought down 4 points for 2 years. If a buyer's income increases 7 percent per year, will the buyer safely qualify for the ending payments, assuming he qualified for the reduced payment at the beginning of the buydown period? (Do *not* use Buyer Qualification Table.)

ANSWERS TO SELF-QUIZ: PAYMENT REDUCTION VERSUS INCOME INCREASE

1. In this instance, the table indicates that the mortgage payments will be 22.4 percent less during the buydown period. In three years, the buyer's income will increase 30 percent. Thus he would safely be able to afford the increased payments.

2. This buyer can reasonably handle a one-year, 3-point buydown which lowers the payment by 17.6 percent.

3. The mortgage payment on this plan will drop (4 points × 6), or about 24 percent (using the six factor since the interest is higher). Dividing this decrease by 2, we can determine that the buyer's income should increase by 12 percent to be able to afford the 24 percent jump in 2 years. The 7 percent increase projected could theoretically cause problems for this buyer.

CASE STUDY EXERCISE: THE BUYDOWN

The following problem will recap the in-depth analysis we've undertaken in this section. To complete the exercise, pretend that you're an agent in consultation with a local builder.

The builder has been having problems selling his new $78,000 homes even though he's been able to arrange 15 percent financing for buyers. There are numerous younger families in the builder's market area. He estimates that they earn an average of about $28,000 to $31,000 per household. Moreover, it's an upwardly mobile market since the income increases of the average family are estimated to be 12 percent.

The builder estimates he can afford a buydown program with a buydown amount of about $5,500 ± $400. However, the lender is standing firm on a mortgage-debt ratio of 28 percent and requires that $8,000 be put down on the home purchase.

What would be the best buydown program that the builder could adopt to attract the most buyers within the qualification standards at the least cost?

To recap the data:
  Price: $78,000
  Terms: $8,000 down, 28 percent debt ratio, 15 percent mortgage money (30 years)
  Buyers: Earn $28,000 to $31,000; increases 12 percent per year
  Buydown maximum: $5,500 ± $400 per unit

SOLUTION TO AND ANALYSIS OF CASE STUDY EXERCISE: THE BUYDOWN

There are two ways to approach this problem: (1) begin with what the buyers can afford, or (2) begin with the assumption that the builder spends all of his buydown subsidy to sell the house. Because you're consulting with him, you decide to see how unaffordable these homes are for the typical buyer.

The homes will require a $70,000 mortgage. At 15 percent, that's a monthly payment of $885. Using the lender's debt ratio, the qualified buyer must earn $3,160 per month or almost $38,000 per year. The average family earns $28,000 to $31,000 or about $29,500. That comes to $2,460 per month. Using the same debt ratio, these families can spend about $690 for their PI payments. So the buyers are about $195 short of what they need to pay per month on the mortgage. In other words, the $885 payment would have to be reduced about 22 percent to $690 to be affordable. However, if a buydown reduced the mortgage on a *one-year* term, the buyers would have some problem with the payments since their income only increases 12 percent per year. A 22 percent buydown with a term of two years, however, would bring the average buyers within range because their incomes would increase 24 percent in the two-year period. So thus far we know the mortgage must be bought down at least 22 percent over a minimum two-year term. Referring to the qualification table, under a $70,000 loan at 15 percent, the number of points that must be bought down to lower the mortgage balance at least 22 percent is the 4-point buydown. This buydown will create a monthly mortgage cost of $667, which most buyers in this market can afford. Referring to the buydown cost chart under a 4-point buydown for two years, this buydown will cost the builder $5,232, which is within his spendable range.

Equity Conversion Loans

The largest source of wealth in the country is the equity that owners have accumulated in their homes. At the end of 1983 there were 43 million owner-occupied homes with a net worth estimated at $769 billion. Over 15.75 million of these homes were owned outright, i.e., without any mortgage debt. In recent years lenders have devised new loan products to tap this huge source of capital. As homeowners in the country grow older and continue to accumulate equity in their properties they will want loans designed to tap this wealth. These loans will probably become an important component in the real estate financing market. In this chapter we will discuss the more common lending techniques that allow owners to convert the current or anticipated equity in their property to cash.

LEARNING OBJECTIVES

After working through this chapter you will

1. understand the characteristics, advantages and disadvantages of shared appreciation mortgages (SAMs);
2. understand the characteristics, advantages and disadvantages of reverse annuity mortgages (RAMs);
3. understand the characteristics, advantages and disadvantages of home equity mortgages; and
4. understand the characteristics, advantages and disadvantages of Grannie Maes.

WHAT IS A SHARED APPRECIATION MORTGAGE?

The shared appreciation mortgage (SAM), or appreciation-participation mortgage as it is called in some areas, is a shared equity arrangement with the lender. The primary attraction to the borrower is that the lender will make the loan with a substantial reduction in the interest rate. In exchange for the rate reduction, the lender requires that the borrower share part of the appreciation of the home. It's not that the lender will receive any less of a return on the loan, rather the lender will receive part of the income in the form of interest and part in the form of profit on the property. Insurance companies have long had this type of equity participation arrangement with developers of shopping centers and other commercial investments.

Differences Between a SAM and a Standard Fixed-Rate Mortgage

There are several important differences between a SAM and a standard fixed-rate mortgage. These are the rate, the term and the use of property value appreciation to increase the yield on the loan.

Rate Reduction.   The interest rate on a SAM is less than the rate on a standard fixed-rate loan. The rate difference could be anywhere from 10 to 40 percent less. Typically the percentage the interest rate is reduced is equal to the amount of the lender's participation in the appreciation of the property. For example, if the lender's SAM rate is 40 percent less than a conventional loan, the lender will earn 40 percent in the appreciation of the property. The reduction in the rate and the corresponding reduction in the monthly loan payments are the main attractions of the loan for borrowers. The difference in monthly payments can be substantial, as shown in the following example:

Borrower's Monthly Payments for a $100,000 Mortgage for 30 Years

$952	Standard loan @ 11%	
− $649	SAM loan @ 6.75% (40% less than the standard loan)	
$303	Difference in monthly loan payment	

For a young couple buying their first home the monthly payment amount may be an obstacle in qualifying for a loan. The reduced monthly payment of a SAM, however, increases their qualifying loan amount and may make the house affordable. In the example above, for instance, if the lender required the borrower's income not to exceed 30 percent of the monthly loan amount, the borrower's income needs to be much less using a SAM loan.

Standard Loan
$38,076 Yearly income ($952 ÷ .30 = $3,173 × 12 = $38,076)

SAM Loan
$25,956 Yearly income ($649 ÷ .30 = $2,163 × 12 = $25,956)
$12,120 Difference

Loan Term.   SAMs are usually amortized on a 30-year basis. (Chapter 2 deals with amortization.) This means that the loan would be fully paid after 30 years. However, most SAMs are due in a much shorter time, usually within ten years. The 30-year payment schedule is used to determine the amount of the monthly payments, but the loan term can be a different length. The remaining balance will be due at the end of the term. This is different from a standard fixed-rate mortgage because the term for a fixed-rate mortgage is the same as the payment schedule (i.e., 30 years). A disadvantage of the SAM is that at the end of the ten-year period the borrower must pay the lender its share of the price appreciation. The borrower, therefore, must come up with the money in cash, refinance or sell the property to pay the lender. This may be a problem if money is tight or interest rates are high.

Property Appreciation. With a standard mortgage the amount of interest collected by the lender is normally based on the loan rate. On a SAM loan, however, there are really two types of "interest" being charged by the lender. The first is the interest actually charged based on the loan rate. The second is the income the lender hopes to realize based on the appreciation of the property. The amount of this income is based on whatever appreciation in value has taken place by the end of the loan term, which is probably about ten years.

For example, a house is purchased for $100,000 and carries a SAM mortgage amortized over 30 years which provides for the lender to receive 40 percent of the appreciation in value after ten years. After ten years the house is appraised for $200,000. The lender would earn $40,000 on the appreciation in value.

$$
\begin{array}{ll}
\$200,000 & \text{Appraised value after 10 years} \\
-\$100,000 & \text{Purchase price} \\
\hline
\$100,000 & \text{Appreciation} \\
\$\ 40,000 & \text{Amount due to lender (\$100,000} \times \text{.40)}
\end{array}
$$

Notice that while the monthly savings for a SAM loan over ten years is $36,360 ($303 × 120), the amount due the lender for the price appreciation is $40,000. If the borrower had purchased a home in an area that experienced greater growth rates, the difference would be even larger. This is one of the disadvantages of a SAM loan to the borrower.

Refinancing and SAMs

A borrower with a SAM mortgage will owe a large amount of money at the end of the loan term. In the preceding example, if the loan amount after ten years was $90,000, the borrower would owe the lender $130,000 ($90,000 + $40,000). The borrower could sell the property at that time and pay the lender, but in many cases the borrower may not want to sell. An alternative is to refinance. Nearly all lenders offer a guaranteed refinancing plan at the end of a SAM loan. The refinancing, however, will probably not be at preferential financing terms. In most cases the refinancing rate will be the current market rate, and the term will be the remaining length on the original loan. In the example we have been using, the lender would refinance $130,000 at current market rates for 20 years.

Other Considerations with a SAM

Property Improvements. Usually a buyer will make improvements and add amenities to the property to make living in it more desirable. With a standard mortgage there are no consequences for the lender or owner, but with a SAM it is not so clear-cut. If the owners add a $10,000 improvement, they will probably increase the value of the property. When the property is sold, how should the cost of improvements by the owners be handled in computing the amount of appreciation? To avoid problems such as this, SAMs usually have provisions that relate specifically to improvements. In most cases the cost of improvements can be deducted from the amount of appreciation.

Another problem with improvements is that the owners may try to justify them by arguing that for their own use a particular improvement is desirable but that the improvement may not add any market value to the property. For instance, an owner might add a fifth bedroom or a fourth bathroom or an elaborate sauna facility. To the lender these improvements are not economically justified and are being made because of the owner's personal reasons or taste. If substantial improvements of this type are made, they will offset much of the appreciation and thus reduce the return on the loan for the lender.

For example, the owner purchased the property for $100,000 with a SAM and agreed to allow the lender to earn 40 percent on the property appreciation. A fifth bedroom is added by the owner for $10,000 that increases the value of the property by only $2,000. The amount earned by the lender is computed below.

	Sale Without Improvement	Sale With Improvement
Purchase price	$100,000	$100,000
Market value at sale	$200,000	$202,000
Gross appreciation	$100,000	$102,000
Less cost of improvement	0	$ 10,000
Net appreciation	$100,000	$ 92,000
Amount due lender	$ 40,000	$ 36,800

Without the improvement the lender would earn $40,000 ($100,000 × .40), while with the improvement the lender earns only $36,800 ($92,000 × .40). To prevent the reduction in earnings by overimprovement, many lenders write SAMs that provide that no improvements can be made by the owner without the prior specific consent of the lender. In this case the owner would have to consult the lender who would make an appraisal and decide whether to allow the improvement.

Destruction of the Property.   Because lenders realize houses and other structures are subject to damage and destruction by wind, fire, flood and other natural causes, they protect their interest in the property by requiring the owner to carry hazard insurance. Normally the amount of coverage required is enough to cover the mortgage (although owners can increase the coverage at their option). If the property is destroyed, the insurance company pays the claim, the loan is paid off and the lender does not lose any money. With a SAM, however, the lender might recover the amount of the outstanding balance but may lose any appreciation in value. To prevent this loss, most SAMs contain a provision stating that the lender will obtain a percentage of any value left after the insurance company has paid the claim. If the property is destroyed, what is left is the land. The lender would then be entitled to a percentage of the land value. The owner could pay this out of the insurance proceeds, if the property is insured for more than the loan amount, or by selling the land.

Calculating the Appreciation Amount.   Calculating the actual amount of appreciation in the property can raise some issues that need to be clarified in the loan agreement. Various costs occur whenever purchasing or selling property. Common purchasing costs include title insurance, recording fees and attorneys' fees. Selling costs can include transfer taxes, real estate brokers' commissions and attorneys' fees. These costs are actual expenses that have to be paid by the borrower and should be included in calculating the basis in the property and ultimately the amount of appreciation.

In the example above the net appreciation with improvements was $92,000 and the amount due the lender was $36,800. The effects of including the purchase and sales costs are illustrated in the following example.

	Sale With Improvement
Purchase price	$100,000
Market value at sale	$202,000
Gross appreciation	$102,000
Less cost of improvement	$ 10,000
Less purchase costs	$ 1,000
Less sale costs	$ 14,000
Net appreciation	$ 77,000
Amount due lender	$ 30,800

The lender now receives only $30,800, a drop of $6,000. It is to the borrower's advantage to ensure that the SAM agreement specifies that the lender's amount will be based on the net appreciation and not the gross appreciation.

If the borrower sells the property the lender is not obligated to accept the net sales price as the fair market value of the property. In that case the market value would be determined by appraisal. The appraiser would be selected by the borrower and the lender from a list of appraisers. If the borrower and the lender cannot agree on an appraiser, each will select one and the market value will be the average of the two appraisals.

WHAT IS A REVERSE ANNUITY MORTGAGE?

While most homeowners are in the work force and pay a monthly mortgage payment to a lender, a growing group of owners exist who are retired and have paid off the mortgage on their homes. Their situations and needs are different, and these retired homeowners are being given more attention as their numbers grow. Older homeowners usually live on fixed monthly incomes with their home as their major asset. On paper, they have built up impressive equity in their homes that gives them an impressive net worth; in reality, they are living on small pensions and social security checks. This income is barely adequate to handle their basic expenses and may not be enough to cover rising real estate taxes, home maintenance expenses, large health care costs and other unexpected expenses. These homeowners have been struggling with an increasingly widespread problem of how to convert some of the equity built up in their home into cash to supplement their other monthly income.

One option is to sell the property, but this is not always desirable because then the sellers must find new places to live, often away from friends and neighborhoods where they are established. Another option is to refinance the property, but this gives the owners one large lump-sum payment rather than a monthly amount. Then they would have to make monthly payments on the new loan and must avoid the temptation of spending more than a prudent amount each month. An ideal loan arrangement would provide them with either a lump sum or a monthly amount without selling their home, without moving and without making monthly loan payments.

The reverse annuity mortgage (RAM) is intended to address this situation by allowing older people to retain ownership of their property and to receive at the same time a portion of their equity in cash to supplement their monthly income. The money is paid out to the borrower in monthly amounts, and there is no monthly loan payment to the lender. The loan becomes payable to the lender when the property is sold, when the borrower dies or when an agreed-upon date is reached. At the end of the loan period the borrower could sell the property and pay off the loan, refinance the house to pay off the loan or, if the property had appreciated, take out a new RAM loan. This process could be continued indefinitely.

Introduced in 1981 when the Federal Home Loan Bank Board authorized savings and loans to write them, RAMs have not been widely accepted and for the first few years were offered by only a handful of lenders.

Negative Amortization

A disadvantage to the borrower in a RAM loan is negative amortization. Each month when the borrower receives a payment, interest is charged on the amount borrowed. Because there is no monthly payment by the borrower, the interest is added to the principal. Interest on the next monthly payment, therefore, will be calculated on a balance that includes both the outstanding principal and the outstanding interest as well. The lender is actually charging interest on interest. While this is not a major concern in the initial months of the loan, it becomes significant as the loan balance increases.

Example of a RAM

A retired couple own a house with no mortgage and wish to take out a RAM loan. The house is worth $100,000, and the lender is willing to give them a loan for 80 percent of the home's value. The total loan amount is $80,000 at a rate of 10 percent, and they will receive $500 a month from the lender.

The borrowers now receive $500 a month to supplement their income. They do not have to make monthly loan payments to the lender, and they can use the equity in their home without having to sell it. The question is: How long will the loan last? Because the interest keeps accumulating, it is added to the principal. So the loan will last only until the interest plus the principal (the monthly amount paid to the couple) equal $80,000. Table 10.1 shows the term of this loan.

Surprisingly it only takes eight and one-half years for the $80,000 equity to be depleted. The rapid buildup in the amount owed is due to interest being calculated on interest. This can be seen by looking at Table 10.1. Because the interest rate on the loan is 10 percent, the first month's interest is $4 ($500 $\times$ .10 $\div$ 12). In the second month the borrower pays interest on $1,004, the amount of the payments made plus the interest from the first payment. Each month the interest amount rises and in month 84 actually is more than the $500 payments being made by the lender.

Annuity Insurance Programs and the RAM

With a RAM the borrower may be in the position of "living too long" and exhausting the equity in the property thus ending the loan and being forced to sell. Lenders tried to correct this by linking the loan to an insurance policy. The policy pays the lender interest that accrues if the borrower "outlives" the mortgage. It continues paying until the borrower dies and the property can be sold. This option has not been popular and is rare.

Disadvantages to the Lender

There are several considerations that make the RAM unattractive to the lender. First, the interest accrues but is not paid until the entire loan is due. This means the lender is getting credit for income that it is not actually receiving but may be subject to taxation. Another problem is that the house may be tied up in probate for a long time if heirs contest

TABLE 10.1: Reverse Equity Mortgage with Monthly Payment to Borrower of $500 (Maximum loan amount is $80,000, interest rate is 10%) (All amounts are rounded to the nearest dollar)

Month	Payment	Interest	Loan Balance
1	$ 500	$ 4	$ 500
2	500	8	1,004
3	500	13	1,513
4	500	17	2,025
5	500	21	2,542
6	500	26	3,063
12	500	52	6,283
18	500	81	9,667
24	500	110	13,233
30	500	141	16,962
36	500	174	20,892
42	500	209	25,021
48	500	245	29,361
54	500	283	33,923
60	500	323	38,719
66	500	365	43,753
72	500	409	49,056
78	500	455	54,623
84	500	504	60,475
90	500	555	66,626
96	500	609	73,091
102	500	666	79,885
Years = 8.5	$51,000	$80,000	$29,551

how the assets of the estate are to be divided. A third problem is that if a borrower defaults on the loan the lender might have a difficult public relations problem if the lender forecloses on an elderly couple.

WHAT IS AN INDIVIDUAL REVERSE MORTGAGE ACCOUNT?

A RAM plan that is gaining popularity is the individual reverse mortgage account or IRMA. This plan includes characteristics of both the reverse annuity mortgage and the shared appreciation mortgage. Under this plan the borrowers can receive a monthly payment for the rest of their lives or a lump-sum amount at settlement. When the house is sold or when the borrower dies, the lender receives the accumulated principal plus interest plus a percentage of the amount of appreciation in the property. The amount the owners can borrow is calculated by taking into account various factors including: the borrower's age, the current value of the house and the percentage of appreciation in the value of the house that will be given to the lender. The appreciation amount is determined from the time the loan is originated until the death of the borrower or sale of the property.

For example, a homeowner is 75 years old and has a house with no mortgage that is worth $100,000. The borrower will receive $500 a month for life, and the lender receives 100 percent of the appreciation of the house from the time the loan starts until the death of the borrower. In addition, when the borrower dies, the house is sold and the lender receives the loan balance advanced to the borrower plus 11.5 percent interest.

A risk for the lender is if the borrower outlives the actuarial tables for additional years. If the borrower in the example above lived for another 10 or 15 years, the lender would be legally bound to continue paying the $500 a month and may take a loss on the loan. This is true even if the debt exceeds the original value of the house at the time of the loan. As might be expected, the age of the borrower will significantly affect the amount of the monthly payment the lender is willing to pay. The earliest age an IRMA will start is 62. A borrower at this age with a $100,000 home might receive a maximum of $243 a month. A borrower who is 87 with a $100,000 home, however, could qualify for as much as $1,000 a month.

In determining the amount paid to the borrower, if the borrower is willing to give the lender 50 percent of the appreciation, they will receive a higher monthly payment than the borrower who will only give the lender 20 percent of the appreciation. The typical sharing ratio is 90 percent. IRMAs usually have a cap on the amount of annual appreciation due the lender. If the annual cap is 15 percent, for instance, the borrower will retain any appreciation in the value of the home in excess of 15 percent per year.

In general, the older the borrower the greater the appraised value in the house; the greater appreciation to be given the lender the larger the amount to be paid the borrower, either as a lump sum or a monthly payment.

GOVERNMENT PARTICIPATION

In an effort to help elderly homeowners take advantage of the equity in their homes the Department of Housing and Urban Development (HUD) started a program to insure home equity conversion loans. The program was authorized by the Housing and Community Development Act of 1987. Beginning in the spring of 1989 and continuing through September 30, 1991, lenders nationwide who are Federal Housing Administration (FHA) approved lenders may make a limited number of insured equity conversion loans. Initially 2,500 loans will be insured by the government, but if the market experience is favorable Congress could greatly expand the program.

The mortgages will be available to homeowners age 62 or older without regard to income level or location in the United States provided they have small mortgages or own their homes free and clear. The amount available to the borrower will depend on the interest rate, the age of the youngest borrower, the value of the house and the maximum FHA loan available for the area where the house is located.

The program will insure three different types of loan plans:

1. Tenure mortgages provide monthly payments for as long as the senior citizen occupies the house as a principal residence.
2. Term mortgages provide for payments for a fixed period of time agreed upon between the lender and the borrower—for instance, ten years from the date of closing.
3. Line of credit mortgages permit the borrower to draw out various amounts of money as needed.

Interest rates on any of the plans can be either a fixed rate or a variable rate tied to an index. The FHA will not regulate rates on the plans. HUD and the Administration on Aging will provide counseling services to assist borrowers in choosing the mortgage that best suits their needs. Borrowers will be required to discuss the transaction in detail with one of these counseling groups and are also advised to review their situation with their accountant, attorney or financial advisor before taking out a loan under any of the plans.

To illustrate the FHA loan plans, consider a homeowner who is in his mid-70s and owns debt-free a home worth $100,000. The owner could take out a term loan (guaranteeing a monthly payment for as long as he lives in the house as his principal residence) for 10 percent and receive a monthly payment of $315. The payments plus interest would accumulate over the years until he no longer used the house as his principal residence. The owner could receive a larger monthly payment and a lower interest rate by sharing a percentage of the house appreciation with the lender. By giving the lender 25 percent of all future appreciation in the house, the owner could get a loan for 8½ percent and receive a monthly payment of $357. The lender could not receive an annualized rate of return on interest plus appreciation that exceeded 20 percent. The owner could receive even higher payments with no appreciation sharing by taking out a term mortgage for five or ten years. A five-year term mortgage at 10 percent interest on the house would enable the owner to receive $690 a month, while a ten-year term would provide a monthly payment of $436.

The Federal National Mortgage Association (Fannie Mae) and the Federal Home Loan Mortgage Corporation (Freddie Mac) who buy mortgages in the secondary market have agreed to participate in the program.

RAMs Summary

RAM loans might someday be used to open up a huge new source of mortgage loans, but they currently do not have much appeal to the elderly, who tend to grow more cautious as they grow older and are reluctant to liquidate their assets. Recent variations of the RAM, such as the IRMA, and recent loan programs, such as the HUD Demonstration Project, however, will probably increase the popularity of these loans, making them a significant factor in the mortgage market.

WHAT IS A HOME EQUITY LOAN?

Real estate has traditionally been considered a nonliquid asset that could be converted to cash by going through the costly and time-consuming process of selling the property or refinancing. Today, however, through the use of a home equity loan, property can be converted to cash very quickly. Equity loans are a new source of credit for homeowners who wish to finance the purchase of large expensive items or pay off outstanding credit card debts, medical or educational expenses, home improvements or other expenses. Home equity loans are being marketed aggressively by banks, and loan volume for this type of financing has grown rapidly as consumers use it to finance everything from cars to college educations.

Home equity loans come in two varieties: the traditional second mortgage and the equity line of credit. With the traditional second mortgage the borrower receives a lump sum of money for a fixed period of time. With the home equity line of credit the lender extends a line of credit that the borrowers can use whenever they want.

There are several ways borrowers may receive their money under a home equity loan. A check can be sent to them, a deposit can be made in a savings or checking account maintained with the lender or another financial institution or a book of drafts that the borrower can use up to their credit limit.

For example, a couple's home is worth $125,000 and has a $40,000 mortgage balance. The couple wish to borrow money to send their daughter to college. A lender may be willing to give them an equity line of credit based on the following typical terms. The loan can be up to 70 percent of the equity in the home. In this case that will be a maximum of $47,500.

$$
\begin{array}{ll}
\$87,500 = \$125,000 \times .70 & \\
-\ 40,000 & \text{Less the Existing Mortgage Balance} \\
\hline
\$47,500 & \text{Maximum Loan Amount}
\end{array}
$$

The minimum equity loan is $5,000 and the minimum loan advance is $1,000. The borrower may have to pay various loan fees that could include a credit report fee, title search charges and points. The loan interest rate is set at 1.5 percent over the prime rate, and the lender has the right to change the rate of interest every three months.

Advantages of Equity Loans

Home equity loans allow the borrowers to convert the equity in their homes into cash relatively quickly and with little up-front costs.

Because the default rate on loans secured by the borrower's residence is lower, the interest rate on home equity loans is lower than the rate on consumer credit.

As a result of the 1986 tax law, interest charged on consumer debt is no longer tax deductible. However, interest charged on home equity loans, up to a loan limit of $100,000, is still tax deductible.

Disadvantages of Equity Loans

The home equity loan is secured by the borrower's residence. If the borrower defaults, the lender could foreclose on the property. This can become a sensitive situation for the lender. Suppose a borrower with a $1,000 balance on a home equity loan becomes unemployed and defaults on the loan. The lender may or may not foreclose on the property. The answer depends on the circumstances of each case and the policies of the lender.

The easy availability of money using a home equity loan may be detrimental for some people. Credit limits on home equity loans can be substantially higher than credit cards, and it is possible that people who overextend themselves on credit cards may be inclined to do the same with home equity loans. The temptation to borrow more and more may be even greater than with credit cards because the monthly payments are likely to be low.

The interest rate on home equity loans is usually variable and tied to the prime rate. This rate can be volatile and when it changes the monthly payment changes.

Home equity loans usually have very high interest caps. If rates rise the borrowers may end up paying much more for the loan than they anticipated.

Federal Regulation

Many borrowers who have arranged equity loans found that the loan agreements allowed the lenders to unilaterally change most of the terms of the loans at any time. Under many of the loan agreements the lender could change the index used for variable rate loans, raise the rates and accelerate the payments. Some lenders tied the interest rate to their own prime giving them complete control over the index, and many have no caps on the rates.

In response to consumer complaints, Congress has proposed new federal guidelines on equity lines of credit and second mortgages. The proposed legislation would require lenders to make full disclosure on home equity loans. Lenders would have to provide information on the annual interest percentage rate, any fees associated with the loan and a description of repayment options when the borrower applies for the loan. Other consumer protections in the bill include:

- prohibiting the lender from unilaterally changing the loan terms,
- requiring the use of publicly available indexes that are outside the control of the lender,
- restricting the lender from calling the loan before the end of the loan term (lenders could only call in the loan for valid reasons such as fraud or default by the borrower),
- requiring the lender to refund application fees, if the lender changes the terms after an application is submitted but before the loan is started.

WHAT IS A GRANNIE MAE?

The Grannie Mae is another method for helping "house rich" and "cash poor" older homeowners to unlock the equity in their homes while allowing them to continue living in the home. A Grannie Mae involves the sale of a home to the owner's child or children. The buyer then rents the home back to the parent at fair market value. The parent receives a lifetime leaseback guarantee on the home and a monthly payment for life that is funded by the proceeds of the sale of the home.

Because the Grannie Mae requires the sale of the property to a child or group of children, the lender never gains title or is put in the position of having to evict the elderly resident. Instead the lender's involvement is limited to issuing a mortgage for the child/investor. The elderly residents are never in any danger of being forced to leave their house because they rent the property at fair market value with a lifetime lease. Even if the children sell the home or can no longer meet the mortgage payments and the lender forecloses, the lease remains in effect.

The child/investor can take tax deductions on depreciation, repairs and maintenance expenses on the house because it is income-producing property. These expenses wouldn't be deductible if the parent owned the home.

The sale proceeds are invested with an insurance company, and the monthly rent is paid directly to the child/investor and an annuity to the elderly person for the rest of his or her life. The annuity could be structured to increase at a predetermined rate each year to cover increases in rental costs. The amount of the annuity is based on the total amount of the investment and the elderly person's age and sex. For example, the annuity for a 55-year-old man is structured to pay out for 22 years. For a 55-year-old woman it will pay out for 26 years. And for a 55-year-old couple it will pay out for 30 years. If the person dies before the payout period is over, the balance is remitted to the estate. If, however, the person outlives the estimated payout period, the annuity continues to pay. The following example depicts the advantage of a Grannie Mae annuity plan for a 55-year-old widower who sells his home to a child/investor.

Example of a Grannie Mae Annuity

Assumptions: Sales price of the home is $100,000 with no outstanding mortgage. There are $4,400 in closing costs leaving the seller $95,600 to invest in an annuity.

55-Year-Old Widower—22-Year Annuity

$ 772	Monthly Annuity
$ 500	Less Monthly Rent Paid to the Child/Investor
$ 100	Plus Monthly Real Estate Tax to be Paid by the Child/Investor
$ 372	Additional Monthly Income
$98,208	Additional Income Over the 22 Years

In this example the widower will receive $372 of additional monthly income from his home that he can spend on living costs.

Disadvantages of Grannie Maes

Like all other types of creative real estate financing arrangements Grannie Maes may not be appropriate for everyone. Disadvantages of Grannie Maes include the following:

- Negative cash flow for the child/investor. The rental payments paid to the child/investor seldom cover the mortgage payments. This means that there will probably be a monthly cash outlay by the child/investor. The child/investor does receive some tax advantages associated with owning investment property that reduce the after-tax loss.
- Higher fees. Lenders usually charge a higher fee for Grannie Maes than they do for conventional loans. The fee may be 1 or 2 points higher for a Grannie Mae.
- Partnership problems. If more than one child owns the house, they may always have the potential problems of deciding who will pay for major repairs or what to do if one of the children needs cash for a personal emergency.

SELF-QUIZ: EQUITY CONVERSION LOANS

1. List some disadvantages to borrowers for a reverse annuity mortgage.

2. How do shared appreciation mortgages differ from conventional mortgages?

3. List some disadvantages to lenders for a reverse annuity mortgage.

4. List any advantages to borrowers for a shared appreciation mortgage.

5. How does an IRMA plan differ from a regular reverse annuity mortgage?

6. List any advantages to lenders for a shared appreciation mortgage.

7. List any advantages to borrowers for a home equity loan.

8. To what extent can a taxpayer deduct interest for a home equity loan?

ANSWERS TO SELF-QUIZ: EQUITY CONVERSION LOANS

1. The common disadvantages to borrowers in a reverse annuity mortgage are negative amortization and the choices faced by the borrowers if they "live too long" and are forced to sell the property.

2. Shared appreciation mortgages differ from conventional mortgages by: rate (which is lower than conventional mortgages), term (which is shorter than conventional mortgages) and the use of property appreciation to increase the loan return to the lender.

3. The common disadvantages to lenders in a reverse annuity mortgage are: the house may be tied up in probate, accrued interest income may have to be recognized while not yet received, the lender may be forced to foreclose on elderly couples.

4. The major advantage to borrowers with a shared appreciation mortgage is the lower interest rate charged by the lender. This may enable the borrower to qualify for a loan they would not have been given under a conventional mortgage.

5. The IRMA plan combines features of both reverse annuity mortgages and shared appreciation loans. The lender receives a portion of the appreciation of the property as well as the interest on the loan and the borrowers do not have to repay the loan until they die or sell the property. They do not have to worry about being forced out of their homes if they outlive the loan.

6. If the property is located in an area that experiences rapid increases in appreciation in value the lender will realize a high return on the loan. Also, because the lender charges a lower interest rate on the shared appreciation loan, the lender may be able to make the loan to the borrower whereas the lender could not under a conventional loan that carries a high rate.

7. There are two primary advantages of home equity loans for borrowers: a lower interest rate than consumer credit and tax deductibility of interest on the loan.

8. Interest on home equity loans can be deducted by borrowers on their tax returns on loans up to $100,000.

Glossary of Financing Terms

Acceleration clause A clause in a mortgage or trust deed that calls all outstanding sums due in the event of certain specified occurrences such as default, demolition, assignment or sale of the property, or any impairments to the mortgage security. To be enforceable, the clause and all its conditions must be stated in the original agreement. See also due-on-sale clause.

Accrued interest The interest payable for the period of time that has elapsed since the previous fully paid period.

Adjustable mortgage loan (AML) The recently authorized name for mortgage loans offered by federal savings and loan associations secured on one- to four-family dwellings on which the interest rate charged is periodically adjustable upwards or downwards. Rate fluctuations must follow the movement of a verifiable economic index not under the control of the lender; for example, six-month Treasury bills. Interest rate changes in AMLs are implemented by (1) changes in the periodic payment amount, (2) changes in the principal loan balance, (3) changes in the term of the loan, or (4) any combination of the three. Other AML variables include how often rate changes are made, whether payment caps are used, how much negative amortization is permitted, how much extension of the term is allowed and how much fluctuation is allowed in the interest rate.

Adjustable-rate mortgage (ARM) The recently authorized name for residential mortgage loans having a periodically adjustable interest rate offered by nationally chartered banks. Similar to the adjustable mortgage loan (AML), with slight differences with regard to interest change caps, negative amortization and loan term. See also variable-rate mortgage and renegotiable rate mortgage.

Adjusted basis The original basis of an asset, plus the costs of improvements, minus the expenses of depreciation, depletion, amortization or other loss. Adjusted basis is used for tax purposes and for deriving capital gains. The latter are obtained by subtracting the adjusted basis at the time of a sale from the net proceeds of the sale.

Agreement for deed See contract for deed.

Alienation clause See acceleration clause, due-on-sale clause.

All-inclusive trust deed (AITD) (also called overriding or overlapping trust deed) See wraparound.

167

Amortization   Repayment of a loan in periodic installments of principal and/or interest. At the end of the loan term both interest and principal will have been paid in full.

Annual percentage rate (APR)   Total finance charges—including fees, interest rate, points and other charges—expressed as a percentage of the total amount of the loan. Must be disclosed to borrower under federal Truth-in-Lending Law.

Annuity   A series of fixed-sum payments paid in a specified number of payment periods, usually monthly or annually.

Appreciation   An increase in the value of real or personal property above and beyond the value of improvements on such property.

Arbitrage   The spread, or difference, between a given set of interest rates, expressed in points. For example, in a wraparound loan, the arbitrage is the difference between the seller's loan to the senior mortgagee and the buyer's loan to the seller. If the seller's loan is 10 percent and the wraparound note is 12 percent, the seller enjoys an arbitrage of 2 points. Arbitrage can be positive income as in the above example, or it can be negative income (loss), as when the above situation is reversed.

Assessed value   The value of real property established for the purpose of assessing real property taxes.

Asset   An item having value. In accounting, assets have a specific, quantified value at any time and are summarized on a balance sheet along with the creditor's claims to the assets (liabilities) and the owner's claim against the remainder (net worth).

Assignment   The transfer of rights or interests in a property by an assignor to an assignee. Nonassignment clauses in contracts expressly limit the right of transfer of the contract.

Assumption   The financing technique wherein a buyer assumes the seller's existing mortgage loan and its obligations for payment. Usually involves a credit check and assumption fee by the lender. May require lender approval. See also due-on-sale clause.

Assumption clause   A clause in a mortgage note or deed that sets forth the lender's conditions and terms for the transfer of a mortgage to another mortgagor. The two concerns of the clause are: (1) the seller's continued liability and (2) possible renegotiation of the terms of the mortgage.

Balloon payment   The final payment of a loan, usually substantially larger than previous installments, which repays the debt in full.

Basis   A quantified value of an asset determined at the time the asset was acquired by its owner. In very simple cases, the basis of an asset is the cash paid for it, or its cost. Deriving the basis of assets, however, can be more complicated, as in the case of gifts, inheritances and real estate exchanges. Professional advice should be obtained when establishing an asset's basis.

Basis point   One-hundredth of one percent (.01 percent). Used to describe the change in value or market price of money assets, including mortgages. Also used to describe changes in yield. Do not confuse with a discount point (1 percent of face value of loan).

Biweekly mortgage   A loan that provides 26 payments a year with the size of the payments equal to one-half of the usual monthly payment. The borrower's equity builds rapidly with this type of loan.

Blanket mortgage   A mortgage loan secured by more than one property pledged as collateral. For example, a homeowner wishing to purchase two adjacent residences may obtain one mortgage by pledging both properties as collateral.

Blended-rate mortgage   See consolidated-rate mortgage.

Bridge loan (also called swing loan and interim financing)   A loan or loan offer, usually of short duration, that is taken out on a property and applied toward the purchase of another property prior to the sale of the first property. The bridge loan can be used to offset the sale of a residence by having the seller named as beneficiary or lienholder of the buyer's junior mortgage (the bridge loan) or trust deed. If the buyer's house is sold prior to or concurrent with the seller's house, the bridge loan can be cashed out before ever being executed (bridge loan option). The bridge loan and bridge loan option can alleviate the timing problem of the buyer's need to close on his or her home before buying another residence.

Builder contribution programs   Financial assistance programs wherein the builder contributes funds toward the homebuyer's debt obligation over a given time period. Can increase the homebuyer's mortgage eligibility and enable the builder to sell the home at less cost to himself or herself than would result from lowering the home's price to the point at which a buyer could qualify otherwise. See also buydown plans.

Buydown plans   Home financing arrangements that provide for mortgage payments to the lender by other parties as well as the buyer. The contributions made by other parties to the buyer's monthly payments reduce the interest amounts that the buyer pays on the mortgage balance. Hence the buyer, in effect, pays a lower interest rate on the loan; the loan's interest rate to the borrower is "bought down." Buydown programs have recently been accepted for purchase by FNMA if certain terms are met. See also builder contribution programs.

Call provision   See acceleration clause.

Capital gain (loss)   The positive or negative difference between the adjusted basis of an asset and the net proceeds resulting from its sale. Capital gains and losses are categorized as long-term (owned more than 12 months) and short-term (owned less than 12 months), and carry different tax consequences. One hundred percent of long-term gains and short-term gains are taxable as ordinary income. Long-term losses, on the other hand, are only 50 percent *deductible* from ordinary income (net of capital gains), at a rate not exceeding $3,000 per year. Short-term losses are fully deductible every year, with $3,000 again the maximum annual deduction.

Cash to loan   A method of acquiring property wherein a buyer assumes the seller's mortgage and pays the seller cash for the remaining balance.

Cloud (on title)   A claim or encumbrance against the title to a property that has the potential of impairing the property's marketability.

Collateral   Assets that are pledged to secure repayment of a loan.

Co-maker   A second party who signs a note with the borrower in order to increase the security of a loan. The co-maker then becomes jointly liable for repayment of the loan.

Compound interest   See interest.

Compounding   The arithmetic process of deriving the end-value of a payment or series of payments when compound interest is used.

Conditional sales contract   See contract for deed.

Consolidated-rate mortgage   A refinancing mortgage, typically offered by lending institutions, wherein a new loan is created carrying an interest rate that reflects the average rate between the old loan and that of a new loan, if it were to be issued at market interest rates. The WAMM (see weighted average money mortgage) also takes into account the outstanding balance and the amount of new money to be advanced. Thus, generally speaking, if an old $20,000 loan at ten percent were averaged with a new $10,000 loan at 15 percent, the resulting WAMM would be a $30,000 loan at 11.7 percent interest.

$$\frac{20,000 \times 10\% + 30,000 \times 15\%}{\$30,000}$$

Contract for deed (also called conditional sales contract, agreement for deed, installment sales contract, land contract, real estate contract)   A method of transferring title to real property wherein the seller (vendor) is paid principal and interest, or interest only, by the buyer (vendee) for a specific period of time. At the end of the loan term the balance of principal and unpaid interest are paid to the seller, who then deeds the property to the buyer. Under the contract for deed, the seller holds legal title to the property and the buyer is granted equitable title and possession. Widely used when a minimum amount of cash is available.

Conventional loan   A term describing the traditional fixed-rate, fixed-term, amortized mortgage loan that is not FHA-insured or VA-guaranteed. (Can be offered by private companies or investors.)

Conveyance   The transfer of interest in real property by means of a deed.

Cross-defaulting clause   A clause in a junior mortgage that specifies that a default on the senior mortgage triggers a default on the junior mortgage.

Debt service   The amount of money needed to meet the periodic payments of a loan, including principal and interest.

Deed of trust (trust deed)   A legal document that transfers title to property to a trustee as security for a debt obligation of the trustor (borrower) to the beneficiary (lender). Differs from mortgage insofar as a third party holds title and reconveys it to the trustor upon satisfaction of the obligation.

Default   Failure to meet a contractual obligation when due.

Deficiency judgment   A judgment levied against the borrower personally for the balance of a mortgage debt when a foreclosure sale fails to generate funds sufficient to satisfy the debt's outstanding balance.

Depreciation   The gradual reduction in value of an asset. For tax and accounting purposes, depreciation refers to a deductible business expense on capital assets that is spread over the life of the assets. Ideally, this tax credit provides the incentive for the business to accumulate capital to replace the asset once it has lost its value. In practice, however, depreciation is a tax deduction that generates funds for any purpose. In addition, the "life" of the depreciable asset is somewhat arbitrary because an asset may in fact appreciate. To qualify for depreciation, the asset must be ruled depreciable. Land and nonincome-producing property are not depreciable.

Discounting   The process of determining the present value of a deposit or series of deposits received at a certain time(s) in the future. A discount is the amount a mortgage has been reduced from its face value to its present cash value. Discounting a loan increases its effective yield to the holder/investor.

Discount points   One percent of the face amount of a loan. Discount points are charged by lenders to raise the yield on below-market interest rate loans to a competitive level. Each face amount point deducted from a loan effectively raises its yield, or interest rate, $\frac{1}{8}$ of 1 percent. For example, a $50,000 loan discounted 10 points bears a new face value of $45,000. If the same loan yielded 10 percent, the new yield would raise 10 points $\times$ $\frac{1}{8}$ percent, or 1.25 percent, to 11.25 percent.

Disintermediation   The act of consumers/depositors withdrawing their savings from banks, savings and loan associations and similar institutions in order to invest these funds directly in stocks, bonds, money market funds and other investments. Occurs when substantially higher yields than institutions can offer are available and easily accessible to consumers. Reduces institutional funds available for loans, for example, mortgage money when disintermediation occurs with savings and loan associations.

Due-on-sale clause   A form of acceleration clause that specifically calls a mortgage loan due—at the lender's option—upon the sale or transfer of the property. The lender's primary concern with a due-on-sale clause is to renegotiate the interest rates if they have increased significantly since the loan's origination date. See also federal preemption.

Effective interest rate   The actual rate or yield of a loan, regardless of the rate stated in the note. Applies particularly to the resulting yield from a mortgage that has been discounted. (See also nominal interest rate.)

Equity   The market value of a property to the owner less all lien amounts outstanding against it. Equity is usually estimated by subtracting debts owed on the property from the property's estimated market value.

Equity participation agreement (EPA)   A mortgage financing arrangement involving a third-party investor who joins with the borrower to finance a (residential) property. The investor/participant's involvement can have the impact of reducing the homebuyer's borrowing needs or of lowering the effective interest rate. The investor can also share in the monthly payment, if this is in the agreement. In return, the investor shares the equitable interest in the property and a percentage of the appreciation. Not to be confused with SAMs. See also shared appreciation mortgage.

Escalator clause   Clause in a loan agreement that sets forth provisions for increases in payments or interest on the basis of some economic index (e.g., T-bill rates) or prescribed schedule. Usually escalator clauses supplant or eliminate the need for prepayment penalties.

Escrow   A disinterested third-party agent who holds and releases money or documents in accordance with instructions given by the parties to the escrow. When the conditions of the escrow have been satisfied, the funds in escrow are delivered.

Fair Housing Law   Title VII of the Civil Rights Act, prohibiting discrimination in residential housing on the basis of race, religion, color, sex, familial status, handicap or national origin. Does not apply to commercial or industrial properties.

Federal Home Loan Bank (FHLB)   The federal regulatory agency that oversees all federal savings and loan associations. The FHLB's principal activity is managing association liquidity and providing reserve funds for members, particularly in local areas where there are temporary shortfalls of lendable funds.

Federal Home Loan Bank Board (FHLBB)   The principal group of regulators within FHLB that issues rulings on regulations and policies.

Federal Home Loan Mortgage Corporation (FHLMC, Freddie Mac; renamed The Mortgage Corporation)   A federal agency formed to purchase mortgages in the secondary market from insured banks and FHLB member savings and loan associations. The Mortgage Corporation also purchases VA and FHA loans. The purpose of the agency is to provide a means whereby lending institutions can sell their mortgages, maintain their liquidity from the proceeds and recycle available funds at market rates. FHLMC cycles its own portfolio by issuing mortgage-backed securities to the general public. Lenders wishing to sell loans to Freddie Mac must use approved forms and follow established procedures and processing guidelines.

Federal Housing Authority (FHA)   A federal agency under the Department of Housing and Urban Development that was formed to standardize home financing and stabilize the mortgage market. FHA's principal activity is insuring approved lending institutions against mortgage loan defaults. Lenders must in turn follow FHA credit guidelines and restrictions. FHA neither buys nor originates loans.

Federal National Mortgage Association (FNMA, Fannie Mae)   A private secondary mortgage market organization regulated by the federal government. FNMA specializes in the purchase of VA and FHA loans but also sometimes buys conventional loans. Its purpose, like that of other secondary mortgage market entities, is to buy qualified loans with bond-generated funds, thereby protecting lender liquidity and stimulating the recycling of mortgage funds. FNMA also stimulates lending by offering lenders commitments to buy as-yet unmade loans that will qualify under one of its commitment programs.

Federal preemption Regulatory or statutory actions taken by federal regulatory authorities, for instance the Office of the Comptroller of the Currency and the Federal Home Loan Bank Board, that expressly limit or overrule the provisions and/or enforceability of state law. For example, the OCC and FHLBB recently preempted state usury laws under certain conditions.

Federal Reserve Board (the banker's bank) A government institution that controls and regulates the operation of all nationally chartered banks.

Federal Savings and Loan Insurance Corporation (FSLIC) The parallel to FDIC, FSLIC insures deposits at member savings and loan associations.

Fiduciary Someone in a position of trust and confidence who acts accordingly as an agent for another.

Fifteen-year mortgage A variation of the fixed-rate mortgage. The interest rate and loan payments remain constant throughout the loan but the loan is paid off in only 15 years. It is usually available at an interest rate lower than a long-term loan rate.

Finance fee See origination fee.

Financial Institutions Deregulation Act A law enacted in March, 1980, authorizing the deregulation of several aspects of the banking and financing industry, in particular the deregulation of interest and earnings limits and the approval for savings and loans to have trust powers and make more consumer loans. One effect of the FIDA law is a lessening of the distinction between banks and savings and loan associations.

Financial intermediary A financial institution that acts as an investor for depositors and a lender for borrowers. Can be described as a loan "retailer" (lends small sums to borrowers) and an investment agent for depositors (pays yields on deposits).

First mortgage A legal document pledging collateral for a loan that was recorded as such before any other mortgages were recorded. Has priority over mortgages subsequently recorded.

Fixed-rate mortgage A mortgage in which the interest rate and monthly payments remain constant over the life of the loan.

Government National Mortgage Association (GNMA) A government agency that participates in the secondary mortgage market. It sponsors mortgage-backed securities programs backed by FHA and VA loans.

Graduated payment adjustable mortgage loan (GPAML) A new financing alternative that is essentially the adjustable mortgage loan's version of the GPM. Provides a graduated payment schedule for the principal and interest, with a variable interest factor built into the payment schedule and/or term and/or principal balance owed. See also graduated payment mortgage.

Graduated payment mortgage (GPM) Also known as the FHA 245 GPM, the financing method in which, under pre-established guidelines, the payments on a fixed-rate and -term, fully amortized mortgage are reduced in the beginning years of the mortgage. Unpaid interest is then added to the principal balance, and payments are increased annually to gradually retire the interest accrued. The graduated payment schedules eventually level off to a fixed payment for the remainder of the term. A standard loan for families with low but increasing incomes.

Grannie Mae   A method for older homeowners to unlock the equity in their property. It involves the sale of the home to their children, who then give a lifetime lease to their parents with a monthly payment.

Gross income   Income generated before any expenses have been subtracted. Often called "the top line."

Growing equity mortgage (GEM)   A mortgage loan where the mortgagor makes extra principal payments every year in addition to the regular PI payments for the purpose of accelerating equity buildup.

Guaranteed loan   A general term for a loan that is backed by payment guarantee from someone other than the borrower.

Home equity loan   A loan based on the accumulated equity in the property. Can be either a lump sum or an equity line of credit, and is usually a junior mortgage.

Housing and Urban Development, Department of (HUD)   The federal department that manages various housing programs throughout the nation; also the parent regulator of FHA and GNMA.

Hypothecation   The pledging of a real property as mortgage security without surrendering possession of it.

Index   The measure used by the lender to determine how much the interest rate on an ARM will change over time.

Individual reverse mortgage account (IRMA)   A mortgage plan that includes characteristics of both a reverse annuity mortgage and a shared appreciation loan. Borrowers receive cash from the lender and when the borrower dies or the house is sold the lender receives the principal, accumulated interest and part of the property appreciation.

Installment sale   A sale in which the seller spreads the receipt of the sale proceeds over two or more years. Installment sales—if certain provisions are met—qualify for deferred capital gains tax treatment.

Insured loan   A mortgage or other loan that is insured against default in exchange for a premium paid by someone other than the borrower.

Interest   Money paid, or charged, or accrued as rent for the use of money.
   Add-on interest. The method of computing interest wherein interest is charged on the entire sum of money over the term of the loan, regardless of any paydowns of principal during the loan term.
   Compound interest. Interest that is computed each period on the original principal as well as the accrued interest on the principal over the previous period.
   Simple interest. Interest that is charged only on the principal balance outstanding.

Interest rate   Interest that is expressed as a percentage of the principal balance, usually the annual percentage.

Interim financing   See bridge loan.

Involuntary lien   See lien.

Judgment lien   See lien.

Judicial sale   A foreclosure sale of property by the court, effected to satisfy a mortgage debt.

Junior mortgage/lien   A mortgage with a right or lien priority that is subordinate to another lien on the same property. The priority is determined by the chronological order in which the liens were recorded. The junior lien is less secure than the first lien or mortgage because upon default the first lien must be satisfied before the junior lien. Junior mortgages typically carry a higher interest rate because of the greater risk involved.

Land contract   See contract for deed.

Lease option (also called lease with option to buy)   A lease that allows a tenant the right to buy the leased property if and when certain conditions are met. Usually the rent payments are applied in part or in full to the purchase price if the tenant opts to buy.

Leverage   The use of borrowed money that, when coupled with one's cash or equity in an investment, increases the investor's return over and above the cost of funds and what the cash alone would have yielded. Reverse leverage in turn occurs when the cost of borrowed funds exceeds the net yield from the investment.

Lien   A legal claim upon the property of another as security for a debt obligation.
Involuntary lien. A lien imposed by law, usually for delinquent taxes.
Judgment lien. A lien placed upon a debtor as a result of a court decree.
Voluntary lien. A lien placed willingly on a property by the owner.

Liquidity   The cash position of an individual or business as it relates to the ability to pay obligations due. Synonymous with degree of cash available. A liquid asset or investment is one that can be converted readily into cash in an amount nearly equivalent to the investment's market value.

Loan constant   The percentage figure in loan constant tables that is used to tell an investor how much money is needed monthly or annually to amortize a loan—of any amount—given a fixed interest rate and period. To determine the cash needed to amortize a loan, the principal amount of the loan is multiplied by the monthly or annual loan constant.

Loan-to-value ratio (LTV)   The ratio between a mortgage loan and the market or appraised value, whichever is less. Used as a standard to measure the borrower's vested interest in the property and his or her consequent willingness to repay the loan. The higher the loan-to-value ratio, the riskier the loan because the borrower has less to lose upon default.

Lock-in clause/provision   A prepayment clause in a mortgage loan that expressly forbids prepayment of a loan in excess of the periodic payment. Practice common to lending policy of insurance companies.

Low-docs   A borrower making a higher down payment (20 percent to 30 percent) may have the loan approved without all or some of the usual credit checks, job and income verifications and tax statements.

Margin   The number of percentage points the lender adds to the index rate to calculate the ARM rate at each adjustment.

Market value   The highest price a buyer would pay for a property, assuming the property has a reasonable period of exposure to the market and that both buyer and seller are informed and not under duress.

Maturity   The date on which an obligation such as a real estate note comes due and payable.

Mortgage   A legal document that conditionally pledges a designated property as security for a loan. See also trust deed.

Mortgage banker   Represent funding sources such as life insurance companies and pension investors. Mortgage bankers locate borrowers, close the loans, and then service them for a fee.

Mortgage broker   An intermediary agent who, for a fee, brings together borrowers and lenders to effect loan transactions. Mortgage brokers also service loans and originate loans on behalf of lenders.

Mortgage constant   See loan constant.

Mortgagee   The party in a mortgage transaction who holds the mortgage as security for a loan, usually the lender.

Mortgagor   The party who gives the mortgage as security for debt; the owner of the debt collateral.

Negative amortization   A loan balance that increases over time rather than decreasing. The result of monthly payments that are smaller than the interest accrued; the difference is subsequently added to the balance of the loan.

Negative spread   The condition of a financial institution in which the aggregate loan portfolio's yield is less than the aggregate interest payable to depositors. Negative spread, usually expressed in percentage points, causes liquidity problems.

Net yield   The portion of an investment's gross yield that remains after all costs have been deducted.

No-docs   See low-docs.

Nominal interest rate   The interest rate stated on the face of a contract, as opposed to the effective interest rate that results from discounting.

Note   A debt instrument stating the loan amount, its interest rate, the term and method of repayment and the promise to repay.

Notice of default   A written notice to a borrower of default on a loan. Frequently there is a clause in a contract for deed requiring the vendor (seller) to give notice of default and specifying a grace period for payment of the delinquent amount.

Office of the Comptroller of the Currency (OCC)   The federal entity that regulates nationally chartered banks; the parallel organization to the Federal Home Loan Bank Board.

Origination fee   Fee charged by the mortgagee for originating a mortgage loan. Covers credit inspection, appraisal fees, inspection of property, loan application processing and other administrative costs.

Payment cap   A limit set on what an adjustable rate mortgage loan's periodic (usually monthly) payments can be. Payment caps may or may not be provided for in the mortgage. Exists as a device to maintain a loan's affordability despite increases in the adjustable interest rate. When payment caps are present, accrued interest is added to the principal, which may result in negative amortization.

PITI   An abbreviation for principal, interest, taxes and insurance, commonly synonymous with the borrower's monthly payment on an amortized loan plus taxes and insurance paid monthly to an impound or escrow account.

Points   See discount points.

Prepayment penalty/charge   Similar to an early withdrawal charge; a levy against the borrower who repays a loan prior to its maturity. Commonly prescribed in an original loan agreement's prepayment clause, the penalty is designed to offset loan charges and loan servicing not recouped by the lender through interest earnings. Not permitted in adjustable rate mortgages after the first adjustment period.

Present value (PV)   Stated in terms of one dollar, PV represents today's value of an amount of money that is not to be received until some time in the future. Can be understood as the current value of money less the compounded interest that would have been earned over the time period during which the money was not received.

Primary mortgage market   The market in which loans are made by institutions or investors directly to borrowers.

Principal   (1) The amount of a loan upon which interest is charged. (2) One of the main parties in a transaction, such as the seller of a home.

Private mortgage insurance (PMI) An insurance policy that protects the lender against losses up to the policy limits on a defaulted mortgage loan.

Promissory note See note.

Purchase-money mortgage The most common form of seller financing; a mortgage loan given to the buyer by the seller as part of the property's purchase price. Usually given in order to bridge the difference between a buyer's down payment and a new first mortgage.

Qualification In real estate finance, the process of obtaining a sufficient amount of information from a buyer and seller to determine the seller's financial objectives and the buyer's purchasing capacity.

Qualified monthly income (QMI) The amount of a borrower's monthly income necessary to qualify for a loan of a given amount at a given interest rate for a given term. Used as a lender's standard to determine how much a borrower can afford to borrow without creating undue risk or hardship. In most cases a QMI must be three to four times the monthly principal and interest payments on the loan.

Rapid payoff mortgage (RPM) An amortized mortgage loan where the loan term is significantly shorter than the customary 25- to 30-year term.

Real Estate Settlement Procedures Act (RESPA) A federal law requiring that all closing costs on a first mortgage be disclosed to the buyer and the seller of a one- to four-family residential property.

Recasting Rewriting a loan with new terms to accommodate a borrower threatened with default. A recast loan may lose priority over previously recorded junior liens.

Reconveyance Transferring title to a property from its present owner to the immediately preceding owner. A necessary practice in title theory states, where the trustor conveys title to the trustee as debt security. Upon satisfaction of the debt, the trustee reconveys the title to the trustor.

Refinancing-to-sell The practice whereby a seller refinances his or her home to maximize its loan-to-value ratio. Thus, when the property is offered for sale, the buyer may be able to assume the loan and purchase the home with a minimum amount of cash.

Regulation Z See Truth-in-Lending Law.

Renegotiable-rate mortgage (RRM) An adjustable-rate mortgage whose recent authorization has since been supplanted by the adjustable mortgage loan (AML) authorization. Because of this, the characteristics and limitations originally established for the RRM may or may not be allowed now. In general, the RRM is a first mortgage with an interest rate that is renegotiable every three to five years. Prior to the new AML regulations, the RRM had a nonextendable term, a maximum interest ceiling (5 percent) over the entire loan term, and an annual interest increase maximum equivalent to ½ percent. These restrictions no longer apply, although it is still possible that RRM-type loans can be made under AML regulations and restrictions. See also adjustable mortgage loan.

Return on investment (ROI) The net yield on an investment's equity, usually expressed as a percentage for a given time period.

Reverse annuity mortgage A mortgage arrangement established for elderly homeowners wherein the mortgagee makes equity advance payments to the mortgagors, then recoups the debt from the proceeds of the sale of the owners' property or estate.

Rollover note A short-term note that can be renewed upon maturity if certain conditions and terms are met. A debt instrument coming into use with adjustable-rate mortgages.

Second mortgage   A mortgage that ranks immediately behind the first mortgage in priority.

Secondary mortgage market   The market in which already existing mortgages are bought and sold. Dominated by major agencies and organizations, which buy discounted mortgages in order to (1) generate a yield for investors, (2) provide liquidity to mortgage sellers and (3) redistribute funds from cash-rich to cash-poor localities.

Security   Something of value deposited or pledged to secure the repayment of a debt.

Seller carryback   An idiom commonly used in real estate for whenever the seller, acting as a lender, holds or "carries back" a first or second mortgage note from the buyer. An example would be a purchase-money mortgage.

Shared appreciation mortgage (SAM) (also called appreciation participation mortgage and equity kicker)   A first mortgage loan offered by a lender to a homebuyer at a lower-than-market interest rate in return for a percentage share in the property's appreciation. In practice, many forms of the SAM are possible—and as many serious legal questions can arise. The key variables in the SAM are: (1) the degree of mortgagee participation in increased value, (2) the degree of mortgagee liability should the property depreciate, (3) the borrower's right of alienation during the loan period, (4) when the appreciation is payable and (5) the quantitative relationship between the degree of participation and the degree to which the interest rate is reduced. The SAM as generally formulated does not confer a shared title interest, as in a joint tenancy, nor does it confer an interest in the original basis of the home at time of purchase. Do not confuse with equity participation mortgages, which involve a third-party investor.

"Subject to" mortgage   A mortgage that confers equitable title on a purchaser without liability for payment of the mortgage note. Upon default, however, the mortgagor could lose his or her equity and the property in a foreclosure sale. The courts cannot order a deficiency judgment upon the mortgagor when there is a "subject to" mortgage. The "subject to" mortgage is similar to a contract for deed sale insofar as the mortgagor's liability is limited to his or her paid-in equity.

Swing loan   See bridge loan.

Term loan/mortgage   Nonamortized loan for a specified period of time in which interest only is paid per the agreement and the entire principal becomes due in full at maturity.

Trust deed   See deed of trust.

Trustee   The third-party holder of the trust for real property as security to the trustor's debt obligation.

Trustor   The borrower whose property is held by the trustee until the debt obligation is satisfied.

Truth-in-Lending Law   Enacted in 1969 under the Consumer Credit Protection Act; implemented by Regulation 7 of the Federal Reserve Board. Ensures disclosure of credit costs by lenders, including disclosure of all fees and charges associated with a loan but separate from its quoted interest rate.

Underwriting   The financial analysis of a borrower made to determine the borrower's ability to repay a loan. Also used to describe the act of purchasing securities for the purpose of reselling or distributing them to investors.

Usury   Charging more interest on a loan than the legal limit. Usury laws vary widely from state to state and in certain instances have been preempted by federal regulations and rulings.

VA-insured loan   A loan made by a VA-approved lender at rates and under conditions established by the Veterans Administration. If the conditions are followed and the borrower has obtained his or her certificate of eligibility, the Veterans Administration will guarantee the lender the first $27,500 of the loan in the event of default.

Variable-rate mortgage (VRM) (also called variable interest rate loan [VIR])   The VRM, like the renegotiable-rate mortgage, is one of the new experiments with adjustable interest rates that have been supplanted by AML and ARM authorizations. See also adjustable mortgage loan and renegotiable-rate mortgage.

Vendee   The purchaser or borrower involved in a contract-for-deed transaction. More simply, a buyer.

Vendor   The seller or lender in a contract-for-deed transaction.

Veterans Administration (VA)/VA mortgage   A federal agency that provides services for veterans of U.S. Armed Forces. In real estate finance, the VA insures lenders against defaults on loans made to qualified veterans. Also assists veterans by guaranteeing higher-risk loans and loans with lower-than-market interest rates.

Voluntary lien   See lien.

Weighted average money mortgage   See consolidated-rate mortgage.

Wraparound (also called all-inclusive trust deed, overriding loan/trust deed and overlapping loan/trust deed)   A junior lien, usually given by the seller to the buyer, for the difference between the selling price and the buyer's down payment. In a wraparound arrangement, the seller continues his or her payments on and liability for senior liens of record, and the buyer's payments flow directly to the seller.

Yield   The rate of return on an investment, e.g., the effective interest rate on a mortgage loan.

Appendix I: Monthly Payment to Amortize a Loan of $1,000

Term of Loan

Interest Rate	1 Year	2 Years	3 Years	4 Years	5 Years	6 Years	7 Years	8 Years
9.000%	87.4515	45.6847	31.7997	24.8850	20.7584	18.0255	16.0891	14.6502
9.125%	87.5095	45.7421	31.8579	24.9444	20.8191	18.0876	16.1526	14.7151
9.250%	87.5675	45.7995	31.9162	25.0039	20.8799	18.1499	16.2162	14.7802
9.375%	87.6255	45.8570	31.9745	25.0635	20.9408	18.2122	16.2800	14.8455
9.500%	87.6835	45.9145	32.0329	25.1231	21.0019	18.2747	16.3440	14.9109
9.625%	87.7416	45.9720	32.0914	25.1829	21.0630	18.3373	16.4081	14.9765
9.750%	87.7997	46.0296	32.1499	25.2427	21.1242	18.4000	16.4723	15.0422
9.875%	87.8578	46.0873	32.2085	25.3026	21.1856	18.4629	16.5367	15.1081
10.000%	87.9159	46.1449	32.2672	25.3626	21.2470	18.5258	16.6012	15.1742
10.125%	87.9740	46.2026	32.3259	25.4227	21.3086	18.5889	16.6658	15.2404
10.250%	88.0322	46.2604	32.3847	25.4828	21.3703	18.6522	16.7306	15.3068
10.375%	88.0904	46.3182	32.4435	25.5431	21.4320	18.7155	16.7956	15.3733
10.500%	88.1486	46.3760	32.5024	25.6034	21.4939	18.7790	16.8607	15.4400
10.625%	88.2068	46.4339	32.5614	25.6638	21.5559	18.8426	16.9259	15.5069
10.750%	88.2651	46.4919	32.6205	25.7243	21.6180	18.9063	16.9913	15.5739
10.875%	88.3234	46.5498	32.6796	25.7849	21.6801	18.9701	17.0568	15.6411
11.000%	88.3817	46.6078	32.7387	25.8455	21.7424	19.0341	17.1224	15.7084
11.125%	88.4400	46.6659	32.7979	25.9063	21.8048	19.0982	17.1882	15.7759
11.250%	88.4983	46.7240	32.8572	25.9671	21.8673	19.1624	17.2542	15.8436
11.375%	88.5567	46.7821	32.9166	26.0280	21.9299	19.2267	17.3202	15.9114
11.500%	88.6151	46.8403	32.9760	26.0890	21.9926	19.2912	17.3865	15.9794
11.625%	88.6735	46.8985	33.0355	26.1501	22.0554	19.3557	17.4528	16.0475
11.750%	88.7319	46.9568	33.0950	26.2113	22.1183	19.4204	17.5193	16.1158
11.875%	88.7903	47.0151	33.1546	26.2725	22.1813	19.4853	17.5860	16.1842
12.000%	88.8488	47.0735	33.2143	26.3338	22.2444	19.5502	17.6527	16.2528
12.125%	88.9073	47.1319	33.2740	26.3953	22.3077	19.6153	17.7197	16.3216
12.250%	88.9658	47.1903	33.3338	26.4568	22.3710	19.6804	17.7867	16.3905
12.375%	89.0243	47.2488	33.3937	26.5183	22.4344	19.7457	17.8539	16.4596
12.500%	89.0829	47.3073	33.4536	26.5800	22.4979	19.8112	17.9212	16.5288
12.625%	89.1414	47.3659	33.5136	26.6417	22.5616	19.8767	17.9887	16.5982
12.750%	89.2000	47.4245	33.5737	26.7036	22.6253	19.9424	18.0563	16.6677
12.875%	89.2586	47.4831	33.6338	26.7655	22.6891	20.0082	18.1241	16.7374
13.000%	89.3173	47.5418	33.6940	26.8275	22.7531	20.0741	18.1920	16.8073
13.125%	89.3759	47.6006	33.7542	26.8896	22.8171	20.1401	18.2600	16.8773
13.250%	89.4346	47.6593	33.8145	26.9517	22.8813	20.2063	18.3282	16.9474
13.375%	89.4933	47.7182	33.8749	27.0140	22.9455	20.2726	18.3965	17.0177
13.500%	89.5520	47.7770	33.9353	27.0763	23.0098	20.3390	18.4649	17.0882
13.625%	89.6108	47.8359	33.9958	27.1387	23.0743	20.4055	18.5335	17.1588
13.750%	89.6695	47.8949	34.0563	27.2012	23.1388	20.4721	18.6022	17.2295
13.875%	89.7283	47.9539	34.1169	27.2638	23.2035	20.5389	18.6710	17.3004
14.000%	89.7871	48.0129	34.1776	27.3265	23.2683	20.6057	18.7400	17.3715
14.125%	89.8459	48.0720	34.2384	27.3892	23.3331	20.6727	18.8091	17.4427
14.250%	89.9048	48.1311	34.2992	27.4520	23.3981	20.7398	18.8784	17.5141
14.375%	89.9637	48.1902	34.3600	27.5150	23.4631	20.8071	18.9478	17.5856
14.500%	90.0225	48.2494	34.4210	27.5780	23.5283	20.8744	19.0173	17.6573
14.625%	90.0815	48.3087	34.4820	27.6410	23.5935	20.9419	19.0870	17.7291
14.750%	90.1404	48.3680	34.5430	27.7042	23.6589	21.0095	19.1568	17.8010
14.875%	90.1993	48.4273	34.6041	27.7674	23.7244	21.0772	19.2267	17.8731
15.000%	90.2583	48.4866	34.6653	27.8307	23.7899	21.1450	19.2968	17.9454

Appendix I continued

Interest Rate	9 Years	10 Years	11 Years	12 Years	13 Years	14 Years	15 Years	16 Years
9.000%	13.5429	12.6676	11.9608	11.3803	10.8968	10.4894	10.1427	9.8452
9.125%	13.6093	12.7353	12.0299	11.4508	10.9687	10.5626	10.2172	9.9209
9.250%	13.6758	12.8033	12.0993	11.5216	11.0408	10.6360	10.2919	9.9970
9.375%	13.7425	12.8714	12.1689	11.5925	11.1131	10.7097	10.3670	10.0733
9.500%	13.8094	12.9398	12.2386	11.6637	11.1857	10.7837	10.4422	10.1499
9.625%	13.8764	13.0083	12.3086	11.7352	11.2586	10.8579	10.5178	10.2268
9.750%	13.9437	13.0770	12.3788	11.8068	11.3316	10.9324	10.5936	10.3039
9.875%	14.0111	13.1460	12.4493	11.8787	11.4049	11.0071	10.6697	10.3813
10.000%	14.0787	13.2151	12.5199	11.9508	11.4785	11.0820	10.7461	10.4590
10.125%	14.1465	13.2844	12.5907	12.0231	11.5523	11.1572	10.8227	10.5370
10.250%	14.2144	13.3539	12.6618	12.0957	11.6263	11.2327	10.8995	10.6152
10.375%	14.2826	13.4236	12.7330	12.1684	11.7005	11.3084	10.9766	10.6937
10.500%	14.3509	13.4935	12.8045	12.2414	11.7750	11.3843	11.0540	10.7724
10.625%	14.4193	13.5636	12.8761	12.3146	11.8497	11.4605	11.1316	10.8514
10.750%	14.4880	13.6339	12.9480	12.3880	11.9247	11.5370	11.2095	10.9307
10.875%	14.5568	13.7043	13.0201	12.4617	11.9999	11.6136	11.2876	11.0102
11.000%	14.6259	13.7750	13.0923	12.5356	12.0753	11.6905	11.3660	11.0900
11.125%	14.6950	13.8459	13.1648	12.6096	12.1509	11.7677	11.4446	11.1700
11.250%	14.7644	13.9169	13.2375	12.6839	12.2268	11.8451	11.5234	11.2503
11.375%	14.8339	13.9881	13.3104	12.7584	12.3029	11.9227	11.6026	11.3309
11.500%	14.9037	14.0595	13.3835	12.8332	12.3792	12.0006	11.6819	11.4116
11.625%	14.9735	14.1312	13.4568	12.9081	12.4557	12.0786	11.7615	11.4927
11.750%	15.0436	14.2029	13.5303	12.9833	12.5325	12.1570	11.8413	11.5740
11.875%	15.1138	14.2749	13.6040	13.0586	12.6095	12.2355	11.9214	11.6555
12.000%	15.1842	14.3471	13.6779	13.1342	12.6867	12.3143	12.0017	11.7373
12.125%	15.2548	14.4194	13.7520	13.2100	12.7641	12.3933	12.0822	11.8193
12.250%	15.3256	14.4920	13.8263	13.2860	12.8417	12.4725	12.1630	11.9015
12.375%	15.3965	14.5647	13.9007	13.3622	12.9196	12.5520	12.2440	11.9840
12.500%	15.4676	14.6376	13.9754	13.4386	12.9977	12.6317	12.3252	12.0667
12.625%	15.5388	14.7107	14.0503	13.5152	13.0760	12.7116	12.4067	12.1496
12.750%	15.6102	14.7840	14.1254	13.5920	13.1545	12.7917	12.4884	12.2328
12.875%	15.6818	14.8574	14.2006	13.6690	13.2332	12.8721	12.5703	12.3162
13.000%	15.7536	14.9311	14.2761	13.7463	13.3121	12.9526	12.6524	12.3999
13.125%	15.8255	15.0049	14.3518	13.8237	13.3912	13.0334	12.7348	12.4837
13.250%	15.8976	15.0789	14.4276	13.9013	13.4706	13.1144	12.8174	12.5678
13.375%	15.9699	15.1531	14.5036	13.9791	13.5502	13.1956	12.9002	12.6521
13.500%	16.0423	15.2274	14.5799	14.0572	13.6299	13.2771	12.9832	12.7367
13.625%	16.1149	15.3020	14.6563	14.1354	13.7099	13.3587	13.0664	12.8214
13.750%	16.1877	15.3767	14.7329	14.2138	13.7901	13.4406	13.1499	12.9064
13.875%	16.2606	15.4516	14.8097	14.2925	13.8704	13.5226	13.2335	12.9916
14.000%	16.3337	15.5266	14.8867	14.3713	13.9510	13.6049	13.3174	13.0770
14.125%	16.4070	15.6019	14.9638	14.4503	14.0318	13.6874	13.4015	13.1626
14.250%	16.4804	15.6773	15.0412	14.5295	14.1128	13.7701	13.4858	13.2484
14.375%	16.5540	15.7529	15.1187	14.6089	14.1940	13.8529	13.5703	13.3345
14.500%	16.6277	15.8287	15.1964	14.6885	14.2754	13.9360	13.6550	13.4207
14.625%	16.7016	15.9046	15.2743	14.7683	14.3570	14.0193	13.7399	13.5071
14.750%	16.7757	15.9807	15.3524	14.8483	14.4387	14.1028	13.8250	13.5938
14.875%	16.8499	16.0570	15.4307	14.9284	14.5207	14.1865	13.9104	13.6806
15.000%	16.9243	16.1335	15.5091	15.0088	14.6029	14.2704	13.9959	13.7677

Appendix I continued

| | | | | Term of Loan | | | | |
Interest Rate	17 Years	18 Years	19 Years	20 Years	21 Years	22 Years	23 Years	24 Years
9.000%	9.5880	9.3644	9.1690	8.9973	8.8458	8.7117	8.5927	8.4866
9.125%	9.6650	9.4427	9.2484	9.0778	8.9275	8.7945	8.6765	8.5714
9.250%	9.7423	9.5212	9.3281	9.1587	9.0094	8.8775	8.7606	8.6566
9.375%	9.8199	9.6000	9.4081	9.2398	9.0917	8.9609	8.8450	8.7420
9.500%	9.8978	9.6791	9.4884	9.3213	9.1743	9.0446	8.9297	8.8277
9.625%	9.9760	9.7585	9.5690	9.4031	9.2573	9.1286	9.0148	8.9138
9.750%	10.0544	9.8382	9.6499	9.4852	9.3405	9.2129	9.1002	9.0002
9.875%	10.1331	9.9182	9.7311	9.5675	9.4240	9.2975	9.1858	9.0869
10.000%	10.2121	9.9984	9.8126	9.6502	9.5078	9.3825	9.2718	9.1739
10.125%	10.2914	10.0790	9.8944	9.7332	9.5919	9.4677	9.3581	9.2612
10.250%	10.3709	10.1598	9.9764	9.8164	9.6763	9.5532	9.4447	9.3488
10.375%	10.4507	10.2409	10.0588	9.9000	9.7610	9.6390	9.5315	9.4366
10.500%	10.5308	10.3223	10.1414	9.9838	9.8460	9.7251	9.6187	9.5248
10.625%	10.6112	10.4039	10.2243	10.0679	9.9312	9.8114	9.7061	9.6133
10.750%	10.6918	10.4858	10.3075	10.1523	10.0168	9.8981	9.7938	9.7020
10.875%	10.7727	10.5680	10.3909	10.2370	10.1026	9.9850	9.8818	9.7910
11.000%	10.8538	10.6505	10.4746	10.3219	10.1887	10.0722	9.9701	9.8803
11.125%	10.9352	10.7332	10.5586	10.4071	10.2751	10.1597	10.0586	9.9698
11.250%	11.0169	10.8162	10.6429	10.4926	10.3617	10.2475	10.1474	10.0596
11.375%	11.0988	10.8994	10.7274	10.5783	10.4486	10.3355	10.2365	10.1497
11.500%	11.1810	10.9830	10.8122	10.6643	10.5358	10.4237	10.3258	10.2400
11.625%	11.2634	11.0667	10.8972	10.7506	10.6232	10.5122	10.4154	10.3306
11.750%	11.3461	11.1507	10.9825	10.8371	10.7109	10.6011	10.5052	10.4214
11.875%	11.4290	11.2350	11.0681	10.9238	10.7988	10.6901	10.5953	10.5125
12.000%	11.5122	11.3195	11.1539	11.0109	10.8870	10.7794	10.6856	10.6038
12.125%	11.5956	11.4043	11.2399	11.0981	10.9754	10.8689	10.7762	10.6954
12.250%	11.6792	11.4893	11.3262	11.1856	11.0641	10.9587	10.8670	10.7872
12.375%	11.7631	11.5745	11.4127	11.2734	11.1530	11.0487	10.9581	10.8792
12.500%	11.8473	11.6600	11.4995	11.3614	11.2422	11.1390	11.0494	10.9714
12.625%	11.9316	11.7457	11.5865	11.4496	11.3316	11.2294	11.1409	11.0639
12.750%	12.0162	11.8317	11.6738	11.5381	11.4212	11.3202	11.2326	11.1566
12.875%	12.1011	11.9179	11.7613	11.6268	11.5111	11.4111	11.3246	11.2495
13.000%	12.1861	12.0043	11.8490	11.7158	11.6011	11.5023	11.4168	11.3427
13.125%	12.2714	12.0910	11.9369	11.8049	11.6915	11.5937	11.5092	11.4360
13.250%	12.3570	12.1779	12.0251	11.8943	11.7820	11.6853	11.6018	11.5296
13.375%	12.4427	12.2650	12.1135	11.9839	11.8727	11.7771	11.6946	11.6233
13.500%	12.5287	12.3523	12.2021	12.0737	11.9637	11.8691	11.7876	11.7173
13.625%	12.6149	12.4399	12.2910	12.1638	12.0549	11.9613	11.8808	11.8114
13.750%	12.7013	12.5276	12.3800	12.2541	12.1463	12.0538	11.9743	11.9058
13.875%	12.7879	12.6156	12.4693	12.3445	12.2379	12.1464	12.0679	12.0003
14.000%	12.8748	12.7038	12.5588	12.4352	12.3297	12.2393	12.1617	12.0950
14.125%	12.9618	12.7922	12.6485	12.5261	12.4217	12.3323	12.2557	12.1900
14.250%	13.0491	12.8809	12.7384	12.6172	12.5139	12.4256	12.3500	12.2851
14.375%	13.1366	12.9697	12.8285	12.7085	12.6063	12.5190	12.4443	12.3803
14.500%	13.2242	13.0587	12.9188	12.8000	12.6989	12.6126	12.5389	12.4758
14.625%	13.3121	13.1480	13.0093	12.8917	12.7917	12.7065	12.6337	12.5714
14.750%	13.4002	13.2374	13.1000	12.9836	12.8847	12.8004	12.7286	12.6672
14.875%	13.4885	13.3271	13.1909	13.0756	12.9778	12.8946	12.8237	12.7632
15.000%	13.5770	13.4169	13.2820	13.1679	13.0712	12.9890	12.9190	12.8593

Appendix I continued

Interest Rate	Term of Loan							
	25 Years	26 Years	27 Years	28 Years	29 Years	30 Years	35 Years	40 Years
9.000%	8.3920	8.3072	8.2313	8.1630	8.1016	8.0462	7.8399	7.7136
9.125%	8.4777	8.3939	8.3189	8.2515	8.1909	8.1363	7.9335	7.8100
9.250%	8.5638	8.4810	8.4068	8.3403	8.2805	8.2268	8.0274	7.9066
9.375%	8.6502	8.5683	8.4950	8.4294	8.3705	8.3175	8.1216	8.0035
9.500%	8.7370	8.6560	8.5836	8.5188	8.4607	8.4085	8.2161	8.1006
9.625%	8.8240	8.7440	8.6725	8.6086	8.5513	8.4999	8.3109	8.1980
9.750%	8.9114	8.8323	8.7617	8.6986	8.6421	8.5915	8.4059	8.2956
9.875%	8.9990	8.9209	8.8512	8.7890	8.7333	8.6835	8.5012	8.3934
10.000%	9.0870	9.0098	8.9410	8.8796	8.8248	8.7757	8.5967	8.4915
10.125%	9.1753	9.0990	9.0311	8.9705	8.9165	8.8682	8.6925	8.5897
10.250%	9.2638	9.1885	9.1214	9.0618	9.0085	8.9610	8.7886	8.6882
10.375%	9.3527	9.2782	9.2121	9.1533	9.1008	9.0541	8.8848	8.7868
10.500%	9.4418	9.3683	9.3030	9.2450	9.1934	9.1474	8.9813	8.8857
10.625%	9.5312	9.4586	9.3943	9.3371	9.2862	9.2410	9.0781	8.9847
10.750%	9.6209	9.5492	9.4857	9.4294	9.3793	9.3348	9.1750	9.0840
10.875%	9.7109	9.6401	9.5775	9.5220	9.4727	9.4289	9.2722	9.1834
11.000%	9.8011	9.7313	9.6695	9.6148	9.5663	9.5232	9.3696	9.2829
11.125%	9.8916	9.8227	9.7618	9.7079	9.6601	9.6178	9.4672	9.3827
11.250%	9.9824	9.9143	9.8543	9.8012	9.7542	9.7126	9.5649	9.4826
11.375%	10.0734	10.0063	9.9471	9.8948	9.8486	9.8077	9.6629	9.5826
11.500%	10.1647	10.0984	10.0401	9.9886	9.9431	9.9029	9.7611	9.6828
11.625%	10.2562	10.1909	10.1333	10.0826	10.0379	9.9984	9.8594	9.7832
11.750%	10.3480	10.2835	10.2268	10.1769	10.1329	10.0941	9.9579	9.8836
11.875%	10.4400	10.3764	10.3205	10.2714	10.2281	10.1900	10.0566	9.9843
12.000%	10.5322	10.4695	10.4145	10.3661	10.3236	10.2861	10.1555	10.0850
12.125%	10.6247	10.5629	10.5087	10.4611	10.4192	10.3824	10.2545	10.1859
12.250%	10.7174	10.6565	10.6030	10.5562	10.5151	10.4790	10.3537	10.2869
12.375%	10.8104	10.7503	10.6977	10.6516	10.6112	10.5757	10.4531	10.3880
12.500%	10.9035	10.8443	10.7925	10.7471	10.7074	10.6726	10.5525	10.4892
12.625%	10.9969	10.9385	10.8875	10.8429	10.8039	10.7697	10.6522	10.5905
12.750%	11.0905	11.0329	10.9827	10.9388	10.9005	10.8669	10.7520	10.6920
12.875%	11.1843	11.1276	11.0781	11.0350	10.9973	10.9644	10.8519	10.7935
13.000%	11.2784	11.2224	11.1738	11.1313	11.0943	11.0620	10.9519	10.8951
13.125%	11.3726	11.3175	11.2696	11.2279	11.1915	11.1598	11.0521	10.9969
13.250%	11.4670	11.4127	11.3656	11.3246	11.2888	11.2577	11.1524	11.0987
13.375%	11.5616	11.5082	11.4618	11.4214	11.3864	11.3558	11.2529	11.2006
13.500%	11.6564	11.6038	11.5581	11.5185	11.4841	11.4541	11.3534	11.3026
13.625%	11.7515	11.6996	11.6547	11.6157	11.5819	11.5525	11.4541	11.4047
13.750%	11.8467	11.7956	11.7514	11.7131	11.6799	11.6511	11.5549	11.5069
13.875%	11.9420	11.8917	11.8483	11.8107	11.7781	11.7498	11.6557	11.6091
14.000%	12.0376	11.9881	11.9453	11.9084	11.8764	11.8487	11.7567	11.7114
14.125%	12.1334	12.0846	12.0425	12.0062	11.9749	11.9477	11.8578	11.8138
14.250%	12.2293	12.1813	12.1399	12.1043	12.0735	12.0469	11.9590	11.9162
14.375%	12.3254	12.2781	12.2375	12.2024	12.1722	12.1461	12.0603	12.0187
14.500%	12.4216	12.3751	12.3351	12.3007	12.2711	12.2456	12.1617	12.1213
14.625%	12.5181	12.4723	12.4330	12.3992	12.3701	12.3451	12.2632	12.2240
14.750%	12.6146	12.5696	12.5310	12.4978	12.4693	12.4448	12.3647	12.3267
14.875%	12.7114	12.6671	12.6291	12.5965	12.5686	12.5445	12.4664	12.4294
15.000%	12.8083	12.7647	12.7274	12.6954	12.6680	12.6444	12.5681	12.5322

Appendix II: Remaining Principal Balance Factors on a $1,000 Loan

For Mortgages with an Interest Rate of 9.00% and an Original Term of:

Age of Loan in Years	5 Years	6 Years	7 Years	8 Years	9 Years	10 Years	11 Years	12 Years	15 Years	20 Years	25 Years	30 Years	35 Years	40 Years
1	0.834	0.868	0.893	0.911	0.924	0.935	0.944	0.951	0.967	0.981	0.989	0.993	0.996	0.997
2	0.653	0.724	0.775	0.813	0.842	0.865	0.883	0.898	0.931	0.961	0.977	0.986	0.991	0.994
3	0.454	0.567	0.647	0.706	0.751	0.787	0.816	0.840	0.891	0.938	0.963	0.978	0.986	0.991
4	0.237	0.395	0.506	0.589	0.652	0.703	0.743	0.777	0.848	0.914	0.949	0.969	0.980	0.988
5	0.000	0.206	0.352	0.461	0.544	0.610	0.664	0.707	0.801	0.887	0.933	0.959	0.974	0.984
6		0.000	0.184	0.321	0.426	0.509	0.576	0.631	0.749	0.858	0.915	0.948	0.968	0.980
7			0.000	0.168	0.296	0.398	0.481	0.548	0.692	0.826	0.896	0.936	0.960	0.975
8				0.000	0.155	0.277	0.376	0.457	0.630	0.791	0.875	0.924	0.952	0.970
9					0.000	0.145	0.262	0.358	0.563	0.752	0.852	0.910	0.944	0.965
10						0.000	0.137	0.249	0.489	0.710	0.827	0.894	0.934	0.959
11							0.000	0.130	0.408	0.664	0.800	0.878	0.924	0.952
12								0.000	0.319	0.614	0.770	0.859	0.912	0.945
15									0.000	0.433	0.662	0.793	0.871	0.919
20										0.000	0.404	0.635	0.773	0.857
25											0.000	0.388	0.619	0.761
30												0.000	0.378	0.609
35													0.000	0.372
40														0.000

For Mortgages with an Interest Rate of 9.25% and an Original Term of:

Age of Loan in Years	5 Years	6 Years	7 Years	8 Years	9 Years	10 Years	11 Years	12 Years	15 Years	20 Years	25 Years	30 Years	35 Years	40 Years
1	0.835	0.869	0.893	0.911	0.925	0.936	0.945	0.952	0.968	0.982	0.989	0.994	0.996	0.998
2	0.654	0.726	0.777	0.814	0.843	0.866	0.885	0.900	0.932	0.962	0.978	0.986	0.992	0.995
3	0.456	0.569	0.649	0.708	0.753	0.790	0.819	0.842	0.893	0.940	0.965	0.979	0.987	0.992
4	0.238	0.396	0.508	0.591	0.655	0.705	0.746	0.780	0.851	0.916	0.951	0.970	0.982	0.989
5	0.000	0.207	0.354	0.463	0.547	0.613	0.667	0.710	0.804	0.890	0.935	0.961	0.976	0.985
6		0.000	0.185	0.323	0.428	0.512	0.579	0.635	0.753	0.861	0.918	0.950	0.969	0.981
7			0.000	0.169	0.299	0.401	0.484	0.552	0.696	0.830	0.899	0.939	0.962	0.977
8				0.000	0.156	0.280	0.379	0.461	0.635	0.795	0.879	0.927	0.955	0.972
9					0.000	0.146	0.264	0.361	0.567	0.757	0.857	0.913	0.947	0.967
10						0.000	0.138	0.252	0.493	0.715	0.832	0.898	0.937	0.961
11							0.000	0.132	0.412	0.670	0.805	0.882	0.927	0.955
12								0.000	0.322	0.620	0.776	0.864	0.916	0.948
15									0.000	0.439	0.669	0.799	0.876	0.923
20										0.000	0.410	0.643	0.780	0.863
25											0.000	0.394	0.627	0.768
30												0.000	0.384	0.618
35													0.000	0.379
40														0.000

Appendix II continued

For Mortgages with an Interest Rate of 9.50% and an Original Term of:

Age of Loan in Years	5 Years	6 Years	7 Years	8 Years	9 Years	10 Years	11 Years	12 Years	15 Years	20 Years	25 Years	30 Years	35 Years	40 Years
1	0.836	0.870	0.894	0.912	0.926	0.937	0.946	0.953	0.968	0.982	0.990	0.994	0.996	0.998
2	0.656	0.727	0.778	0.816	0.845	0.868	0.886	0.901	0.934	0.963	0.978	0.987	0.992	0.995
3	0.457	0.570	0.651	0.710	0.756	0.792	0.821	0.845	0.895	0.942	0.966	0.980	0.988	0.992
4	0.240	0.398	0.510	0.594	0.658	0.708	0.749	0.782	0.853	0.918	0.952	0.971	0.983	0.989
5	0.000	0.208	0.356	0.465	0.550	0.616	0.670	0.714	0.807	0.893	0.937	0.962	0.977	0.986
6		0.000	0.186	0.325	0.431	0.515	0.583	0.638	0.756	0.864	0.921	0.953	0.971	0.982
7			0.000	0.170	0.301	0.404	0.487	0.555	0.700	0.833	0.903	0.942	0.964	0.978
8				0.000	0.157	0.282	0.382	0.464	0.639	0.799	0.883	0.930	0.957	0.974
9					0.000	0.148	0.267	0.364	0.571	0.762	0.861	0.917	0.949	0.969
10						0.000	0.140	0.254	0.497	0.720	0.837	0.902	0.940	0.963
11							0.000	0.133	0.416	0.675	0.810	0.886	0.931	0.957
12								0.000	0.326	0.625	0.781	0.869	0.920	0.951
15									0.000	0.444	0.675	0.805	0.881	0.927
20										0.000	0.416	0.650	0.787	0.869
25											0.000	0.400	0.635	0.776
30												0.000	0.391	0.626
35													0.000	0.386
40														0.000

For Mortgages with an Interest Rate of 11.00% and an Original Term of:

Age of Loan in Years	5 Years	6 Years	7 Years	8 Years	9 Years	10 Years	11 Years	12 Years	15 Years	20 Years	25 Years	30 Years	35 Years	40 Years
1	0.841	0.875	0.900	0.917	0.931	0.942	0.950	0.957	0.972	0.985	0.992	0.995	0.997	0.999
2	0.664	0.736	0.788	0.825	0.854	0.877	0.895	0.910	0.941	0.969	0.983	0.990	0.995	0.997
3	0.466	0.581	0.662	0.722	0.768	0.805	0.833	0.857	0.907	0.951	0.973	0.985	0.991	0.995
4	0.246	0.408	0.523	0.608	0.673	0.724	0.765	0.798	0.868	0.931	0.962	0.979	0.988	0.993
5	0.000	0.215	0.367	0.480	0.566	0.634	0.688	0.732	0.825	0.908	0.950	0.972	0.984	0.991
6		0.000	0.194	0.337	0.447	0.533	0.602	0.659	0.777	0.883	0.936	0.964	0.979	0.988
7			0.000	0.178	0.314	0.421	0.507	0.577	0.724	0.855	0.920	0.955	0.974	0.985
8				0.000	0.165	0.296	0.400	0.485	0.664	0.823	0.903	0.945	0.969	0.982
9					0.000	0.156	0.281	0.383	0.597	0.788	0.884	0.935	0.963	0.979
10						0.000	0.148	0.269	0.523	0.749	0.862	0.923	0.956	0.975
11							0.000	0.142	0.440	0.706	0.838	0.909	0.948	0.970
12								0.000	0.347	0.657	0.812	0.894	0.940	0.965
15									0.000	0.475	0.712	0.838	0.908	0.947
20										0.000	0.451	0.691	0.824	0.899
25											0.000	0.438	0.680	0.817
30												0.000	0.431	0.674
35													0.000	0.427
40														0.000

Appendix II continued

For Mortgages with an Interest Rate of 11.75% and an Original Term of:

Age of Loan in Years	5 Years	6 Years	7 Years	8 Years	9 Years	10 Years	11 Years	12 Years	15 Years	20 Years	25 Years	30 Years	35 Years	40 Years
1	0.844	0.878	0.902	0.920	0.933	0.944	0.953	0.960	0.974	0.987	0.993	0.996	0.998	0.999
2	0.668	0.741	0.792	0.830	0.859	0.881	0.899	0.914	0.945	0.972	0.985	0.992	0.996	0.998
3	0.471	0.587	0.668	0.729	0.775	0.811	0.840	0.863	0.912	0.955	0.976	0.987	0.993	0.996
4	0.249	0.414	0.529	0.615	0.680	0.731	0.772	0.806	0.875	0.936	0.966	0.982	0.990	0.994
5	0.000	0.219	0.373	0.487	0.574	0.642	0.697	0.741	0.834	0.915	0.955	0.975	0.987	0.993
6		0.000	0.197	0.343	0.455	0.542	0.612	0.669	0.787	0.891	0.942	0.969	0.983	0.990
7			0.000	0.182	0.320	0.429	0.516	0.587	0.735	0.865	0.928	0.961	0.978	0.988
8				0.000	0.170	0.302	0.409	0.495	0.676	0.835	0.912	0.952	0.974	0.985
9					0.000	0.160	0.288	0.392	0.610	0.801	0.894	0.942	0.968	0.982
10						0.000	0.152	0.276	0.535	0.763	0.874	0.931	0.962	0.979
11							0.000	0.146	0.452	0.720	0.851	0.919	0.956	0.975
12								0.000	0.358	0.672	0.826	0.905	0.948	0.971
15									0.000	0.490	0.729	0.852	0.919	0.955
20										0.000	0.468	0.711	0.841	0.912
25											0.000	0.456	0.701	0.835
30												0.000	0.450	0.696
35													0.000	0.447
40														0.000

For Mortgages with an Interest Rate of 13.00% and an Original Term of:

Age of Loan in Years	5 Years	6 Years	7 Years	8 Years	9 Years	10 Years	11 Years	12 Years	15 Years	20 Years	25 Years	30 Years	35 Years	40 Years
1	0.848	0.882	0.906	0.924	0.937	0.948	0.956	0.963	0.977	0.989	0.994	0.997	0.998	0.999
2	0.675	0.748	0.800	0.837	0.866	0.888	0.906	0.921	0.950	0.976	0.988	0.994	0.997	0.998
3	0.479	0.596	0.678	0.739	0.785	0.821	0.849	0.873	0.920	0.961	0.981	0.990	0.995	0.997
4	0.255	0.422	0.540	0.626	0.692	0.744	0.785	0.818	0.886	0.945	0.972	0.986	0.993	0.996
5	0.000	0.225	0.383	0.499	0.587	0.656	0.711	0.756	0.847	0.926	0.963	0.981	0.990	0.995
6		0.000	0.204	0.354	0.468	0.557	0.627	0.685	0.803	0.905	0.952	0.975	0.987	0.993
7			0.000	0.188	0.331	0.443	0.532	0.604	0.753	0.880	0.940	0.969	0.984	0.992
8				0.000	0.176	0.314	0.424	0.512	0.695	0.852	0.926	0.962	0.980	0.990
9					0.000	0.167	0.300	0.408	0.630	0.821	0.910	0.954	0.976	0.987
10						0.000	0.160	0.289	0.556	0.785	0.891	0.944	0.971	0.985
11							0.000	0.154	0.472	0.744	0.871	0.934	0.966	0.982
12								0.000	0.376	0.697	0.847	0.922	0.959	0.979
15									0.000	0.515	0.755	0.874	0.935	0.966
20										0.000	0.496	0.741	0.866	0.930
25											0.000	0.486	0.733	0.861
30												0.000	0.481	0.730
35													0.000	0.479
40														0.000

Appendix II continued

For Mortgages with an Interest Rate of 14.00% and an Original Term of:

Age of Loan in Years	5 Years	6 Years	7 Years	8 Years	9 Years	10 Years	11 Years	12 Years	15 Years	20 Years	25 Years	30 Years	35 Years	40 Years
1	0.851	0.886	0.909	0.927	0.940	0.951	0.959	0.965	0.979	0.990	0.995	0.998	0.999	0.999
2	0.681	0.754	0.805	0.843	0.872	0.894	0.911	0.926	0.955	0.979	0.990	0.995	0.998	0.999
3	0.485	0.603	0.686	0.747	0.793	0.829	0.857	0.880	0.927	0.966	0.984	0.992	0.996	0.998
4	0.259	0.429	0.548	0.636	0.702	0.754	0.794	0.827	0.895	0.951	0.976	0.988	0.994	0.997
5	0.000	0.229	0.390	0.508	0.598	0.667	0.722	0.767	0.858	0.934	0.968	0.984	0.992	0.996
6		0.000	0.209	0.362	0.478	0.568	0.640	0.697	0.815	0.914	0.959	0.980	0.990	0.995
7			0.000	0.193	0.340	0.454	0.545	0.618	0.767	0.891	0.948	0.974	0.987	0.994
8				0.000	0.182	0.323	0.436	0.526	0.711	0.865	0.935	0.968	0.984	0.992
9					0.000	0.173	0.310	0.420	0.646	0.835	0.921	0.961	0.981	0.990
10						0.000	0.166	0.299	0.572	0.801	0.904	0.953	0.977	0.988
11							0.000	0.160	0.487	0.761	0.885	0.943	0.972	0.986
12								0.000	0.390	0.716	0.863	0.933	0.967	0.983
15									0.000	0.534	0.775	0.890	0.945	0.973
20										0.000	0.517	0.763	0.883	0.942
25											0.000	0.509	0.757	0.879
30												0.000	0.505	0.754
35													0.000	0.503
40														0.000

Index